WRAPPED IN RUGBY

DOUGLAS SCOTT BRUCE

ISBN: 1492154326
ISBN 13: 9781492154327

Foreword

I often wonder what gets into people when they feel the need to write a book about themselves, especially when they have not been seen on Big Brother, The X Factor, Crimewatch UK or some other profile raising affair. Memoirs are widely read if they are written by, or about, some famous sportsman or politician but I have always thought that the readership of "Mr Man In The Street" would be of minimal interest..... until now.

Dougie Bruce has written his memoir and has asked me to write the foreword. I have known Dougie since before my first Cap for Scotland and have shared some great times with him after rugby Internationals and many other rugby orientated occasions involving both Heriot's Rugby Club when he was Secretary and General Manager and Mackie Academy FP Rugby Football Club when he was their President. We have never, however, indulged in any discussion about literature, though Dougie did tell me on one occasion that he had something in common with authors, he said that he once read a book!!

Well I have now read *his* book and although he has made it clear that he was never a rugby star, Dougie has had the fun of less competitive amateur rugby with all the hilarity that goes on at that level. I think you too will have fun reading about his escapades in the world of Rugby Union and the importance that George Heriot's

School placed upon the fifteens game. His time with Mackie Academy FP Rugby Club, Stonehaven, of which my brothers, David, Kenny and I are honorary members, is well documented in a style that any rugby fan will recognise. You will have a smile if not a belly laugh at some of the stories Dougie tells of his humble experiences as a schoolboy at Heriot's, in other sports and indeed some of his lifetime experiences in the workplace and as a family man.

— Iain "The Bear" Milne

Table of Contents

Introduction ·· i

Chapter 1   I Discover the Game of Rugby ····················· 1

Chapter 2   In Which I Discover Additional Exposure
            Problems; Hastie Bye-Laws of the Game of
            Rugby; Touring···································· 7

Chapter 3   Playing School 1st XV Rugby; A First Flight;
            Touring to Ireland; International Athletics;
            Melrose Sports Day ······························ 14

Chapter 4   Sundays ·· 42

Chapter 5   In Which I Learn About Rugby Etiquette ·········· 53

Chapter 6   I Discover A Sporting Mentor; I Become A British
            Junior Champion and A Schoolboy
            Internationalist··································· 58

Chapter 7   From Junior Athletics to Scientific Torture and
            I Don't Belong to Glasgow by the Way ············ 64

Chapter 8   I Leave School and Start a Career ················ 79

Chapter 9   George Heriot's School (FP) Rugby Club Beckons ··· 99

Chapter 10 I Get Married and Join New Clubs in Nottingham·· 127

Chapter 11 On My Own in Aberdeen ························ 165

Chapter 12 In Which I Join Ken Scotland's Old Club and
            Help Found Mackie FP··························· 169

Chapter 13 I Help Form A New Club; Club Dinners; Famous
Visitors; History and Traditions; Community
Spirit; Stockholm Exiles, Heriot's Cavaliers · · · · · · · 179

Chapter 14 New Clubs in the North; A Madcap Coach,
Mackie Minis · 214

Chapter 15 In Which I Become An Administrator; I Meet
Jo Maso · 227

Chapter 16 Fun with A Bear · 243

Chapter 17 Withdrawal Symptoms of the Retired
Rugby Player · 252

Chapter 18 Edinburgh and Heriot's Rugby Club · · · · · · · · · · · · · 257

Chapter 19 A Pre-Season Tournament; Embracing Sponsors;
Special Players; Fund Raising, Rosemary and
I Tour Paris and Rome · 261

Chapter 20 In Which Touchline is Born, Championship
Win and Civic Reception · 271

Chapter 21 Lord MacKay and the SRU; Grumpy Ground
Staff and Irritating Interruptions · · · · · · · · · · · · · · 278

Chapter 22 World Cup 1999; Springboks, Samoa and That
Man Bill McLaren · 285

Chapter 23 More from My Office Window; Touchline and
the Back Office · 292

Chapter 24 Kenny Scotland and Pies; The Job Just Gets
Bigger; How Mean Can Supporters Get · · · · · · · · · · 299

Chapter 25 The Losing Battle to Keep Membership Numbers
Up; More Experiences with the Three Bears······305

Chapter 26 New Coaches; Sir George Mathewson; Local
Residents ································· 313

Chapter 27 Bad Weather; The Cup; Sympathy for Hawick;
Gala and Dod Burrell; Matt Williams and Todd
Blackadder ······························ 318

Chapter 28 Reunions; SRU Changes Again! Another Mackay
Leads the Way; Radical Changes Planned at
Goldenacre································324

Chapter 29 Clark Cup; Summer Rugby; Pro Rugby and
Our Lights; Possible False Dawn at the SRU;
The Truth About Numbers of Players in
Scottish Rugby.··························329

Chapter 30 SRU's Strategic Advisory Group; Fund Raising;
BBC Rugby Special at Heriot's; Pro Rugby
Blamed for Rift in Scottish Rugby; Andy Irvine
and the Moonies!! ······················ 335

Chapter 31 Community Rugby; My meeting with Harlequins
CEO at the Stoop; Friends of Scottish Rugby;
The London Caledonian Club and My First
Plateful of Partridge; Mini Cab Fiasco in London.···342

Chapter 32 SRU Meltdown, Jock Millican to the Rescue;
A Dream Vanishes; Skye Beckons ···············349

Introduction

As I was nearing the end of my time as secretary and general manager of Heriot's Rugby club it occurred to me to write a book about my rugby experiences both on and off the field. That was the latter part of 2004.

Going by the date of publication, you will realise that I am a slow writer.

My story, or rather stories, began in 1958 when I was introduced to rugby. I participated in other sports and was actually better at most of them compared to my rugby efforts, but rugby dominated because it was hugely important at my school, George Heriot's in Edinburgh. As I started to recount my early experiences in rugby union, lots of other boyhood, adolescent and later, more adult, moments came to mind. Some stories have nothing to do with the game of rugby union but I thought they might bring a smile to the faces of some people as they may see themselves in similar circumstances. So far as my rugby playing is concerned, I never reached the top of the game, nowhere near it in fact but like thousands of other men with rugby in their blood, I had a huge amount of fun from just being involved in the small way that I was. My rugby accounts are a bit like life; they start off with gay abandon to use an old description and develop a more serious slant as the years go on, especially as I report my administrative days in the Premier league during the massive upsets that beset the SRU. Sadly, rugby has become a bit too serious for my liking as it strives for perfection on the pitch but it's something that I think the young players will be coping with, if only because it's all they have known. Hopefully they will find a similar sort of fun in the modern game to the very amateur game which I enjoyed. Young lads are seeking contracts to play the game professionally and my club, Heriot's, has played an important part in the careers of many aspiring pros.

So, here is my humble autobiography which could just as easily be your book if you are male and were born shortly after the Second World War. The book has a beginning, a middle and an end. The former and the latter concern rugby so I have called my book "Wrapped in Rugby"

WRAPPED IN RUGBY

*Dedicated to the memory of my dear Rosemary
who had a lot of rugby to put up with!!!!*

CHAPTER I

I Discover the Game of Rugby

It is early September 1958:

What a relief, a rugby afternoon. Goldenacre, home of Heriot's rugby beckoned. A short bus journey away in reality but in my mind it was light years distant from sums, spelling and, more importantly, my class teacher Cruella DeVil. I didn't appreciate, at the tender age of ten, that rugby would become one of the biggest influences on my life. The oval ball game would teach me sportsmanship and teamwork; open many social and business doors and give me many lasting friendships together with oceans of fun.

A couple of Edinburgh Corporation double-decker buses were waiting for me and my wee pals outside the school's Lauriston Place gates, right opposite the Royal Infirmary. The site of that hospital was, in the mid eighteenth and early nineteenth centuries, the home of George Watson's School. The Watson's boys were serious rivals of Herioters then, and nothing has changed much since those Victorian times except that Heriot's v Watsons street scuffles have been replaced by healthy games of rugby on well-kept pitches. Like the Royal Infirmary however, Watson's school has moved away. In the case of the former it was for health reasons in the latter, probably for both health and safety reasons!

Heriot's and Watson's have produced many famous Scottish Rugby Internationalists, none more so than the Hastings brothers, Gavin and Scott of Watsonians and Andy Irvine, Kenny Scotland, Iain, Kenny and David Milne of Heriot's. Kenny Scotland was already, at this time in my story, a hero of mine and all my wee pals at Heriot's; he was about to become a massive part of Heriot folklore, a legend in his own life time. A year later, the 1959 Lions hailed this quiet little rugby genius.

The bus at Lauriston place soon filled up with boys eager to get down to their beloved playing fields at Goldenacre.

We pulled up at the entry to the driveway on Warriston Gardens which led to the Red Pavilion, a beautiful red brick Victorian building which was erected as the HQ of Heriot cricket. In the winter, it was where all the rugby cadets were based. Like a good wine it had a complex aroma about it that one could almost bite through. I can still sense that smell to this day; it consisted of the odours from: real rubber mats, chipped and well stud-marked wooden floor boards seasoned with earth, line chalk, dead grass, dubbin-drenched leather rugby balls, linseed oil, boot polish, cricket boot whitening, a musty whiff of stale sweat and, paying lip service to personal hygiene, there was a hint of carbolic soap.

Most of us little blighters just could not get off the buses quick enough; we ran like hell up the drive, school bag in one hand, kit bag in the other, quite determined to win this unofficial weekly race. By the time we had covered the hundred and fifty yards or so to the Red Pavilion, our arms were stretched like those of orang-utans, our lungs were gasping for oxygen and pulses were racing. If the run up the drive was done in record time, then the change out of our school uniforms into the famous blue and white hooped rugby jerseys was a blur. We could not wait to get on with it and win a cap for Scotland. Some of us actually did go the whole way but others simply got wrapped up in the game at various lower playing levels and then, later in life, in the administration of the game. I was one of those latter lucky guys.

Once changed into rugby kit, a rabble of excited wee boys ran about outside the Red Pavilion chasing each other and making a hellish racket. A whistle blew. Mr Hastie, would gather us all in to organise some teams. We played a strange form of rugby which our teacher called Balmoral. God only knows why it had that name, I never got to the bottom of that; but, Balmoral it was and Balmoral we played. It seemed very like the rugby I had seen the former pupils play on Saturday afternoons, same ball, same direction to run, ball in hand but no kicking, well not of the ball anyway, no scrums and no line outs. All we wanted to do was score tries.

For me this was a great game, so much more fun than football and much easier, for me anyway. I was not very good with my feet, at least in the finer arts of dribbling, passing and shooting. Okay, okay, I was totally incompetent at the beautiful game. But hold on a minute, this handling game was different. It was something that I could really express myself in, and, because I had quite a good turn of speed, once the ball was firmly planted in my hands and I had set off, no one could catch me. Who cared about lessons and Cruella DeVil, my Dominie.

After a few weeks Mr Hastie advanced the process a bit and we started to take proper positions and the plumper boys found them-selves in the front two rows of the scrum and from those positions backwards to full back it seemed the thinner the players needed to be. In fact, the first full back in my team, William Dishington, was so thin, if he turned sideways he disappeared from sight and would probably have dropped down the proverbial street drain. Bill's physical appearance however, belied his skill both as a rugby player and as a cricketer. It was at that stage, I think, for all backs, that the darker side of the scrum, particularly the front row, started to become a closed shop, a secret society so to speak. These props and hookers developed skills that no back could ever understand. They were the workhorses of the team, striving as one solid unit to get the ball for us brylcream boys to run about daft with, scoring brilliant tries against Daniel Stewarts and Melville College. We seemed forever to be playing only those schools in the very junior teams.

Those of us who are now parents, indeed grandparents, and who played rugby at primary school in the fifties and before, will no doubt wonder what parents and school authorities at that time were thinking about. To make it in time for the Saturday morning kick-offs for the youngest teams, you were up before the milk man was about. The fixtures were always played on the most baltic of days of the winter; Edinburgh Corporation buses were few and far between; streets were near deserted, so it was difficult to find anyone to ask for directions to some unknown rugby ground. In those days, when there were no people carriers or Trinity tractors to transport the legions of kids to rugby venues, our naïve parents seemed to be blissfully unaware of what so concerns today's parents: funny sorts of men we now commonly call paedophiles. Perhaps our folks had a sixth sense which told them that such monsters were not due to be a serious threat on the Edinburgh streets until the eighties or nineties; or at the very least until their little sons of the fifties had returned home safely of a Saturday morning in the Corporation bus from, say, Watsons ground at Myreside or Meggetland, home of Boroughmuir school rugby and near neighbours of Watsons. Meggetland was far enough away and unseen from the district of Goldenacre where I lived, for my Elie-born mother to have it all but proved to her that the world is indeed round.

After such a Saturday morning adventure I would generally return to the bosom of my family physically intact, all limbs fully functional, complete with my coat, scarf, gloves, all of my rugby kit and, be fully recovered from exposure to the elements. Long before the advent of "risk assessment" our parents and school teachers, perhaps subtly, were not so daft about allowing us wee boys to find our own way around town. Is it just possible they had a good idea of what was going on out there and just wanted us kids to be adventurous, experience a wee bit of life and learn how to be independent?

Remember also, as part of this subliminal toughening process, there was absolutely no way rugby boys were allowed to take simple precautions against the fierce wind-chill factor that existed on Scottish Saturday mornings. One was labelled a complete sissy if, in an effort to remain compus mentus whilst waiting for the rare pass out on the wing, two rugby jerseys were worn or indeed any kind of supplemental upper undergarment.

Some years after my early beginnings in rugby, I was selected to play on the left wing for the School 1st XV in the annual match against Edinburgh Academy at Newfield, their school ground. It was a Wednesday afternoon in the depths of December and the Polar North seemed to have got fed up being in the north and had travelled down for the day to Newfield. There I was, quivering, non-sissy-like on the left wing, in front of the whole of both senior schools' supporting pupils, who, needless to say were all wearing heavy overcoats, woolly hats, scarves and gloves. After about forty-five body and mind numbing minutes and into the second-half I lost the plot altogether. I hadn't had one pass all fff.......... freezing afternoon. I remember coming to in the showers thinking how similar my encounter with the freezing temperature had been to the last walk that Captain Oates, the famous colleague of Scott of the Antartic, had taken. Of course, the major difference was the fact that Oates had deliberately sacrificed himself for the good of his team. According to Gibby Galloway my English teacher whose class I attended first period the next day, I had suddenly, and with no explanation, taken off down the left wing, minus ball and put in a bone shattering tackle on my dumbfounded opposing wing. This action left everyone at Newfield nonplussed, especially the now traumatised Academy right winger as the play was way behind me and on the other side of the pitch.

'Bruce,' said Gibby 'Had you taken leave of your senses?' Well actually I suppose I had but, like paedophilia, exposure to the elements wasn't due to be fully recognised until later in the second-half of the twentieth century.

The Red Pavilion

CHAPTER 2

In Which I Discover Additional Exposure Problems;
Hastie Bye-Laws of the Game of Rugby; Touring

Some years later, in the early eighties when I was a member of the Stonehaven club, Mackie Academy FPRFC our 1st XV played a match against Panmure 2nds. It got very cold and after the two captains pleaded with the referee for mercy, the match was abandoned. Lower team matches always seem to be played miles from the changing rooms, Panmure was no exception. Stiffened by the severe wind chill factor, we trudged into the comparative warmth of the breeze block building, or was it freeze block, where we noticed that the full back of Panmure 1st XV had retired early too. He looked like one of those ice sculptures and had to be defrosted. I can only imagine the pain the poor guy went through when his blood started to course round his veins.

Around about that time, one of the Mackie players was due to be married. A special North East of Scotland ceremony called a blackening was laid on for lucky future husbands. The poor guy in this case was stripped down to his underpants and blackened with whatever came to hand, often the main ingredient, as featured in this case, was smelly waste sump oil. Our blackee was then chained to a lamp post outside the pub where the celebration was being held. Sadly the guys forgot all about the poor chump as they sat pouring beer down their faces. A passer-by saw the restrained groom and called into the pub to see if anyone had lost the "chilled kinna guy attached to the post roon the front ken ". The plastered mob ran out to unchain what was a now frosted hostage ; he didn't look that bad but that was because they couldn't see his true hypothermic, deoxygenated blue colour for the black oil.

An hour or so steeped in a warm bath helped the sadder and wiser captive resolve to be married only once, no matter what, or, at least if things didn't work out, he would remarry elsewhere in Scotland. All of this sorry tale occurred in the area of Stonehaven harbour where the next blackening was re- jigged because of the hypothermia implications. Logically the lamp post wheeze was dumped. Instead, after the mandatory blackening, the recipient was, in the dead of night, thrown off the pier into what everybody assumed was the sea. Big miscalculation. Instead of hearing a big splash a horrible kind of crump noise was audible followed by a great deal of bad language as the now badly battered, bruised and blackened hubby to be, extracted himself from amongst a fishing boat's winch and other blunt but bruising deck machinery.

Those readers that were scholars in the early fifties will also recall that the school rugby season was relentless. None of this namby pamby going away with the family for Edinburgh holiday weekends. Oh no, the show had to go on every Saturday, decreed Mr Hastie and his counterparts at all the other rugby schools. Presumably, the view taken was that the Monday was the holiday not the Friday evening, the Saturday or the Sunday. Most folk had nowhere to go anyway and probably possessed very little money to spend even if they had gone away.

Ah! the luxury of being a sports master at an independent school in the days when the cinema reigned as Her Majesty's subject's main form of entertainment. There were no computers, play stations, nor any other serious rival sports to rugby football. Rugby was a religion at Heriot's and the attitude towards it was dogmatic. Upon arrival in the senior school, Heriot boys were offered two main choices of winter sports: rugby or cross country athletics. It was fashionable to consider cross country as a bit girly and so rugby was the main choice. In fact, some of the young men who were not interested in any sport at all chose to play rugby because they really did not fancy putting in the requisite miles running round and round Goldenacre playing fields. Rugby seemed the easier option; it was a bit of a gamble because the Games Master, when addressing the school at the beginning of the season, told the boys what their options were:

'Boys, there are two games options for you, rugby or cross country. Choose wisely,' he warned.

The man spoke out the side of his mouth, with the occasional glance over his shoulders as if to check no unwanted ears were about. It was a presentation that had a bizarre feel about it, at least it seemed that way to me and my pals. A normal impression of a male PT teacher is one of a man in a track suit and trainers or in a pair of black trousers, an open necked white, short sleeved shirt and white gym shoes. Unless he was on the rugby pitch, our man Hastie always wore light brown slacks, a shirt, a bow tie to match the shirt, a brownish tweed sports jacket with some pens in the breast pocket (one also behind his right ear) and beetle-crusher, bullet-proof brown shoes. I don't believe the soles ever wore out in the thirteen years I was at school. For a games master, his habits were anomalous; he occasionally smoked a pipe when he was not puffing on a hand-rolled cigarette. His unusual attire and unhealthy tobacco addiction added a certain eccentricity to the man whilst also lending an air of importance to proceedings. He was a kind of Wizard of Oz .

When Heriot boys reached the senior school there was no choice really for the lads looking for what they thought was an easy life. These guys had all forms of energy sapping exercises sussed, so it had to be rugby; cross country would definitely be too much like hard work for them.

'Before you make your choice,' Hastie went on with complete confidence, 'If you opt for rugger then you must be available every Saturday for the entire winter sports season.' "Hmmmmm," thought the lads who fancied a Saturday morning in bed at least now and again. In the end rugby won the day for these boys because they figured that they would be so useless at rugby they would never be picked to play on Saturdays. They were sadly disillusioned; Hastie, it seemed, would field dozens upon dozens of teams. Luckily for all games masters in both the private and state schools, this was a time when no Supermarkets were looking for land to build new stores on. There was more than enough grass to go around for zealous rugby masters to fit up with pitches and lots of rugby matches with hundreds of wretched little boys to put on them. Unsuspecting Heriot parents were plunged into a Sunday only weekend whether they liked it or not. Never mind the fact that they were the customer, so to speak; paying a chunk of their net incomes towards school fees, there was no questioning the supplier, there was absolutely no going back on the decision. Nothing desperate ever really happened but, being kids, we took teachers' statements to the limit of our extremely vivid imaginations and had mental pictures of just how far our masters might stretch their rules. 'I am awfully sorry Mrs Bloggs, whilst I fully sympathise with your position, we really cannot let your son Horace away for his grannie's funeral on Saturday; he is in the umpteenth fifteen who are down to play away against Glasgow Academy twentieths.' Other bye-laws surrounding the rigid governance of fixtures included the potential postponement of matches. Such postponements were never announced and they were only likely to occur if the weather deteriorated making the pitches unplayable. The state of a pitch was decided by the groundsman and any parent second guessing him was ignored. Even trying to get at the facts was forbidden. The possibility of summary execution awaited a pupil if he or his caring mummy called up the groundsman's office at Goldenacre to ask about the prospects of matches taking place. So, wee Johnny and his team mates would have to get up as usual at the crack of an Artic, to be snowy or rainy Saturday dawn, head for the corporation bus to Goldenacre and only then to be told they had endured a wasted journey.

The reason for this behaviour was to avoid clogging the one and only phone line when the ground staff were engaged in apprising referees and the opposition teaching staff of the conditions, especially if they were coming from afar. Technology had not begun to provide us with a second TV channel never mind a helpful answering machine; butter had probably only just become un-rationed and young people were staring at bananas wondering what to do with them! A website with up to date information was not even a ridiculous fantasy.

Now, one may think that this policy was draconian, to say the least, but, in actual fact, it was good for the soul, and an excellent habit to get into for later rugby life. A married Herioter, due to turn out for his rugby team, upon eyeing the three feet of snow in his back garden would have been crestfallen at the possibility of a flat Saturday if had not been for the "turn up at all costs" Hastie tradition. Such a fellow would instinctively apply the standards laid down at school and could, with a crystal clear conscience, say to his wife, who was having costly visions of an afternoon in John Lewis,

"Dash it all and help my Bob darling, it's Saturday and no matter what the weather looks like here, and in all fairness to my team mates, I must get to Goldenacre/ Myreside/ Meggetland/Raeburn Place or wherever lest I suffer the most horrible of consequences, you know how it is pet lamb."

From the point of view of a coach such an approach is a bit of a boon as some extra training can be put in with the lads instead of the match; from the players point of view, his traditional Saturday remains pretty well intact and minus the usual bruises. Whilst downing his fifth pint by 4.30pm, not to mention a fair share of both the home and away pie trays, he can reflect on how his fitness level has been maintained and how his Saturday routine has not been mucked up. That was the case up until the eighties. Since that fateful decade, in the case of most clubs, wives can insist that their husbands call up their club and check the message on the telephone answering machine about the likelihood of the match being off. In some more hardened and cynical cases, the wife will make the call herself just to be on the safe side. Either way the machine will likely have a message from some spoilsport or other that explains the pitches are unplayable and the player might just as well resign himself to the fact that not only is rugby cancelled, that particular Saturday has gone west also; so, Sunday effectively has now begun.

Andy Irvine and our girls, Kirsten (left) and Sarah

CHAPTER 3

Playing School 1ˢᵗ XV Rugby;
A First Flight; Touring to Ireland;
International Athletics; Melrose Sports Day

George Heriot's School Games master Donald Hastie never actually coached any of the three School 1ˢᵗ XV's that I played in. My coaches in the senior team were two of our PT teachers, Malcolm(Molly) Hunter and Willie Waitt. Both were former pupils of the school.

My first senior XV season, 1963/64, was when Molly Hunter was in charge. We played 22 games, won 7, lost 12 and drew 3. Our pretty dismal record wasn't Malcolm's fault, rather, the team was just too young and inexperienced in practically all positions. The Captain, Bruce Welton, was one of only two players from the previous season who stayed on at school. I was only fifteen and in my third year in the senior school when I was asked to play in the school fifteen. I was so young that my dad was asked to write a letter to the school giving them permission to select me for the firsts. My dad was so chuffed that I had been selected for the top team he wrote the necessary missive with great haste lest the school change its mind.

Molly wasn't helped by the school's Headmaster, William McL. Dewar, who, upset at the performances of the school flagship fifteen and, no doubt, with the best of intentions, began to involve himself with team selection. Willie Waitt got the benefit of that team the next year when we were a bit older and wiser; our game stats were an improvement on the previous year : played 20, won 10, lost 8 and drew 2. Points for 189 and against 134.

In the season of 65/66 Willie Waitt had an even better time with our team. The record was : Played 16, won12 lost 3 drew 1. Points for 246, points against 80.

We also won a number of fairly prestigious sevens tournaments that year, namely our own one at Goldenacre, then Murrayfield, Hillhead in Glasgow and Morpeth in Northumberland. We were beaten finalists at Paisley. The Paisley tournament final where we were playing Paisley Grammar looked like it was ours too as we were a try ahead at what felt like the twentieth minute. There had been no injuries; the referee seemed to be running the second half well beyond the allotted time. It did look as if the ref was playing on until our opponents scored or we killed it off with one more score. We kicked the ball off the park expecting that to be that. But, no the ref called the lineout which we won. We were working our way up to their line but a Paisley lad intercepted a tired pass and we were done for. Paisley scored under the posts, they converted, the ref blew the whistle and that was that. Or rather it wasn't! One of our props, Jimmy Burnett, had to suffer the embarrassment of listening to his mum berating the referee at the prize-giving. What a dressing down that fellow got. Jimmy's Dad was also there and after he had let his wife fire a number of shots across the bows of officialdom he moved in and gently persuaded her that that was enough. I have to say that none of the Heriot teachers present nor the players were quick to stop our Mrs Burnett. I think we all thought that a grave injustice had been done that day. By the way Mrs Burnett, brolly in hand, for years followed whatever team Jimmy was in shouting words of encouragement to Heriot's and the opposition got, well, you can imagine. Jimmy was eventually joined by his brothers Robbie and Harry in the Heriot's FP firsts and their loyal mum was in seventh heaven.

But for the Paisley hiccup we would have had a clean sweep of the major school sevens circuit that year. Our team was Jo Clark, Dave McDougall, Jimmy Burnett, Graham Pettigrew, Derek Lee, Jimmy Craig and myself.

Jimmy Burnett went on to play FP rugby, broke his neck in a 2nd XV game against an Edinburgh University side, recovered after neuro surgery and months of hospitalisation then went on to play for the FP 1st XV, Edinburgh and ultimately for Scotland. His was a remarkable story of determination and courage.

My last two school rugby seasons were periods that gave me such a lot of satisfaction. Not being academic in the least, rugby and, of course, my athletics gave me a great sense of achievement. I think sevens was a favourite of mine, especially our campaign at the end of the fifteens season in 1966. It was easy, you see, because the forwards never failed on our ball and won most of the opposition's ball. Our scrum-half had a long rifle like pass, our stand-off was a great wee general and my centre was simply a bullet from a gun. When we won ball from set pieces it was in my hands before you could say George Heriot. This often meant I had huge long runs if the scrum or lineout was deep in our territory. Nobody in the side could have been described as a slouch; my centre and future FP Rugby Club President, Jimmy Craig and I could break evens for the hundred yards.

Good though that season's seven was, Wullie Waitt had an abundance of reserve talent in the stage wings, many of whom could have been in that team and I think, with the same success. My close friend Fraser McRitchie, who played the previous season on the wing whilst I was at centre, was very unlucky not to have been in the side. He was definitely a much better footballer than me but I guess I had the edge on him for pace and, once the ball was planted firmly in my hands, it was difficult to catch me with the space that there is to run around in on a "sevens pitch"

The year Fraser played in the sevens team I remember vividly the tournament at Morpeth and especially the final. Much was against us in that North East England game. The weather was atrocious which meant handling was very difficult. The ground was a swamp of mud and the refereeing again was strange. That particular tournament was the one and only time in my rugby career when I saw a ref blow for the kicker being out of time with the kick. In an early round we had scored a try and Derek Lee went through exactly the same routine as he always did and was just about to take his run up to convert the try into a goal when the ref called time. Later on in that tie Fraser McRitchie cleverly using the slippery surface to his advantage, dived at a player's ankles to tap tackle him. He was like a torpedo as he dived on to his front, slid furiously and accurately to his target, hit the target and then carried on off the pitch and smacked head first into a brown leather bag that was sitting on the touchline. There was a clunk and a Oooooooyah as Fraser battered into the bag. Leaping to his feet, rubbing a very sore head Fraser opened up the bag and, would you believe it, inside there were four shot puts! Fraser made more than a few unseemly comments.

My stand-off in that sevens team was a fellow called Derek Lee. Derek played stand-off in both sevens and fifteens all the way through school from primary five and was never dropped. Some thirty-five plus years after I left school I met a Herioter who I played against regularly in school practice matches over the years

17

and who, as a very good stand-off, tried his best to oust Derek Lee from his place but never quite managed. This man, however, became one of the most famous and important people in the world of golf. His name is Peter Dawson, secretary to the Royal and Ancient Golf Club. Peter left George Heriot's around the age of thirteen; his dad had taken up an appointment in the south of England but Peter returned to Scotland at the age of fifty to take over the big job at the R&A from Sir Michael Bonallack. Shortly after Peter's R&A appointment I went over to meet him at the Royal and Ancient and we had a great deal of fun reminiscing. Despite Peter's early departure from Heriot's, he remembered very clearly all his old school rugby pals. I was impressed with that, given his very full life after his stint at Heriot's. One of the lads he remembered distinctly was the aforementioned Fraser MacRitchie. Fraser came down to Heriot's at the primary six stage from Dingwall in the Highlands. At the age of nine, he was a huge fellow. A natural ball player with pace, great balance and a very high knee action, Fraser was tough to beat or catch and extremely difficult to tackle head on. Fraser gained a schoolboy cap in a match against the English schools in his last year and, in the early days of his career in the Metropolitan police, he played in their, then, top class 1st XV. Before moving to London, Fraser patrolled the right wing of Heriot's Former Pupils Rugby Club 2nd XV and I looked after the left side of the pitch.

Donald M Hastie, known as DMH, had overall charge of all games at Heriot's school hence his games master title. Throughout the primary and senior school Hastie would continue to influence pupils in all sports but I mostly came across him, so far as rugby was concerned, when the weather was bad and games periods were cancelled. When that happened we would sometimes go to the gym to practice tackling; this exercise was not performed on tackle bags as is the modern practice, but on real live breakable boys. Despite the rubber mats on to which we thought we were being fraudulently lured to perform our tackle drills, it was quite a painful exercise. One could see boys counting their fingers, shaking their rattled heads and rubbing their limbs and joints after "nailing" and being "nailed" on the mats; nailing was a Hastie term meaning a good tackle, for those of you with mucky minds. Suspicious that they had just been at the wrong end of a Hastie shady deal they would sneak over to inspect the quality of the so called fall breaking paraphernalia only to discover that, on picking up a corner of the mat, it was wafer thin and about as much use as an ash tray on a motorbike. It toughened us up a tad though!

On other bad weather days we would repair to the OPLR (old physics lecture room) and watch ancient loop films of rugby players scrummaging and taking part in lineouts. I swear Hastie did that in the hope that we would forget how painful the tackle mat practice was the last time it was wet and, the next rainy day, we would go back to the gym with our bad memories erased. For those of you who don't know, a loop film was exactly that, a film with no end to it, just a constant repetition of its limited and usually very boring content.

To us youngsters, the players in these loop films were hilariously attired. They had muckle great boots with yards of laces wrapped round and round the built in ankle protectors, their shorts looked like they had been tailored, jodhpur-style, out of a heavy absorbent material that resembled remnants of Royal Navy great coats; neck ties were used to hold them up. Whatever was used to suspend these shorts would have had to be strong because, if the shorts were to be worn during a heavy shower of rain, the wearer could easily have doubled in weight. Heaven knows when these loops were filmed and what fashion house it was that sponsored the kit. The latter question is of course a silly one because don't forget we are still in the days when rugby was so amateur the players paid for absolutely everything including all their kit.

My favourite loop film was the one where a pack of very stiff-backed forwards would demonstrate how to collectively dribble the ball forwards. This dribbling was at one time considered to be a great skill and nearly resembled a sort of modern day dynamic ruck but, given the eccentricity of the bounce of the rugby ball, acceleration of the pack of forwards was well-nigh impossible. I suppose the skill was keeping the bobbing and weaving ball going forward as fast as possible, not to mention staying behind the player who was next going to boot the ball on. The dribbling pack of attacking forwards would, therefore, present a nasty battle front for the defending team; the only way the opposition was going to stop this dribbling was for some heroic fool to make a futile gesture by diving on the ball; the result being a kicked in face. The black eye, split lip and busted nose would at least show some lucky girl at the Plaza dance hall that night what a hero he was.

Scottish rugby players were renowned for this skilful forwards' footwork. I remember watching this ploy at Murrayfield in the early fifties the racket from the home support was unbelievable as they shouted "feet Scotland feet" My Mother-in-Law, during a rare phase and, when I think about it, the only phase when she liked me, confessed that, before the Second World War she had a boyfriend who was a Watsonian and who sometimes took her to Murrayfield to watch Scotland. It was a kind of double confession; the first and most important part being that it was with a Watsonian she attended the games; the second part was that she thought for many years that there was a player in the Scottish XV called Feet!

After the loops were finished we would get some sort of story from Hastie. The subjects were varied and included: best sporting behaviour, general health hints, brainwashing reminders of how awful professional sport was and the escapades of famous capped Herioters. On the health subject we would be warned of the dangers of smoking and that was seen by us clean living young lads as a bit beyond the pale, given that our presenter was a roll-up fag and wal-nut- plug-pipe man. He used to say to us that he would give a thou-sand pounds just to know he had healthy lungs. The professional sport remarks always included the sneering jibe about Heart of Midlothian Football Club Limited, sometimes the Hibs got a blast-ing. Rugby players regularly set up as examples to us all were sixties Scottish rugby icons, Kenny Scotland and Eddie McKeating. They were both playing for Scotland in the mid-fifties and the beginning of the sixties and DMH usually found something to say about them that was intended to be inspiring and, of course, it was. They were big time heroes of the whole Heriot community, a community that existed in most parts of the world, and cared greatly about their rugby stars. Kenny Scotland was the Eric Liddell of his time.

When starting or wrapping up a wonderful story about Kenny Scotland, our games master always gave the man his full name, Kenneth James Forbes Scotland; during the story he was referred to as simply KJF. It was quite important to us lads for a proper rugby player to have a decent set of initials, minimum two. D and S were mine and to me they had a certain ring to them; they are very Scottish: Douglas Scott. It was difficult for those of us with great initials to imagine what was running through the minds of parents that stopped short at one Christian name for their son/s. What were these poor guys going to do if they got into the FP 1st XV; the match programmes would publish a team list which would expose his par-ents thoughtless omission.

Having been regaled with so many KJF stories, and hav-ing those fabulous initials stamped in my memory, it didn't take me long after I became secretary and general manager of George

Heriot's FP Rugby Club, some forty years later, to notice that the photograph of Kenny on the club's caps gallery had his name down as K F J Scotland. It had been like that for over forty years and not even Kenny had noticed!

Senior schoolboy rugby was a simple game with a simple formula: forwards win the ball as quickly as possible from lineout or scrum, get it out to the backs immediately, backs pass the ball along the line to the winger who scores a try. Yes, school rugby was simplistic but good fun, especially if you were in the backs and even more especially if you were a winger. My school 1stXV had some excellent fixtures, mostly in the central belt area but sometimes we went on great adventures to what we thought were far off romantic places such as Aberdeen, where we played Robert Gordon's College, Dollar, the home of Dollar Academy and Dublin where we had a whale of a time on, and off, the pitch with the Belvedere College boys. Our annual encounters with Belvedere were home and away fixtures. Belvedere came to Edinburgh around the October mid-term break and we travelled to Dublin between Christmas and New Year. The Belvedere lads had, what I thought to be a very tame time in Presbyterian Edinburgh, but Dublin for me was completely wild. I was there three times and it just got better each time. Belvedere College have many famous former pupils. Two will be familiar to most readers, namely Tony O'Rielly, the famous Irish and British Lions winger, and Terry Wogan, the television and radio broadcaster.

The first time I was selected to play in this overseas fixture was December 1963. Our method of transport was to be by air. It would be my first commercial airline flight. It was not however my first venture into the skies.

In the summer of 1962 as a cadet in my school's Combined Cadet Force, I had flown with the Edinburgh University Air Squadron in a single engined monoplane called a de Haviland Chipmunk.

A chipmunk was effectively a Tiger Moth without one pair of wings. The experience was a complete nightmare and I decided, there and then, that flying was strictly for the birds.

Thinking back on it I suppose it could be seen as quite comical but at the time it was very far from being funny. The Combined Cadet Force was structured in such a way that it gave schoolboys the opportunity to experience a year in the army section. Then a cadet could either stay in the army section or transfer to the RAF or the Royal Navy sections. The overall purpose of the CCF was to teach young lads how to be independent and how to lead men in later life, either as an officer in Her Majesty's Armed Forces or, indeed, in any other environment that needed well-organised decision makers. Joining the CCF was not compulsory at my school but the headmaster, in his annual recruiting drive, suggested that any future university applicant would be looked upon favourably if his school CV showed membership of the CCF. I suppose the initial year in the army section was meant to cover the basic square-bashing and instil the various elements of discipline, map reading, weapon handling and so on. During that year small tasters of the other services were provided in order to help a young lad make up his mind about what branch of the CCF he would prefer to join. Flying with the Edinburgh University Air Squadron sounded very exciting to a number of us young army cadets and so, as green unsuspecting fools, we duly signed up for a morning flight. Some of us were to become sadder and much wiser cadets after the event.

Arriving at RAF Turnhouse fresh-faced, innocent and eager, we disembarked the big truck that had taken us from the Edinburgh University Air Squadron's HQ just around the corner from Heriot's school. An RAF officer briefed us on what was going to happen which included the flight plan, how to put on our parachutes, helmets and how to climb into the aircraft. I hadn't realised that the parachute, once strapped tightly to my body, would leave me in the shape of a dining room chair. Suitably togged up, my pilot and I, resembling drunks with severe back problems, staggered out to the chipmunk. Climbing on to the reinforced part of the wing with some difficulty, given that I was severely hampered with my chute, I made my way along the wing and into the front part of the cockpit. I thought it a bit illogical and scary that the pilot was to sit aft of me. Suitably strapped in, the next step was for the pilot to talk to flight control and get permission to take off. My imagination by this time was in full Reach for the Sky and Dambusters mode, various epic film music scores were running through my head and, just as I was imagining myself as Guy Gibson, Da da da dum diddy dum dum da da da dum diddy dum dum, permission was granted for us to take off.

'Hold on old boy,' said my pilot as we tottered down the runway and eventually started to climb unsteadily up into the Midlothian sky. What an odd sensation followed. The de Haviland Chipmunk is a fairly light machine and for every three feet we climbed we seemed to drop two feet. It was as if we were being lifted up by a giant pair of very elastic braces, a perpetual bunji jump with no end scheduled. Chipmunks flew at heights way below a modern airliner and so we felt every bit of turbulence going. After finishing our climb, and about ten minutes or so into the flight, the pilot said to me, 'Cadet Bruce, would you like to do some aerobatics?'

Squeakily I replied 'Sir I thought that that was what we had been doing for the last ten minutes!'

'Oh no no no Bruce, come on old chap, how about it?' he taunted.

The romance of the occasion was fast bleeding away and I replied: 'Eh, no thanks sir, maybe the next time'

'Oh well then Bruce would you like to take the controls?'

'Whaaaaaaat was that sir?'

'I said would you like to fly the kite?' replied the determined flyer.

'Oh well sir if you think it will be safe.'

A very brief explanation was given to me as to what the foot pedals and the joystick did. Given that I thought that I had my life and the pilot's life in my hands plus the lives of a large chunk of the central belt's population not to mention a few thousand quids worth of plane at my mercy, I listened very attentively to the instructions.

"Tally Ho!" and off I flew. What an amazing feeling it was. I was just getting the hang of it when the skipper shouted,

'There is a lot of cloud ahead keep her level and straight.'

I was so disorientated I pleaded with the skipper to take over as I was terrified we were going to hit the Forth Bridge or plunge into the Forth itself, or worse still, end up in Glasgow!! Anyway we got over all that and flew down to the west of Grangemouth, crossed the Forth and came back along the coast of the Kingdom of Fife. We crossed back again from somewhere around Kirkcaldy and headed for home. Now feeling quite Douglas Baderish and smug about the whole affair as we headed for Corstorphine Hill, I was looking forward to regaling all my non-Cadet Force chums with Biggles-like daring-do tales.

'So sorry old chap,' rang in my ear. 'Can't land for the mo, a British European Airways Viscount bound for the smoke is getting ready for take-off, so we will just circle the Corstorphine Hill until the civvie gets out of our bally way. Please keep radio silence meantime, my good fellow.'

Round and round we went. There was a landmark radio mast top-dead centre of the hill which was affecting me as if it were a hypnotist saying "look into my eyes." We were so close to the ground I was initially distracted by the animals in the Zoo at Corstorphine.

But eventually, as we seemed to be flying faster and faster in ever decreasing circles round the mast, I had to break radio silence.

'Sorry sir I am getting really dizzy and I am going to be sick.'

Whilst grabbing a brown paper bag designed for such occasions up came the massive breakfast my mother had told me I would have to have if I was going flying. How she knew that I'll never know as my mum, to my certain knowledge, had never been in an aircraft.

Thankfully we soon got the all clear and down we came.'Well did you enjoy that Bruce?' enquired the pilot.

'Oh yes sir.' I lied unconvincingly and, was just about to shamble back to the hut where I had been issued with my parachute, when I saw "Cadet I-Wish-I-Had-Never-Been-Born" climbing rather awkwardly off his chipmunk. Looking desperately miserable and covered in sick, he was carrying, with great difficulty, a bunch of sick bags to my single which made me feel instantly better. I waited until he waddled up to me before I asked him what on earth had happened.

'Well,' he burped. 'I was getting on fine until my pilot decided to do some aerobatics over Kirkcaldy. Suddenly we were upside down and I vomited all over the canopy. When we returned to the upright position, meals I recognised from months back cascaded all over me. That prompted a constant filling of bags.'

Poor bugger, I thought. I believe Cadet-I-Wish-I-Had-Never-Been-Born opted to stick with the foot soldiers. I went on to the Navy section and vowed never to fly again.

All of this flying malarkey took place before lunch which, understandably, I did not feel up to eating, but, worse still, I had to run a couple of heats in the afternoon for my school games championships. What a preparation for such an important day in my athletics career. I went home first after being dropped off by the RAF truck and explained to my flying expert mother that I had been terribly sick.

'Here son,' she said handing me a large brandy. 'That will sort out your unsettled tummy.'

It did help. I turned up in a very merry state for my heats which, incidentally, I won handsomely. Thinking back on it now, it's just as well there wasn't any dope testing in those days. I wonder, after this confession, if I will have to hand back my medals.

To be picked to play for my school in a foreign land was so important to me I relegated my previous flying experience to the back of my mind. The arrangements for accommodation were reciprocal; some boys stayed with my family during the Irish guys visit to Edinburgh and I stayed with one of their families in return. So, having already met the Irish lads and shown them what Edinburgh was all about, it was our turn to experience the delights of a rugby tour in a foreign city, Dublin. My father, like my mother, was from Earlsferry, the magical East Neuk of Fife village. My dad was filled with gallons of that fabulously acid sarcasm that is common to all Fifers. When I asked him if he would pay for my trip to Dublin he asked me if I would like to take a friend whilst I was at it. The remark, whilst Fife tongue in cheek, was made nevertheless, just so that I would not take such a special trip for granted.

Dublin here we come.

There was an air of tense anticipation as we boarded the Aer Lingus Fokker Friendship at Edinburgh Turnhouse Airport minus parachutes this time. After settling into our seats a stewardess came round with a tray of lemon drops. The sweets were supposed to relieve the pressure that seems to build up in your ears. In any event it was the only food we were to get on the flight. I don't think there was much time for a meal anyway as we were hardly up in the air when we were down again.

Of my three trips to the fair City the first,1963, was the most enlightening; I suppose that's logical but I was so ignorant of the politics and culture of the Republic of Ireland that, to get me up to speed was quite a task for my hosts. I have no doubt that the parents of the boy I was staying with had many a chuckle at some of the remarks I made and the questions I asked.

I thought Dublin was a curious capital. In retrospect, it was just like a city in one of those parallel universes that cropped up from time to time on Star Trek, that wonderful television series about space travel which was broadcast in the latter half of the sixties. In Dublin, people, places, and time seemed, at first, quite normal, until I had a chance to take a closer look. The people seemed quite parochial for a major city. Everybody talked to everybody unlike the citizens of cold Edinburgh. The Roman Catholic religion dominated. I had never really noticed religion, any religion out with a church building. In Dublin it manifested itself in all sorts of ways, but a few features really stuck out : the streets were full of priests either walking or cycling; the passengers on buses shook every time they passed a church, this was caused by the passengers crossing themselves in unison.

The buses looked absolutely ancient and smaller than Edinburgh Corporation buses. Clothing fashions for both men and women seemed about ten years behind the UK and the cafes, whilst cosy and very hospitable, had a look about them that was, in my imagination, pre World War Two; nothing like the new coffee bars in Edinburgh such as the "New Yorker". There were beggars in the street, something unheard of back home then. The beggars I saw in Dublin in the early part of the sixties were seriously poor looking souls, dressed in rags, shoeless and dirty. They could be seen begging as families.

Our trip to Dublin started on the 27th December. So far as I was concerned Christmas was well and truly over, but when I arrived at my host's house for the first time on my very first Dublin tour,

I discovered that it was still going on with them. I remember the house where I was billeted, as it were, had a huge kitchen with work tops still groaning with turkey, hams and all sorts of goodies. I had never seen the like and I suppose that was because I had come from a very Presbyterian household to that of a very Roman Catholic domain. Frankly, I didn't really know the difference between the two faiths. What I did find out was that Irish Catholics made a point of going to church on Sundays and my hosts were no exception. They also thought I was as religiously devout as they were so they insisted upon taking me to a Presbyterian church in Dublin. I would have thought that such places of worship would be as scarce as hens' teeth but no, there were some and I was taken to the very biggest. To me, at that age, it was the only time I had ever been to church on my own. It was a surreal experience . I tried very hard to hide at the back and at the end of a pew so I could make a break for it once everybody was praying, and find a café nearby; but, the Irish being the Irish, whether Catholic or Presbyterian, are very friendly. A small group, realising I was a stranger amongst them, went out of their way to make me feel welcome and so I found myself stuck in a pew down near the minister. So that was that, an hour or so cleansing my soul whether it needed it or not. The one big advantage Dublin had over Edinburgh was after the main morning mass everywhere was open, by that I mean cafes and pubs.

After the church experience my host met up with me and started to show me around. In addition to the various pubs and dance halls he and some of his team mates took me to a number of places of historical interest in Dublin; none more so than the Dublin General Post Office. This particular building is famous but not for any postal reason. The GPO achieved its fame, or notoriety, for being the base of the Easter Rising which occurred on Easter Monday, April the 24th 1916. The aim of the uprising was to achieve political freedom from British rule. A man called Padraic Pearse seized control of the General Post Office in Dublin and from the steps of that building he announced the establishment of a provisional government of the Irish Republic. Bitter fighting followed between the Republicans and the British forces but by the 29th April, Pearse had to surrender. My host's interest in the location of this famous uprising was certainly sincere but the historical implications played second fiddle to the attention they drew to the marksmanship of both sides. Amazingly accurate but erotic shooting was evidenced by neat bullet holes through what were once the nipples of maidens on a large statue in front of the GPO!

Later, during that trip to Dublin I decided to send some postcards home. I needed some stamps and so I popped into what we would call a Crown Post Office i.e. a big one. This building was quite long and wide. It had a large U-shaped counter which supported little booths that had no identification on them so far as I could see. Each booth was shut. My Dublin friends told me to knock on any one of the booth doors and someone would come and attend to me.

I walked up to the first booth on the left . Knock, knock, there was no buzzer.

A little lady opened up her wee doors.

'Well now, hello there, I'm Mary and how are you, what can I do for you today?'

'Oh, my name's Douglas and I'm fine Mary, could I please have some stamps for my postcards which I want to send to Scotland.'

'Well you see Douglas, you've come to the wrong person,' she explained 'You'll have to go to the middle booth at the very bottom end of the office and the assistant who's up there will help you.'

'Oh, ok then, thank you Mary.'

Watched by my pals I strode off to where I had been directed. I knocked on the relevant wee door and it was some time before

I heard movement from behind the barrier. It sounded as if a lot of ledgers and other stationery were being cleared out of the way. Silence for a bit, then, suddenly, the doors opened to reveal the same little lady who I had just spoken to at the earlier booth!

'Well now, hello I'm Mary, how are you, what can I do for you today?'

I was beginning to think that I was on the set of a Laurel and Hardy film. Perhaps the lady was an ancestor of Mrs Doyle from the TV series Father Ted. Politely I asked again for my stamps, Mary smiled sweetly and rewarded me both with stamps and change from my one punt note.

One very important feature that I could not compare with Edinburgh was the Dublin pubs.

My first visit to the Irish capital coincided with my introduction to public houses. Oh I forgot! That is apart from a diversion from my Scouting 1st class badge hike in Selkirk.... I have to say all of the Dublin city- centre pubs were extremely lively with folk musicians and stout drinkers. By stout I don't mean fat drinkers but those fellows who drank Guinness, Murphy's and other variations of the theme. There was a most amazing etiquette in the Dublin pubs that was strictly adhered to whenever performers struck up. No one dared talk, shuffle feet, sneeze, break wind, blow their noses or do anything that might distract the artistes or the audience. Breathing had to be muffled and, tough-luck if you were asthmatic, no pubs for you; the atmosphere in the pubs was thick with cigarette smoke.

Being in such a different country and culture, I couldn't help but ask questions of my hosts, such as "Are these guys in army uniforms the IRA?" and, "Why is there a Nelson's column right in the centre of Dublin?" The first question was met with stifled laughter coupled with "Can ye please tell yore man to keep his voice down." The second was answered with, "Ye know we wonder about that too."

The IRA must also have wondered why such a symbol of English Imperialism featured so obviously in the Republic's capital; it really must have annoyed them because they dynamited it off the face of the earth in 1966. I have often wondered if poor old Horatio had gone honourably upwards into orbit like a rocket or had he just collapsed ignominiously into a heap of rubble on the street.

Our encounter with the Belvedere lads on the park was not exactly a game that one would have written home about but, nonetheless, we won.

I remember putting in a cross kick from the right wing and Murray Wylie our tight head prop and pack leader running on to it catching it in the air and then sprinted over the line for a try. I had never had a cross kick gathered like that and had a score off it. I was very pleased with that piece of work.

We had a most enjoyable dinner at Belvedere College after the game. I remember Donald Hastie, who had travelled with us, made a speech which included a thanks to the Belvedere people for their wonderful hospitality and an apology that his wife had been unable to accompany him as her sinuses had blown up, as he put it. We all had visions of the poor Mrs Hastie minding her own business and suddenly her face explodes, synovial fluid everywhere! The following day we flew out of Dublin and back to Edinburgh. I think my Dad felt that he had had his money's worth.

The December 1964 tour was blighted by bad weather. Sadly, the pitch we were due to play on froze over causing the match to be cancelled. We played tip (touch) rugby instead. Returning to Edinburgh, the weather having thwarted our last game of that year, we eagerly looked forward to the next trip.

The remainder of our domestic campaign was still in front of us and a game that sticks out for me was, what I think was probably the last game of that season, when we played Glenalmond School near Gleneagles in Perthshire. This fixture turned out to be quite daunting and, unusually for us, it was played on a Saturday afternoon. The daunt, so to speak, for me was John Frame, not much later to play for Gala and Scotland. He was already well known to us as a big dangerous centre but I had high hopes that he had already left school.

Our coach pulled into the school grounds and we disembarked to a big welcome from the Glenalmond school pupils. Of course being a boarding school all their boys were available to shout encouragement for "School".

They were also all there in the dining room where we had lunch with our opposition for the afternoon. To be honest, I was allowing the thought of this huge man, Frame, spoil my lunch which consisted of an ice cream scoop of mashed potatoes and a couple of slices of spam garnished with some peas. I was sitting next to our captain Colin "Mugs" Malcolm and asked him if he knew if there was any truth behind the rumour that Frame had left school already. Mugs turned to this massive bloke sitting beside him and asked him if John Frame had left school. This monster of a fellow had just opened his huge face and stuffed an entire slice of spam into it. After a couple of quick chews the spam was gone and he turned to Mugs and said in a loud bear like growl 'I'M FRAME!'

"Gulp" went I, and taking one look at my lunch I shoved it away and started praying.

After some welcoming speeches from the Glenalmond games master and others we filed out of the dining room and headed for the dressing rooms. Mugs was doing his best to boost morale as we changed; we went through the usual good luck routines before leaving the dressing room for what seemed like a fairly long trot up to the pitch which was built up on a plateau. Up we climbed on to the playing surface to be greeted with a rousing cheer from "School".

If that was unnerving, what was to come next put the tin lid on it. Stretcher bearers appeared with two stretchers and laid them out by the side of the pitch. The only other time I had seen a stretcher was in an ancient Hollywood movie based on the book "All Quiet on the Western Front".

"Gulp" again, and a further gulp, as the "School" team appeared amidst a hell of a racket from their support. The only relief I got was when I found out, as we took our positions on the field, that John Frame was to be marked by our other centre that day. But I had to cope with an equally big lad whose name I never found out. We won the game and I was so relieved when the final whistle went. I had never been so knackered in a fifteens game in my life thanks to the tackling we had to put in that day.

Back to touring.

My last tour to Dublin was in December 1965. This tour had anti- English connotations which managed to sail right over my head. A group of our Irish pals together with some of us Scots lads were crossing, I think, the O'Connell bridge when we were regaled by a fellow who was carrying a big board which had written upon it "Stay away Margaret" .

When I first saw the sign it crossed my mind that this fellow was going to extraordinary lengths to keep his wife or girlfriend away, however it wasn't anything so close to home for the protestor. In the early days of June 1963 Princess Margaret and The Earl of Snowdon made a visit to Northern Ireland and some Republican citizens really didn't want her there. The Princess made nine visits altogether to Northern Ireland between 1947 and 1996. Perhaps our slogan carrying Republican thought another tour was imminent.

My team mates and I were not particularly bothered one way or the other about this mono protest. However, our hosts had some local chums with them who were apparently embarrassed by the protestor. Relieving him of his offensive board they grabbed him by the ankles and made to hang him over the parapet of the bridge, demanding as they did so, that he apologise for the demonstration in front of such important guests of the country. The poor fellow begged to be brought back to the safety of the pavement. There was no way back until he shouted his apologies. Shout them he did in fairly quick time.

A few years later, that Liffey bridge incident became something more than just a tour story. My brother-in-law to be, come 1966, one Flt. Lieutenant Derek Sinclair McCracken had been the Princess Margaret's aide-de-camp for her 1963 visit to Northern Ireland. Thank goodness I didn't know him at the time and, crucially, neither did my Irish hosts otherwise the relationship might have turned a rugby prank into a diplomatic crisis, and the Liffey into a bath for the Anti-Royalist.

My 1965 trip to the republic was marred by the October visit to Heriot's by the Irish boys. During the match I was at the end of a thumping good tackle by a Belvedere lad and, falling awkwardly, I twisted my knee and that caused a lot of ligament damage. I did not recover before the return match in Dublin but my rugby master Willie Waitt allowed me to travel with the team as touch judge.

I was becoming a bit of an old hand at this particular tour and Dublin was by now familiar territory. Running the line however was not something that I had had any experience of but, although it is an important job, it is simple enough; at least I thought it was. Including International sides, all teams back in the sixties and all the preceding years provided their own touch judge. The Laws of the game of rugby required the referee to be independent but not the second officials. Touch judges were expected to be honest about their decisions.

Being a school holiday my touchline sojourn was in front of a few rugby masters, some press men, the players themselves and, of course, the referee. Belvedere College honoured the Heriot lads by inviting the Irish International referee Kevin Kelleher to officiate. Kelleher was to become famous for sending off Colin (Pine Tree) Meads in a test match at Murrayfield when the All Blacks toured the UK in 1967. There was a huge crowd at Murrayfield to witness Meads rushing out from a maul trying to charge down a Davie Chisholm touch kick; Chisholm dummied the kick and then tried to side step Meads who was hopelessly beaten but he stuck his leg out and kicked or tripped Chisholm; Kelleher sent him off amidst roars from the crowd imploring him so to do. Full attention was being paid by the braying masses to the unsporting incident on the pitch; it was high drama at the time and hilariously punctuated by my brother- in-law (remember- Princess Margaret's aide) exclaiming loudly that he was terribly sorry for something. I wondered what? As Meads was leaving the field in front of an enraged Scottish crowd my brother in law, in the excitement, had accidentally kicked a shooting stick from underneath a fairly portly spectator. Succumbing to gravity, said heavy weight plunged to the deck as if he had been shot at point blank range. The poor fellow was, in one minute, along with thousands of ranting Scots, demanding the expulsion of Meads, and the next, scrambling about amongst the feet of the lynch mob, dazed and wondering what on earth had happened to him.

Back to that match at Belvedere:

The score was even shortly before full time; after an exchange of tries in the last few minutes, the match would remain drawn if the Heriot kicker could not make the conversion. Derek Lee, the Heriot marksman, lined the ball up to the right of the posts but picked his spot quite far back to reduce the angle. There was a following wind.

Taking a shortish run up he stroked the ball beautifully; it looked good as it soared onwards and upwards. Referee Kelleher took his lead from the Belvedere touch judge who lifted his flag too early indicating a successful kick, but I noticed the ball fade at the last second thanks, possibly, to a gust of wind and it drifted past the right-hand post. I waived my flag to show no goal. Kelleher and the teams had all seen the Belvedere touch judge, but not me. The whistle had been blown to signal a successful conversion and blown again for no side. Some touchline support tried to draw the ref's attention to me and my no conversion flag waving but it was to no avail. Heriot's won the match and it was official. My team mates gave me a tough time after the match but, more importantly, I was summoned to the referees room where Kevin Kelleher asked me what made me want to disallow the kick. I had to tell him that everyone, including himself, had not waited to see the whole journey of the ball and that it had faded at the last moment drifting wide of the post, albeit only marginally.

The next day to my embarrassment and no doubt Kevin Kelleher's, the incident made it to a corner of the front page of the Irish Times. Thankfully we were off to Blighty that afternoon.

After saying farewell to our wild Irish friends, for me the last time, we returned courtesy of Aer Lingus to the old Turnhouse airport and on to welcoming in 1966 and the start of the countdown to my school-leaving celebrations. I didn't much care for the classwork part of my time at George Heriot's school, just ask any of my academic teachers; well you can't because by now they have probably all gone to the classrooms in the sky. I did, however, love the sports bits. So what was there to look forward to? Well, I hoped that my knee would fully heal up soon and if it did there was the remainder of the rugby term to catch up on and, at worst, I would at least make the sevens team. Then there was the athletics to look forward to.

As it turned out my knee eased up quite a bit and fairly quickly. It never completely recovered as it probably needed surgery then and, for whatever reason, nothing more permanent was done at that time. Anyway, I got my place back at centre. The wings were two very talented lads namely Derek Gartshore and my pal Fraser MacRitchie. Derek was not the fastest of wings but he had wonderful footballing skills and a great talent for avoiding tackles. Derek had also been a member of the Scottish Schoolboys International Athletics side in the previous summer of 1965. Derek high- jumped and I ran in the 100 yards and the 4x 110 yards relay. There were seven Heriot schoolboys in the National athletic squad that year. The event took place at a stadium in Brighton and all the teams stayed in Ovingdean Hall, a boarding school nearby. I did not have much success on the track and I think the team as a whole was well beaten especially by the English contingency. Obviously, the schools down south had a much bigger choice of athletes and, so far as I could tell, English school leavers were a year older than us Scots so there were more mature English athletes in a number of events. Barbara Inkpen, a famous senior English high jumper, still at school, was competing that day. Three years later she was competing for Great Britain in the Olympics and won gold in the Commonwealth games in 1978. At the time of this schools international she had probably just finished her final term. I had never seen such a tall slender, graceful girl.

Speaking of maturity or rather the lack of it, one Scottish field events competitor had been watching some girls competing in the female version of his event. After they finished he persuaded them to come and watch him. A number of the boys, including me, were aware of this lad's advances towards the girls and thought that it would be a good idea to watch proceedings from the embankment above the throwing net. His female audience was down near the event. It was time for our colleague to throw. With great aplomb he stood up in front of the girls to remove his track suit. First off came the top. Flamboyantly, and as though he were a male stripper, he cast it aside then slowly he turned to his track suit bottoms; suddenly a shout came up from one of the judges for our man to get a flaming move on. He was a bit startled at this and hurriedly pulled down his track suit bottoms. Hysteria followed as the poor guy, now flustered, managed to not only pull down the track suit but his shorts and indeed jock strap went south with them. I expect he has never forgotten that moment and neither, clearly, have I!

The 65/66 rugby season for me was crowned by the sevens tournaments that we won and which I have already covered. It could easily have been topped if it had not been for George Heriot's School protocol.

I had travelled down to the Melrose Sevens with Derek, my brother-in- law to be. The Heriots FP seven was doing quite well having got to the third round. The second round had been a difficult one and, because of injury, they were short in the backs. They could only put another forward from their squad into the side for the next round but had learned that I was in the crowd. They found me and asked me if I would play. Of course I said I would but the school would possibly have something to say about it all.

'We will check,' said the committee man. They checked, how I don't know; it was a resounding NO. The team lost the tie and I lost a wonderful opportunity to play in the most famous sevens tournament in the world.

Just prior to the Heriot team being knocked out of the tournament, Gala had suffered a similar fate to Hawick. This state of affairs was irrelevant to us, or so we thought as my brother-in-law, me and other Heriot supporters made their way to a pub for a whistle-wetting before the final of the tournament. If it was against the school rules for me to play in FP rugby matches it was certainly against the rules for me to be drinking in a pub. Och, what the hell. Derek was first into the pub followed by a Gala supporter. Mike Hutton, one of the FP 1ST XV props and I followed but just as we were squeezing into the packed pub, a Hawick man spotted the Gala fellow coming in and made an innocent, but unknown to him, very stupid, enquiry of the Gala man:

'Hoo did Gally get on in the last round?'

Whoosh! The Gala man thinking the Hawick man was taking the proverbial made to hit the Hawick questioner a punch but Derek got in the way. He saw the punch coming, ducked, but still caught it on the shoulder. Down he went under the feet of the two borderers who were by now in a fury of exchanged punches. Some others took sides and joined in. Mike Hutton and I were in the thick of it when Mike shouted sarcastically to Derek, who was helplessly stuck fast on the ground,

'Come on Derek, why are you not getting torn in?'

Derek gave a great reply, 'I am waiting to see who is winning!'

'Here's the Polis comin doon the road!' shouted someone. He was probably taking bets on the outcome, but was also looking out the door for such a lawful appearance. Apart from the main protagonists we all scattered about the pub and acted innocently. Even Derek managed to scramble to his feet. The fighters continued exchanging blows when the local bobby strode in and, without breaking his stride, kicked the Gala chappy up the bum. As he fell out the way our man in blue delivered a similar kick but this time the recipient got it in his marriage tackle as the Royal Navy would say.

'Right, ootside the pair oh ye,' commanded the constable. He gave them a huge dressing down and told them to leave Melrose immediately and if he saw them again in the town that day he would arrest them. Off they went and we in the pub carried on. It was a great fight though!

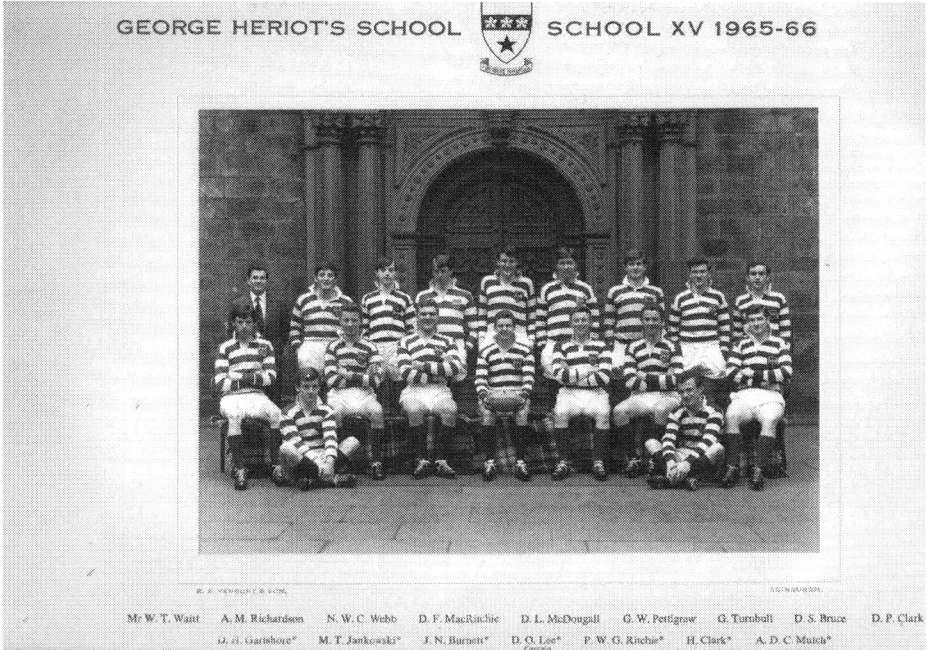

Heriot's School 1st. XV Season 1965/66
Back Row, Left to Right: Mr W T Waitt, A M Richardson, N W C Webb, D F
MacRitchie, D L McDougall, G W Pettigrew, G J Turnbull, D S Bruce, D P Clark
Sitting: D H Gartshore, J Ingles, M Jankowski, J N Burnett, D O
Lee (Capt.), P W G Ritchie, H Clark, J A B Craig, A D C Mutch

CHAPTER 4

Sundays

For my part, a Sunday has always been a kind of surreal day; a limbo day. As a young boy every Sunday seemed to be exactly the same. Little in the way of regulated sport was allowed on the Sabbath, certainly no rugby was permitted by the SRU. They were always dreich days even if the sun shone. In the fifties my Sabbath would kick off with a riveting session at Sunday school followed by lunch whilst listening to the wireless broadcasting the news incorporating the weather forecast and the shipping forecast, with particular worries about North Utsire, South Utsire and Viking. The main worry for me, and I suspect most folks was, where the devil were these places and what awful weather they always seemed to be enduring. Those announcements were then hotly pursued by the Two-Way Family Favourites show with the conscripts in BFPO Germany. Then, the wireless switched off, came the final Dad bonus:

'Because it is now bucketing with rain son, let's go and spend a couple of hours in the museum in Chambers Street or the National Library on George the 1V Bridge' .

On such Sundays my father, ex RAF Bomber Command (ground crew) during Hitler's war, always took me to the exhibit of a working model, in section, of a Merlin engine, the power unit of a Lancaster bomber and the Spitfire. By the time I was about nine or ten I could have stripped the thing down and put it back together again blindfolded, or even better, flown a Lanc and bombed the museum. I just couldn't wait for the school week to start and to get out on to the rugby pitch.

It was fifteen years later when I was twenty-five that I realised the significance of those Merlin visits. The Nazi's war had probably left a mental scar with my Dad as it must have done to many of the dads of my wee rugby pals. Two years after retiring, my Dad died of kidney cancer. He spent his last few moments, my Mum at his side, counting in the Lancs from some hellish raid or other; F Fox, V Victor, B Baker and so on. I guess it troubled him whether a Lanc was lost with all its crew thanks to German flak or the failure of an engine because an important check had possibly been missed or completed incorrectly. This counting in story was to crop up thirty plus years later when I became Heriot's Rugby Club manager.

As I reflect upon those childhood days when I was not supposed to have a care in the world, Sunday being a rugby free day seemed to me to be repetitious, mildly religious and often boring, but, looking back, I realise my dad spent precious time with me. I do recall some experiences with my Dad that I can now have a chuckle at. When the weather was ok, Dad sometimes took me to Granton harbour to check out the huge trawler fleet that was based there; I loved that. In the early fifties all the trawlers were coal-fired steam-driven craft. Believe it or not, it was quite an interesting experience to see these filthy, rusty, but at the same time, quite graceful looking boats lining up to load on tons and tons of coal. An enormous tube protruding from what was a very surreal giant-sized refrigerator then injected ice into another hold on each trawler. The trawlers would be at sea for ten days to a fortnight, perhaps even longer, so their catches had to be kept as fresh as possible.

Sometimes we would go to either Granton harbour or Leith docks to meet up with Jimmy Barclay, an old Waid Academy school pal of my Dad's who was a very successful trawl skipper with a company called Croan. Jimmy would radio a message from, say, somewhere off the Faroe Islands to Croan's office in Edinburgh, asking them to advise Dad that he would be docking at whatever harbour at 2pm on such and such a Sunday. I loved that kind of afternoon and I thought that being a trawler skipper would be an ideal job for me when I left school. I did wonder however how I would be able to fit in rugby and athletics if I was going to be away at sea for a few weeks at a time.

Kids often have these romantic ideas about what they want to be after leaving school. For many it was a train driver, a pilot or something similar; for me it was off to sea commanding a Croan's trawler like Jimmy Barclay. I was soon to be disillusioned big time.

One Sunday afternoon Dad and I took a bus down to Leith docks and went aboard Jimmy Barclay's trawler which, coincidentally, was called "The Bruce". I had been aboard trawlers before and they had an amazing blend of smells: fish, obviously, then, coal, hot oil, seriously stale sweat, cigarette smoke, salty sea and tarry rope. We got the usual warm welcome from Jimmy who made full use of the east Fife dialect. My Dad often slipped into that mode when in the company of his fellow Fifers and I just loved to hear it. Jimmy took us up to the bridge. Normally our visit was a short one as our host was usually keen to catch a train to Anstruther where he lived but, on this occasion, he asked us if we would like a mug o' tea and a biscuit whilst he showed us his new technology for finding fish. 'Yes that would be great' we both replied with excited anticipation.

Jimmy took a hold of a tube with an attached whistle. He blew loudly on the whistle down to the galley and then shouted down the tube to a person he called Wullie.

'Yes skipper,' replied Wullie.

'Three mugs o' tea and a puckle biscuits.'

'Aye, aye skipper, comin' up.'

As Dad and I took turns to look through a tube like instrument we could see a circular screen which showed images in the water under the boat. It reminded me of the X-ray machine in Allan's shoe shop, kids department, in Edinburgh's Princes Street. Not fully appreciating the dangers of X-rays mums were quite happy for us kids to regularly stick our feet under this Flash Gordon like wonder machine. It let the mums and the sales person get a good view of how much space our feet had in our prospective new shoes. Jimmy explained that his machine worked on the same principle as sonar which was developed during the 2nd World War by the Royal Navy to track down German U-boats. If we had been at sea and if there were any shoals of fish around they would show up quite clearly. Jimmy would order his crew to let out the trawl net and catch them. That of course was the fine tuning. A skilled skipper would firstly have to find the general area of sea that contained fish.

During this wee scientific tutorial a loud cough at the open bridge door signalled the arrival of the tea.

'Come in Wullie.'

In lumbered the biggest man I had ever seen holding three huge mugs of tea full to the brim with the fingers of one hand and some biscuits in the other. This was a guy that should never be allowed near the sonar I thought, for fear that the fish might see him and scatter to the four corners of the globe. Wullie looked just like Bluto from the Popeye cartoon series. Wullie's hands were massive and, if he ever clutched a water melon, his digits would have made it look like an apple. That was the good bits. Wullie had a lantern face, the jaws of which held, loosely, some very bad teeth with a few missing in the front; he clearly hadn't shaved for many days and obviously used a whole bucket of grease from the engine room to tamp down his massive mop of hair. He also smelt of a giant mouldering haddock that had BO and bad breath!

'Thank you Wullie,' said Jimmy and off Wullie went back down the gangway to his galley. Jimmy Barclay had already made it clear that I was to ask as many questions as I liked about trawling as my Dad had told him I wanted to be a skipper when I was older. Completely mesmerised by the giant of a man that had just brought the tea to us I had to ask a question about him.

'Mr Barclay, does Wullie the cook always bring you a mug of tea that is full to the brim like the ones he has just brought to us today?'

'Oh aye,' said the skipper, 'richt to the tap o the mug.'

'Does he manage to do it when there is a gale on and a heavy sea?'

'Oh aye, in aw weathers the foo mug comes up frae the galley.'

Uneasy, I asked how it was possible for him to get the mug full of tea up the gangway without spilling a drop. I glanced to my left and spotted a concerned look on my Dad's face.

'Ye ken,' said Jimmy 'I wondered aboot that tae and, one day efter I asked Wullie for a mug, I had a wee sly like keek oot the door and doon at the fit o the gangway I saw Wullie tak a big slurp o tea oot ma mug. I quickly shut the door and waited ahin it. Just afore the knock I heard Wullie spit oot the moothfoo ai tea back intae the mug.'

At this point my Dad and I looked at each other and were nearly sick all over the bridge.

On a less nauseating note, quite often in the summer months my Dad used to take me golfing on Sundays after church. My Dad, being a Fifer, was born a very good golfer. He wasn't a big hitter but had all the other shots. He could fade or draw at the drop of a hat- it was all too easy for him and a joy for me to watch and learn. Dad was a member of Bruntsfield Links Golfing Society which is a beautiful golf course near Cramond in Edinburgh. Summer Sundays there were usually quiet and we had little difficulty with tee times. It seemed to me that on most Sunday afternoons we ended up playing with a gentleman called James Letham. Mr Letham and Dad were both elders in St Serf's Church in the Edinburgh district of Trinity. My Dad, although a senior official of the then National Commercial Bank of Scotland, was outranked by Mr Letham who was the treasurer of the Bank of Scotland. Although they were fellow elders in the same kirk, and friends, so far as I know, they did not socialise together other than on the golf course. Actually both my Dad and James Letham probably worked so hard and long that they had little time to do the kind of socialising that goes on nowadays! So, why was it that we seemed to play golf together so much?

It was purely and simply coincidence. Dad, although licensed to drive a car, was never confident about his eyesight after he had a terrible argument with a Westland Lysander aircraft during the war. Lysanders were used mainly to carry agents and supplies between Britain and the resistance forces in the occupied countries. Lysanders were amazing little aircraft that were able to land quietly in small rough fields. I believe that their Bristol Mercury engines were fairly quiet and that the pilot could feather the propellor to dampen further the aeroplane's noise upon landing. Dad was walking across a runway at one of the aerodromes he was stationed at and got knocked down by a Lysander that he never saw or heard. This accident injured him severely and affected his eyesight. Public transport was therefore the Bruce's main method of getting from A to B.

To get to Bruntsfield we took the number 1 bus across the road from our house and after alighting at the little village of Davidsons Mains we walked the fifteen minutes or so through parts of Barnton to the golf course. After we had picked up Dad's caddy car from the shed and his clubs from his locker we would proceed to the starter's box; I already had my clubs. The starter was a fellow called Johnny. Johnny, an ex-Guardsman, was always very smartly turned out with particularly shiny, black shoes. The man was extremely courteous, very tall and had a back as straight as a flagpole. He would see us coming, welcome us and tell us to go straight to the first tee or the tenth depending on how busy the course was. Then, as if by magic, James Letham would appear from the side of the club house suitably kitted out with plus fours, white shoes, white shirt, short sleeved dark pullover and with his caddy who always looked like he had spent the night in the caddies' shed accompanied by a couple of manky donkeys and some very smelly pigs.

I stayed out of the adult's conversation but, if I know my Dad he would have kept the subject firmly on golf or perhaps the kirk. Banking would not have been on the agenda. After the eighteen holes were over we would all shake hands then Dad and I would go through the arrival routine exactly in reverse. No stopping in the clubhouse for refreshments, even when I was over eighteen. Apparently he would tell his fellow members I didn't drink!!! We would almost be at Davidsons Mains when Mr Letham would swoop down on us like Batman in his enormous black Austin Princess with a back passenger space of about par 4 in length. I suspect it was normally chauffeur driven but his man probably had the weekends off. Mr Letham stayed quite near us and so we got a lift the whole way home. I could never understand why this return lift wasn't arranged on the 18th green. I thought it was probably something to do with protocol and rank. Sometimes Mr Letham was not to be seen at

Bruntsfield and this meant long walks both to and from the golf course. The upside of that was Dad would usually give me a couple of threepenny bits to put in a Milky Way machine at the newsagents just by the bus stop. One Sunday I put in my two threeppeny bits and out came two Milky Way chocolate bars. The two threepenny bits were also returned to me. My Dad told me to put the coins back in the slot. I explained to him that somebody else would come along and take out the next two Milky Ways and pocket his two coins. Surely nobody would be so dishonest exclaimed my father. The bus came and just as it pulled away from the stop, two fellows who had been watching us came along, pulled out the chocolate bearing tray collecting the bars and the coins. They duly repeated the exercise no doubt until the Milky Way supply was exhausted.

Sundays on the golf course eventually developed the sort of monotonous and repetitive tone to them, just like most of the other types of Sundays. Dad had a reasonable amount of patience with me on the course as I gradually mastered the rudiments of the game, well some of it. However, to this day bunker shots give me the jitters. Dad would never allow me to play out of the bunkers. I think he was afraid that I would empty the hazards of all their sand and cause the secretary of the club to write to him. In a funny kind of way such a sanction made me think much more carefully about my shots in an attempt to avoid sand and save me the humiliation of having to lift my ball and place it behind the bunker.

One Sunday, during the school holidays, was a bit different. The late great Dai Rees was visiting Bruntsfield and he stopped to exchange pleasantries with me in the locker room as he was passing through the clubhouse to meet the club pro, a big broad-shouldered man called Ian Anderson. During a very long golfing career, Dai Rees won thirty nine tournaments, finished second in the Open Championship on three occasions, and played in nine Ryder Cups, captaining the side no fewer than five times, leading the team to victory in 1957. The presence of Dai Rees came as a bit of a surprise to my Dad and he was just as pleased as punch to shake the man's hand. I, of course, didn't have a clue who he was but was apprised of the great man's history on our walk to Davidson's Mains prior to the regular pick up by Mr Letham. No Milky Ways that Sunday.

Later that week I was to experience a big golfing disaster. I used to practice chipping into an upturned golf umbrella in our back garden . I always used an ancient mashie niblick which had a shortish hickory shaft and an old and very shiny leather grip on it. When I was a youngster I didn't bother with a glove and so it would have been quite difficult to play a full-blooded shot with the club; keeping a hold of it would have been tricky. I was about to prove that day just how difficult. I had some lightweight plastic practice balls and thought that I would just have a good old belt at them. The first shot that I took seemed to have a very light through swing and suddenly I realised that my mashie had parted company from me. I couldn't think at what point the club had decided to desert me, so I ducked, covering my head for a few seconds. Then realising that I had not been knocked out or injured in any other way, I couldn't see where the club had gone. I looked skyward just in time to see the sixty-odd year old, hand-forged warhead with wooden tail flying onwards and upwards and straight through the first floor window of a house two down from ours. The club's trajectory caused it to just miss the top of our near neighbour's brand new television set and land at his feet. The poor man, a Mr Drew Paterson, was taking an après lunchtime nap and was, needless to say, very rudely awakened. It took him a moment or two to connect the loud tinkle of smashed fenestration with the ancient looking golf club that now lay at his feet. Once the fellow had realised what had caused the window to be shattered he then had to sort out in his mind why and how such an event could have taken place. One can only imagine what was being computed in his brain. Clank whirr- "First I hear a crash and awaken with a start and there, at my feet, is an old golf club and a large hole on my window and shards of glass everywhere. Why is there a club at my feet right in the middle of my traditionally peaceful and rejuvenating afternoon nap?"

Had I perpetrated this stupidity elsewhere I would probably have been far, far away in only moments but, given the fact that the incident had occurred in my neighbourhood and in the interests of goodwill between my parents and this poor neighbour who was not easy to get on with, I ran up to check the damage. By the time I got to the scene I found that nobody had been injured, at least not physically. Mr Paterson was, however, in a state of speechless shock. The only noise at that time was coming through from the other side of the house. It was Mr Paterson's old mother shouting,

'Drew, you have smashed all the lunch dishes. Why have you smashed all the lunch dishes ya bally fool that you are?'

Drew shouted back, 'I haven't smashed the dishes mother. Douglas has flung a golf club through the window'

This was obviously the worst excuse Mrs Paterson had ever heard from her fool of a son.

'Oh stop annoying me. You have smashed all the dishes,' Mrs P bellowed back .

'I am telling you, Douglas has flung a golf club through our window and it just missed the television set,' Drew protested.

Through the racket of Mrs Paterson's accusations I started to try to explain that I had not actually pre-meditated a flinging of the golf club through the window and meant the Paterson's no malice. Rather, it was simply a freak accident. Drew took some convincing but I got there in the end. What a carry on. I consoled the pair of them by promising that I would pay for the repairs to their glazing.

I didn't have any money so my next worry was telling my Dad, who did, what had happened when he came home from the bank. I told him the whole sorry tale. With absolutely no hesitation he said that he understood that that sort of mishap could happen to anybody, in fact it happened to golfing icon Dai Rees only the day after we met him. His driver flew out of his grip on the first tee and smashed through a greenhouse causing extensive damage.

Dad took the view that if it was good enough for good old Dai it was good enough for his son.

Heriot's School VII Season 1965/66
Back Row, Left to Right : D P Clark, G W Pettigrew, D L McDougall, D S Bruce
Seated: J N Burnett, D O Lee (Capt.), J A B Craig

CHAPTER 5

In Which I Learn About Rugby Etiquette

There were a number of boys at Heriot's who were not really inter-ested in playing rugby seriously but who did plod on at the game to the best of their ability; they respected those lads who did take the game seriously and who were good at it. Many of the "not very good at it brigade" realising the social value of rugby union went on to become administrators of the senior game or even referees. The lads who excelled at the sport played for the FP's and went on to play for their districts and in some cases, their country. Herioters along with the former pupils of many a Scottish rugby playing school have popped up all over the world and introduced the game to areas hitherto bereft of the sport. It is a sport that welcomes play-ers of all abilities who seem to stay with the game, and at its very heart, one way or another, until death they do part.

Strangely, I think most Herioters of my era look back on those austere post World-War Two times with a huge amount of affection, quietly thanking Donald Hastie for making rugby more compulsory than breathing. Not only did we have an opportunity to experience the lasting camaraderie that rugby afforded us, we learned an awful lot about playing the game of life with a sound set of principals.

Incidentally, as the boys who chose rugby matured, they built up a respect for those lads who opted for cross country as their winter sport. The senior XVs at the school were obliged to enter the school annual cross country championships and were always well and truly hammered by, so called, weaker pupils.

From a very early age many hundreds of young Heriot boys were taught how to be sportsmen by Donald Hastie. It was chiselled into our skulls that, when a try was scored, it was scored by all fifteen members of the team, not just the lad that carried the ball over the line. Additionally, the try scorer was expected to display the body language of that of a player, thoroughly ashamed of himself for having the audacity to touch down for, what was then, a meagre three points. Three points that, nevertheless, caused a deficit in the opposition's score bank account. Bowed, guilty looking figures would return from the scene of the crime, cringing with embarrassment, trying so hard to avoid eye contact with proud parents on the touchline. By the time they got back behind their own lines, the action of scoring a try had assumed the magnitude of a capital offence. Whilst this "dead man walking" was going on, God help anyone in his team who would dare to emulate the actions of professional footballers. You know the kind of palaver, it's the scene where the goal scorer is virtually gang-banged by his team mates in front of an extremely pissed-off opposition. Such behaviour, we were told by Hastie, head sunk into his shoulders as he looked around checking that no unwanted persons were about, was the conduct of, for example, employees of the Heart of Midlothian Football Club Limited. Great emphasis was placed upon the word *limited* as if it equated to some dreadful, filthy disease.

Some thirty plus years later I attended the annual dinner of the Mackie Academy FP Rugby Club in Stonehaven. The main speaker was Jim Telfer, the then amateur SRU coach, eventually to become professional director of rugby at the SRU. He proclaimed that the strength of the game of rugby union lay in the fact that it was an amateur sport unlike the higher levels of association football, where, at the top level the players were paid a ridiculously high wage. He went on to say that football was in dire straits because of its "professionalism"; if we were ever to pay rugby players our game would suffer a similar fate. So, as well as being probably one of the best coaches the rugby world has ever seen, he was also, ironically, a bit of a Nostradamus. For the Rugby Unions throughout the World at that time rugby league, indeed any form of professional rugby, was considered to be tainted, but things were changing quietly in the background. The first Rugby World Cup in 1987 could be seen as the catalyst for that change when the game "outed" itself.

The host countries for the inaugural competition were New Zealand and Australia and much was going on down in the Antipodes that stirred up players from the Northern Hemisphere. It was alleged that some of the better known Aussies and New Zealanders were being paid for making television adverts whilst still playing amateur rugby. Autobiographies were being written by star players and payments, it had been rumoured, were being taken by these fellows for their books. The guys from the Five Nations got to thinking about what they were doing with their lives, their careers, their families. Rugby seemed to be taking up so much of their lives. I asked Iain Milne, tighthead from the 1984 Grand Slam side, what it was like to play for his club and Scotland in the amateur days. He said it was not difficult when he was playing his club rugby for Heriot's but it was a nightmare when he moved south to play for Harlequins. Attending Sunday International squad sessions meant he had to get up to Edinburgh from wherever he was playing his rugby in England. "The Bear" often had to get in a car with Bill Cuthbertson, another Harlequin and 84 slammer, straight after a game, say, in Bath and drive to Edinburgh, have some sleep, train with the Scotland squad on the Sunday and drive straight back to London ready to start the week's work. On top of all of that Iain, when he was based in Edinburgh, frequently came up to Stonehaven to help Mackie Academy FPRFC with all sorts of training sessions and the likes.

A lot of the boys Donald Hastie was influencing were already devout fans of one or other of the two professional football sides in Edinburgh. It was probably genetic, their fathers and grand-fathers before them having been Jambos or Hibbies. Although lots of these boys were following the weekly progress of the local pro football teams, copying their antics never seemed to manifest itself on the rugby park. The two game codes were poles apart. Hastie's lectures seemed to have a hypnotic effect on his young charges. We were like Pavlov's dogs; as soon as we recognised a rugby pitch, our sporting manner was triggered. I know I can speak for every pupil that was ever under the spell of Hastie, that spell will still be cast over them, even after all these years which in my case is more than a half century. I can still see our rugby master laying down his laws, one after the other and in such a manner that they should probably have been tacked on to the ten commandments. Probably the most important one was "Thou shalt never even think about challenging a referee's decision." Again, that law has stuck and it really does make it easier for a game to be played in the proper spirit and also easier for the ref-eree to remain impartial. "Thou shalt not boo nor tolerate booing" was another really important law. All my school PT staff loathed booing; so then did their pupils.

Kids are so easy to impress. In Donald Hastie's case he impressed his young pupils with only good; but how old fashioned some of his ideas have now become. If it had been up to Hastie I reckon John McEnroe the tennis player, would have had a career of early baths.

CHAPTER 6

I Discover A Sporting Mentor; I Become A British
Junior Champion and A Schoolboy Internationalist

I have a lot more to thank Donald M Hastie and Heriot's school for
than just instilling sportsmanship in me. DMH, as he was nicknamed,
spotted the sprint in me when I was only ten. Unbeknown to me, he
kept an eye on my progress in the winter on the rugby pitch as a winger
and as an athlete on the track in the summer. Heriot's had a couple
of British Junior Athletic Champions during Hastie's time as games
master and he had a yearning for another. DMH approached me one
day in the school playground when I was a raw fifteen year old,

'Bruce'- one didn't get called by one's first name at my school
until you were in the fifth or sixth year. 'Bruce,' he said 'I think you
could be a pretty decent hurdler, you know, and I am sure that, with
some extra coaching after school in the gymnasium on a Monday
and a Wednesday, you could be the school's next British Junior
Champion in three year's time.'

Not being academic in the slightest and in no rush to get home
to do homework, I jumped at the opportunity.

In those days indoor hurdles practice was akin to taking up Kamikaze flying. The hurdles were of a very simple construction: a crossbar placed on top of a wallbar on one side at the relevant height and held up at the other side by a wooden upright with a peg slotted in it at right angles. Three such simple erections were placed down the length of the south side of the gym where the wallbars were. That was also where access to the gym was from the changing room! In line with the flight of hurdles was a long corridor stretching from the swimming pool boiler room. That corridor was the run-up to the hurdles. A heavy door at the end of the run-up corridor and a few yards from the first hurdle was left open. A pile of the wafer-thin rubber mats, as described in an earlier chapter, was placed at the other end of the hurdles. They were supposed to act as a buffer should I run out of stopping space. A few difficulties there then.

The first worry was, that upon acceleration in to the gym, some tidy person may have decided to slam the heavy door shut so, like the cartoon cat, Tom of Tom and Jerry fame, I get flattened and then scraped off the door panels. The second, and very real worry, was the possibility that some unsuspecting person may decide to walk into the gym through either one of the two entrances off the dressing room, broadsiding me. The third was the gym itself. The floor had a hard cork surface; falling on it, I thought, would be a fairly unpleasant experience. Finally- and that was an adverb in this instance that had a couple of meanings - finally there was the so called cushioning at the end of the event.

Anyway, after a few, practical slow-motion demonstrations from a fully-dressed and bow-tied DMH about leading and trailing legs, three strides between each stick and so on, I was sent off on my first solo flight.

I started walking down the corridor towards the boiler house door. Sandy Rafferty the school head-jannie appeared from behind it. Sandy was always smartly dressed in an immaculate dark blue uniform with polished brass buttons on the jacket and a peaked hat. Shaking his be-hatted head like a naval captain unhappy about an admiral's sea battle plan, he asked,

'Hastie hasn't got you running into that hurdles death trap as well has he?'

As well as who? I thought, but never found out. What did he mean by death trap? Good God the door, the dressing room entrances, the rough cork floor and the crappy mats suddenly conjured up in my mind a horribly painful end to a very young, innocent life. The gym seemed so casually fraught with danger that I imagined the possibility of javelin throwing practice going on in the place, caber tossing and the school pipe band marching up and down, even before I had finished my stint. What was I doing there? Suddenly academia seemed like a very good idea.

I tried to get a mental picture of me running up to the hurdles, taking off for the first one with my left leg leading, snapping it down and pulling my trailing leg bent at the knee and parallel to the ground, three strides, repeat the hurdle clearance a second time and so on. Sandy, still shaking his head and now tut tutting in a disparaging manner, disappeared back into the bowels of the boiler house.

In one seamless motion I turned, forgetting to shout for runway clearance from air traffic control i.e. Hastie, then immediately started my take off. Short strides in first gear, second gear, third and then full throttle in fourth. Hastie, who was guarding the door lest it slam into me as per my first worry, had been keeking round the wall to give me the chocks away sign and was startled to see me already winding up to a fair old sprint pace. I just could not cope psychologically with the first hurdle and had to abort my take off with a spectacular side step off my left foot to my right which led to me crashing into the back of a startled and hastily retreating hurdles coach. Apart from nearly swallowing his unlit pipe, which he had been casually blowing through as part of a cleaning process, he hit the deck face first. He was ok but I had a number of cork burns, yes cork burns, on my left thigh, the underside of my left arm and the left side of my face. It looked like I had been in a road traffic accident without a car. I began to wonder at the wisdom of the whole thing.

After DMH got up, dusted himself down, gathered all his pens and straightened himself out, he decided that an alteration to the coaching plan was necessary to give me confidence and so he took away the first hurdle and lowered the other two. The effect of this was to give me a practice run that was entirely in the gym. No boilerhouse run up. We did this for the first two weeks and then raised the hurdles . A week or two more like that and I was ready to go back to three hurdles, the corridor and the tut-tutting jannie. I had many a grazing fall but three winters of DMH's coaching and encouragement, not to mention three seasons of rugby, the last of which dealt me a bad injury to my right knee, saw me approaching the summer of 1966, aged eighteen, basically fit and ready for competitive hurdling. DMH duly entered me as a Heriot's pupil in the UK Junior Championships to be held at the Hurlingham stadium in London.

The Scottish Junior Championships took place shortly before the British event and for some reason my stride pattern had gone a.w.o.l. and I managed only third place. That did not augur well for the big one. Because the school holidays had started I couldn't call upon my mentor, Donald Hastie to sort me out. George Sinclair, the coach of a local senior athletics club called Octavian's came to my rescue. He asked Herioter and Octavian, Tony Hogarth, to spend a couple of evenings running over hurdles with me to get my rhythm back. I was really grateful to Tony, especially as he was still recovering from a groin injury at the time. Between George and Tony they got me back on schedule at what was then called New Meadowbank.

Tony was a British Junior champion in the high hurdles and a Scottish men's' High and 440 yards hurdles champion.

Earlier that summer, though still a schoolboy, I had been invited to join Octavians by George Sinclair who was their senior coach. George was also the coach for the Scottish Junior Athletics team. He had not been involved with my entry to the British Championships until I asked for his help with my stride pattern. During this remedial coaching session he asked me how I was travelling to the competition. I told him my plan was to travel to London overnight, after my sister's wedding, in a train to Kings Cross, and then get myself over to the track. He took it upon himself to include me in the official Scottish contingent and fly me to London on the morning of the championships. Everyone involved in this manoeuvre, especially me, knew that it had the potential to cause a bit of a political storm at George Heriot's School once the holidays were over. George Sinclair, himself a Heriot former pupil, was sympathetic to Donald Hastie's feelings. Knowing DMH had spent the guts of three winters with me, George made sure that I was written up in the programme of events as a Heriot School boy and I was allowed to wear my school athletics vest. That I did very proudly. I never expected to do all that well but, to my astonishment, I won my heat in the fastest of the first round times. When the final came around my astonishment and that of a couple of million BBC Grandstand viewers reached a new level when, totally overcome with nerves whilst hammering my starting blocks into the cinder track, I filled my pants in front of the TV cameras. I was given about five minutes to go and clean up. I had to rinse out my jock strap and borrow a pair of shorts from my team mate, Jimmy Craig, who wasn't too keen, for obvious reasons, and also he needed them back quickly for his 220 yards sprint.

Thoroughly drained of adrenalin, which I had just proved beyond all doubt was brown, I suspected that I had had it but no, the gun went and I scampered off and won the thing. I was chuffed but I do believe that DMH got just as much pleasure out of my win as I did. I hope that was so as he deserved most of the credit for persevering with probably the stiffest hurdler that ever staggered over the obstacles. I tell this story not as if I was some accomplished athlete but more because it is a story about a dedicated school teacher who was prepared to give up hours and hours of his spare time to a pupil in whom he had faith and from whom he thought he could bring out the best that was in him.

Back Row, 5th from left: My mentor and Heriot's School Games Master, Donald "DMH" Hastie minus bow-tie

CHAPTER 7

From Junior Athletics to Scientific Torture and
I Don't Belong to Glasgow by the Way

My schoolboy international team mate in the 200 yards hurdles, Freddie Warder, was a typical, slightly built and excellent Royal High School 1st XV stand-off. At the High School he followed in the footsteps of Colin Telfer, Hawick and Scotland. Freddie in later life became an actor and starred in a TV series about a prison governor, I think, but it may have been a policeman. The race was split into a series of heats and a final. I got to the final but sadly Fred didn't make it. The outcome was: first, England, second Scotland (yours truly), third England, fourth Wales and fifth Northern Ireland, I think. Twenty years later I was sitting up in bed reading a book written by Gareth Edwards, the famous Welsh, Lions, Barbarians and Cardiff scrum-half. Amongst all the rugby stories was a reference to a 200 yards hurdles race he had taken part in as a schoolboy at an international athletics meeting held in Belfast in 1966.

The hairs stood up on the back of my neck and, much to the amazement of my wife, Rosemary, I jumped out of bed shouting

"I was in that race" and ran down the stairs to get out my old scrapbook. I was pretty sure the dad of another of my team mates had taken a photo of that race. There it was glued into my book of memories. The image was taken just as we were coming off the bend and into the straight. Good God, right enough, there was Gareth Edwards in an English vest behind me in third place. Gareth Edwards, like many school kids with top class sporting potential went to a famous English school by the name of Millfield. Well well, there it was in black and white, me and Gareth Edwards. Funnily enough, I also beat J. J. Williams that day in the 4x110 yards relay. J. J. was the famous Welsh winger of the seventies. Actually, to be fair, I was running last man in the Scottish relay team as was J.J. for our Welsh counterparts; my three colleagues, Jimmy Craig of Heriot's, Ian Turnbull of Merchiston Castle School and Peter Thomson of Penicuik High, had built up a very good lead. It was just as well as I had to run like blazes just to scrape home in front! It was some day but, amazingly, it was to come to life again all those years later, but in a rugby context.

My senior athletics experiences however, were to suffer a big reality check. I soon discovered that athletes no longer at school and spending their days in the workplace missed their routine daily fitness exercise.

At George Heriot's school, which was a complex of four large buildings spread over a very large area, we only had a few minutes to get from one class to another and this usually meant running like hell because our subject classes varied from building to building. Fat kids, thin kids, spotty kids, asthmatic kids, short-legged kids, long-legged kids, geeks and gawks either turned into Olympic sprinters or they would suffer the consequences. Understandably, no teacher tolerated tardiness, given he or she had only forty minutes in a single period to din a lesson into his or her charges.

At one period of senior school life I had what I thought was a reasonable justification for being late for some classes. The injury I sustained to my knee while playing against Belvedere College caused my right leg to be plastered from crutch to ankle thus rendering me incapable of running at a pace much faster than a sedated tortoise. Indeed, even if I did try to accelerate I tended to go into a sort of clumsy pirouette as if I was a Panzer tank with a busted caterpillar track. When I think about it, a journey from, say, Mr Robertson's engineering drawing class in what was known as the New School, involved a lung bursting sprint up two flights of stairs then, if you were of a cavalier nature or just plain stupid, a long dash the length of the art department corridor. I use the adjective "stupid" because everyone knew that the art department stage of a journey to and from the Old School was often covertly patrolled by its head, an artist who went by the name of Mr McHardpaintbrush. He caused the whole classroom changeover to resemble a sort of Russian roulette. The classroom entrances along the corridor were like the firing chambers in a revolver. One of them could be loaded with the bullet i.e. McHardpaintbrush who was likely to shoot himself out and give said stupid boy six of the best for running dangerously along his corridor. After the punishment the punishee was released to await the fate that would be dished out by the next master who understandably was not going to be pleased at having his class interrupted by a young man with a swollen, throbbing superheated hand.

The departure from McHardpaintbrush could not be accomplished by running. No, it was more of a ludicrously speeded up walk straight out of Monty Pythons Ministry of Funny Walks. You know the kind: it's where you become elasticated at the waist and neck. A belted pupil could have been mistaken for a chicken mime. A punished pupil, after leaving the art department's radar range, was then in the general region of some primary school classes so, a balance of care with reasonable speed, dictated tactics. This involved a kind of wind-up run until the open playground was reached then, it was full steam ahead across the no- speed-limit expanse of tarmac, up the terracing steps and into the three-hundred and fifty year old senior School. Whether muscle straining and gut-wrenching athleticism followed, depended on the next academic subject and the style of stairway that led to the relevant classroom. Given the foregoing, readers could be forgiven for thinking that my school was founded and designed on ancient Presbyterian principles and its architecture from some dark Transylvanian Count's castle. Not so, at least insofar as the architecture went. I recall that all pupils and staff were proud of their school. The main building is beautiful with a turret at each of its four corners. The two turrets on the north side of the building had been altered somewhere between 1659, when it opened as a Hospital, and the year I entered the establishment which was 1954. The alterations included the installation of modern staircases. The turrets on the south side of the building still had the original seventeenth century spiral staircases. Mostly, thank God, I only had the Northern parts of the building to contend with and they were bad enough. If I was particularly unlucky during a class changeover between the new and old schools I could, for example, have received a McHardpaintbrush belting and then a vertical run up a south turret after the long tarmac straight. The whole thing was like one of these modern computer games. Worse still, any of that could have been compounded by my plastered and immobile leg.

To make matters even worse at the plastered leg time, I was obliged by an English teacher, by the name of Mr Hilariously-Sarcastic, to ask permission from the teacher of the class prior to his one, to leave a few minutes before the period end, thus affording me enough time to make it to the beginning of his class.

This usually caused the earlier teacher to explode and ask me who Mr Hilariously-Sarcastic thought he was. I could have hazarded a guess but that would probably have come back to haunt me. It was amazing the physical and mental conundrums a Heriot pupil could get into in my days at the venerable establishment. It didn't do me any harm though, in fact it probably helped stave off a potential heart attack in later life!!

So anyway, there I was, in senior athletics with Octavians all stiff and likely to get flabby because I was standing around all day working in a bank. My first proper training session with George Sinclair was on the New Meadowbank track. Old Meadowbank in the sixties was a speedway track and New Meadowbank was adjacent. I remember the speedway track well. I once went to a meeting with some school chums. The place was packed and I spotted an area near the track that was completely empty and from which a great view, I thought, could be had. After the first circuit of the first race we were sadder and wiser young men. The reason our spot was empty was because the track at that point was at the first bend where a lot of jockeying for places occurred as the riders slid their bikes and worked hard to get grip. As they did so an avalanche of cinders was thrown up by the rear wheels of the bikes and all over me and my ex pals.

The Bruce training debut at New Meadowbank was a major turning point in my life. Boyhood to manhood in one not so easy lesson. It was, in fact, a nightmare. Coach Sinclair put me with a group of fellow sprinters. Sprinters included those poor souls who ran the 440 yards. I had always thought such an event was a middle distance race! Later on in my athletics career I was seduced into running that insane event but with hurdles in the way!!

My first new manly exercise involved repetition sprints starting at around the point where a 220 yards sprint would begin.

On the word "go" we had to run as fast as we could for as far as we could over a period of I think about nineteen seconds. A marker was thrown down where the fastest bloke got to in the allotted time. This was to be the benchmark. Well, I thought that was not too bad until I realised we had to jog very quickly back to the start where, again, on the word "go" we had to try and reach the marker within the benchmark time. This process carried on until we dropped.

There was a very good scientific reason for this form of torture. All living cells require a source of energy to survive. Carbohydrates are stuffed full of it so athletes such as marathon runners load themselves with them for several days before a race. But cells need oxygen to efficiently break down carbohydrates ultimately producing carbon dioxide and water. However, if there's not enough oxygen the breakdown halts prematurely producing lactic acid in muscle cells causing athletes to writhe in agony! Besides building muscle, athletes train to improve their lung capacity. i.e. improve their oxygen intake. Inadvertently, school provided me and my classmates with lots of exercise as, summoned by the bell and burdened by books, we raced from classroom to classroom trying to dodge the likes of Mr Mchardpaintbrush.

After about four repetition runs I found myself in a daze, excused myself and went off in search of the gents toilets as I did not feel at all well. I was found sometime later by a group of retired men who had taken a wander into the stadium toilets in order to run off their Saturday lunchtime pints. I was lying on the lavatory floor, unconscious, thanks to a huge oxygen debt. They brought me round and I staggered off to the changing rooms waving bye bye to athletics, or so I thought. Next morning, a Sunday, a persistent coach Sinclair turned up at my door and talked me into having another go. Training from there on in was mandatory. I cannot remember ever training for Octavians and not being horribly sick at the end of, or even, during a session. Heaven knows what Olympic athletes put themselves through; I salute them all.

Both Old and New Meadowbank were demolished to make way for the Commonwealth Games in 1970.

During my period with Octavians, along with my pal Fraser McRitchie, I also ran for the school FP athletic team and trained under the Scottish National coach, John Anderson. John was later to become the starter of events on the popular television pro- gramme "Gladiators" Our old friend Donald Hastie was in charge of the FP athletic team and he suddenly decided to bar those of us who made Octavians our first choice of club from competing for the FP team. I am sure it was not a personal thing. DMH just put Heriot's first. Fraser and I were out in the cold. It was a silly thing to do because it would have been very unlikely that any major ath- letics event would have been on at the same time as a minor FP club contest and so we would always have been available for the FP team. I suppose what really upset Donald Hastie was the fact that we were obliged to compete in the National championships as Octavians not as former pupils of George Heriot's School. There was to be no dispensation such as that afforded me at the earlier British Junior Championships.

So barred we were, and it hurt both Fraser and me. We did however believe that we could greatly improve as athletes with Octavians whereas the likelihood of that happening if we remained as purely FP athletes was zero. It saddened us that Donald Hastie and a number of school teachers just could not see our point of view but we lived with it until one fateful evening at the grounds of Edinburgh Athletic Club. Octavians, as I have men- tioned already, did not have their own track and so we had to use the tracks belonging to The Edinburgh Corporation as the Toon Cooncil was then known. We alternated between The Edinburgh

Southern Harriers track at Fernieside in the deep south of the town, Edinburgh Athletic Club's ground at Balgreen in the west side of the city and Meadowbank just off the city centre towards the east. On the occasion of this story the FP's were in a three-way contest with Edinburgh Southern Harriers and Edinburgh Athletic club. The venue was Balgreen, home to Edinburgh Athletic. Heriot's were a man short for the 440 yards. This was Fraser's event but of course he wasn't in the team because of the ban. Hastie spotted us and we wondered if he would bury his pride and ask Fraser to run. We should have known better – DMH stuck to his rigid conservative principles. It so happened Fraser and I had turned up at Balgreen to do some training and had no idea that this contest was on.

There was little we could do but either go home or sit and watch the match. We chose the latter. The main reason for that was Jimmy Craig, our old school pal and rugby team mate, was due to run in the 220 yards with another mutual school friend, Gill Borthwick. Both Gill and Jimmy were speedy over the furlong. They were also highly competitive rivals.

Gill, by the time of this story, was quite a star in Scottish club rugby as a high try scoring winger for Heriot's FP. I think he was perhaps unlucky never to have been capped for his country. In our minds Jimmy was the faster of the two and I guess Jimmy thought that to be the case also. Jimmy would be cool about the race but we knew that Gill had a quite different temperament and would take the event as a personal challenge as well as a race with his club-mate to get maximum points for his team. Fraser and I sat on the embankment around the track and watched the evening's events unfold.

Eventually we got to the 220 yards and the draw saw Gill in lane one and Jimmy further out. These occasions were, of course, strictly amateur and all the clubs had to provide judges, starters, long jump pit rakers and so on. The starter that night was John Craig, Jimmy's dad. I don't know where it came from but, for all the time I was a school athlete, Heriot's races were started with an officer's revolver out of The Great War and it was a pretty impressive means of starting a race. None of these namby-pamby percussion cap starter's pistols. Oh no, we had to have a serious weapon. Our starters meant business, don't you know.

Well it was apparent, due to his prancing about, arm waving and other flamboyant physical jerks that Gill was in the mood for a race. Jimmy was much less obvious in his last minute loosening exercises. 'Take your marks,' commanded John Craig. Into the blocks went the athletes. 'Get set.' BOOM! the gun erupted, flames and smoke shot out of the barrel. Gill in his wound up excitement had jumped the start by the tiniest fraction of a second and John Craig sensed it. Conscious of his responsibility to be fair, John pulled the trigger to fire the recall. We were not so far away that Fraser and I couldn't hear the hammer on the six shooter going "click", then "click, click". There was no military style bang though. The blank cartridges in the revolver's firing chambers were duds. Now, if you were as fanatical a Herioter as John Craig was, and you were biased towards your own team man, in this case Gill, you could have forgiven John for turning a blind eye to Gill's error. Any athlete, including myself, that got away with a false start like that one would be unlikely to own up. It really was not that obvious but John, showing true impartiality and proper sportsmanship, did his damndest to bring those athletes back to start all over again. However, no matter how hard he tried recalling the men in the conventional manner the runners failed to respond. Having gone through the orthodox route and failed, John, no mean sprinter in his day, took off down the track after the sprinters; they all by then had a full head of steam up and didn't hear the recalls, being only clicks. John shouted his unashamed demand,

'Come back, can't you hear me? Come back you deaf bastards.'

His screaming was followed by the wartime hand gun arcing its way hopelessly towards the runners. John's desperation to right a wrong was in vain. Because of a shortage, all the remaining volunteer officials were acting as time keepers and, inexplicably, they chose to ignore John's antics. So the result stood: Heriot's first and second, I have no idea who was placed where after that. John didn't, by then, care because Jimmy and Gill were yards ahead of the opposition and the false start probably made no difference to the result. All in all it was one of the more interesting training nights for me and Fraser.

From Octavians, three Herioters, Fraser McRitchie, Tony Hogarth and I were included in the initial Scotland track events squad for the 1970 Commonwealth Games. I never felt that I had any real chance of making it to the team and as it happened none of us did in the end.

The formation of this squad was a couple of years before the event took place so that meant additional training from the Scottish coach John Anderson. We would go on residential weekend courses from time to time and the first one was hell, sheer unadulterated hell. If I had known just how bad it was going to be I would have done some extra training for it. Imagine having to train to be properly fit for a training session.

There wasn't a lot of money in the Scottish Amateur Athletics Association at that time. At least I guessed that to be the case as we stayed in a school somewhere in Glasgow. No flash hotels for us. The beds were erected in classrooms. The bed springs and mattresses were too soft and everybody developed distinct curvatures of the spine over the two nights we stayed there. We arrived on a

Friday and assembled in the gym to hear from the National coach what tortures we would be subjected to over the following two days. On reflection waterboarding would have been a cakewalk compared to what coach Anderson dished out.

After a sleepless night we all got up and, remembering the torture schedule, we declined breakfast and after the first session couldn't look at our lunch. Leslie Piggot, the then national 100 yards sprint champion, preparing for some repetition sprints was berated by John Anderson for smoking! Can you imagine Usain Bolt having a fag during a training session.

'Leslie Piggot why on earth do you smoke, it's bound to affect your breathing?' enquired the coach.

'Actually, I don't breath during a hundred yard sprint, there isn't the time !' came the Piggot retort.

Head shaking, the coach moved off to take out his wrath on poor devils like me.

The first nightmarish day finished and Fraser and I were already into the later stages of our escape plan. I think it was at that point I started thinking about just how much I really wanted to be a senior international athlete. The sacrifices that would have to be made, was I good enough, could I get better with my knee problem always being a niggle?

The Plan: Fraser and I decided that we couldn't take a second night of watching loop films of sprint starts and the like so we approached John Anderson and asked if we could go out into Glasgow for our evening meal rather than stay in for dinner. No, absolutely not was the reply.

So, we went anyway. Walking calmly out of the school we headed for the gates and a bus stop. Guessing the direction that would take us to Glasgow city centre we climbed aboard the first bus that came along. It took us to Sauchihall Street which was, in any event, the only Glasgow street we had heard of. I mentioned earlier that although both of us had been to Glasgow many times to play rugby or compete in athletics matches we had always returned immediately to Edinburgh in our coach thus any exploration of Scotland's second city was always denied us.

Although we did not want to endure another evening in that school we didn't want to be doing anything daft in town such as spending our freedom in a pub. Sunday training would be horrible enough without the complication of a hangover. We just wanted something nice to eat and maybe one beer. A Reo Stakis steak house suddenly appeared and in we went. The steak was delicious and that, followed by a vanilla ice cream cost us each ten shillings and six pence. The beer was one shilling and six pence. The total in new money was sixty pence. Sounds cheap but we were both on around £425.00 per annum at that time as junior employees of The Edinburgh Savings Bank. No bonuses back then.

Feeling satisfied, and knowing that by the time we got back to the school everybody would be in bed, we felt that the evening had been a worthwhile exercise.

We found a bus stop relevant to our destination and in due course a bus came along. There were three people before us in the queue. At the front a teddy boy with all the regulation gear on: the long black jacket with velvet lapels and huge side pockets, white shirt with a black shoe lace tie, tight trousers and beetle crusher shoes. His hair was styled in the fashion of the then recently deceased "Big Bopper". Standing behind the ted were a couple of ladies with new huge hair-dos, I think they were called beehives, large fur coats, proportionately large handbags and stiletto-heeled shoes. Just as we got on behind I noticed that the ted was a bit wobbly on his feet, pished as they say in Glasgow. He was carrying what

75

looked like a fish supper in his right hand and with his left hand he pulled himself up on to the bus deck.

We all had to go up the stairs as there was no room on the lower deck . There were three empty rows of seats one after the other starting at the front pavement side. The women sat in the first two seats, Ted next, then me and Fraser. We had no sooner got comfortable when Ted started to demolish his fish supper. The women at the front were oblivious to anything other than what had happened on their Saturday night. They were gabbling on, as I suppose Fraser and I were, when the lone diner finished his meal, screwed up into a greasy ball the newspaper that his smelly cuisine had been wrapped in and threw it casually over his head, narrowly missing us but hitting the people in the seat behind. They obviously thought that the very best thing that they could do was to ignore what had just happened to them and carry on with a nonchalant air.

'Gabble, gabble, gabble!' continued the fur coated ladies.

Our man from the mid-fifties then projectile vomited his partially digested haddock and chips all over the woman immediately in front of him.

Well we were all stunned into silence and our breathing was momentarily arrested, apart from the lady whose fur coat was now harled with chipped potato, brown sauce, pickled onion and the catch of the day. The poor woman was sobbing uncontrollably.

'Effie, that man has just been sick aw ower yer coat!' screamed the hitherto untouched one.

'A ken, shut yer face Ina, Christ knows whitl happen noo!' squealed the now very stinky lady. She looked like the contents of the stomach of a gigantic Artic Skua.

Whooooooosssssssh. Ted did it again, but this time covered Ina's coat and her lovely new hairdo.

'Ina, he's dun it tae you noo!'

Stating the bleeding obvious seemed to be the way these women worked.

Fraser and I just could not believe that this was all happening.

Thank God the bus slowed down and we realised it was our stop. Fraser made to get up but I suggested that it might be prudent to let the fellow who had just relinquished the rental of his evening meal get off before us. By the time the scunner had got to his drunken feet the poor women had made their way to the back of the bus and the stairs down to the exit platform. Ted followed them and then me and Fraser. The three of us had just made it to the top of the stairs and looking down we could see the two women standing on the pavement in hysterics and floods of tears. The conductor looked up at us and in the nick of time swung round on the platform pole thus avoiding the third volley of puke which, exocet style, battered into the wretched women, this time down their fronts.

Ted scrambled down the stairs, negotiated spectacularly, the step off the bus and staggered past the distraught women as though nothing had happened. We asked them if there was anything we could do to help them but they just howled their eyes out. We took that as a no. The bus conductor dinged his bell and off the bus went.

Fraser and I got back to the school thanking God that we didn't have to present ourselves to our coach covered in vomit. The next day John Anderson gave us the mother of sessions after which neither of us could walk, never mind run, for about a week such was our oxygen debt!

Schools International, Belfast 1966
England in the lead, 2nd Scotland (yours truly), England 3rd- Gareth Edwards

CHAPTER 8

I Leave School and Start a Career

After leaving school in July 1966 I was officially due to start work immediately at the old Edinburgh Savings Bank. James Thomson, chief accountant of the bank and one time Heriot's FP stand-off, agreed to let me begin my banking career at the Haymarket branch of the bank after the British Junior Athletics Championships later in that month. Mr Thomson was a keen sportsman and happy to help me, a fellow FP, prepare for the athletics event of my life. Mr Thomson's brother, Ian, was one of the famous eight Herioters that played for Scotland at full back.

The day soon came round for me to start work at the bank. The manager and staff at the Haymarket branch gave me a generous welcome and congratulated me on being a British Junior Champion. My celebrity lasted approximately five minutes and then it was down to the serious business of banking. My very first boss was called James Shannon Baxter. My initial impressions of him were that he had an air of authority about him; he looked like he wouldn't suffer fools gladly; a man not to be trifled with, I thought. Not that I had ever trifled with anyone in authority before. I had tried to trifle in another context with the odd Mary Erskine girl and in some cases they trifled with me - I was only too pleased to be trifled with like that but that's another story. If I was ever going to contemplate trifling behaviour it certainly wasn't going to be with James Shannon Baxter. The first instruction I got from the boss was,

'Young Bruce, will you please go to the bank.'

Funny, I thought I was already in a bank. Mr Baxter handed me two big leather bags and a Bank of Scotland withdrawal chit.

'I am sorry sir, I don't understand'

'We bank most of our money with the Bank of Scotland at the close of business each day because we are not insured to hold more than a few thousand pounds overnight,' came the reply which was delivered in a tone, and look, of despair.

'Oh I see.' I felt like a bit of a fool.

I was so scared of making a further fool of myself, I was frightened to ask where the nearest Bank of Scotland was. So, I set off, thankfully in the right direction but I could feel Mr Baxter's laser like eyes burning holes in the back of my neck. I hadn't really made a fool of myself, it was just that Mr Baxter seemed to be such a scary person that, at the tender age of eighteen, and because he was sighing and shaking his head a lot at me, I just assumed I was a natural born clot and that nothing could be done to help me. I have to say that I did feel a bit like a penny bank clerk as I stood in a queue each morning and afternoon, withdrawing from, and paying money into, the Bank of Scotland. My humiliation was compounded by the smell of gas that appeared to be under the teller's nose as he dealt with my transactions.

It's funny isn't it how things that go round come around. The Savings Bank network was, in the not too distant past, taken over by Lloyds bank to become Lloyds TSB and then in the very recent past that organisation took over The Bank of Scotland!

One day I was to find a redeeming feature in myself. There were bigger clots than me going around town. Mr Baxter told me I had to get a National Insurance number and in order to obtain the necessary reference I was to report to the National Insurance Offices, somewhere in an area of Edinburgh called Fountainbridge. I duly set off for what I considered to be a bit of a skive.

I was filling in a form in the social security department when a young lad, about my age, approached me. I guessed he was an apprentice tradesman, given his blue overalls, a foot rule sticking out a side trouser pocket and a pencil behind his ear.

'Hello pal,' he said with a very puzzled look on his face. 'What's your surname?'

'Bruce,' I replied to this very formal request.

My new found friend now sported an even more puzzled expression. He looked at his form which, I noticed out of the corner of my eye, was still completely blank, he had entered nothing.

'What do you mean?' he enquired.

'What do you mean what do I mean ?'

It then dawned on me that the poor lad didn't know what surname meant. I asked him what his full name was.

'Wullie McNohandle,' he said.

'Well Wullie, McNohandle is your surname.'

'Oh, ok,' and off he went back to his desk to complete the task.

He was still there as all the new contributors to the UK economy left the room. Wullie is probably now a millionaire property developer with a big house in Barnton and a yacht and villa in Cannes.

Just as I was congratulating myself on not being the dumbest guy in town I found myself in another one of those awful Baxter moments. The next day after my encounter with the joiner, Mr Baxter, who had decided to help out with ledger posting let out a bellowing,

'Whose writing is this?'

The whole staff had to go and look at the handwriting on a ledger card. Guess what: it was mine. The ledger cards had a lot of important information on them including the nature of the depositor's employment.

Mr Baxter, waving the card at me said,

'Douglas, what on earth is an armchair winder?'

'I don't know sir, but an awful lot of them have been coming in to the bank and opening accounts so that their employer can send their wages to the bank.'

'Well what do you *think* an armchair winder is ?'

'I have no idea sir, something to do with the construction of armchairs I suppose,' came the clueless and nervous reply.

It was becoming horribly obvious to me that good old Baxter knew perfectly well what an armchair winder was.

'Look, this fellow has never had anything to do with furniture, he is an armature winder at the newly opened up factory that manufactures electric powered motors, you clot.'

By the time I left school I had experienced summer jobs, well actually only one type of job but it was over a period of three summers. Like every kid up until about the age of fourteen to fifteen. I had gone on holiday with my parents but, by the age of fifteen, that experience was not one I wanted to go through again and I guess it was the same for my folks. I usually spent a couple of term holiday weeks away with the school's Combined Cadet Force and after that the remainder of the holiday was just complete boredom.

My folks happened to mention to a friend of theirs that I was bored and could do with something to fill in my lengthy holiday time. The friend was a member of the Scottish Liberal Club on Princes Street. He said he would have a word with the club secretary to see if he needed any summer help. This secretary fellow happened to be the uncle of my hero Kenny Scotland, Jim Scotland. He told my folk's friend to ask me to call him for an interview. I did that, and before you could say Kenny Scotland, the world's first running full back, I was interviewed and duly taken on at The Scottish Liberal Club HQ as the assistant handyman and occasional cocktail waiter. My experiences in this job made it very difficult for me to take working for a living seriously. The whole set up was quite bizarre with sprinklings of hilariously extraordinary experiences; at least they appeared that way to me at the time. Talking of time, it's amazing where it has all gone. The Liberal Club, as I knew it, is no more. It was sold, along with the adjoining Scottish Conservative Club building to Debenhams many years ago. Prior to all those big changes there was a fever of activity during the morning hours in these buildings which were steeped in history. Such activity was not really noticeable at the front, that is to say Princes Street, it was all round the back in the little lanes off Rose Street. Amongst a variety of deliveries to the back doors of many an establishment, a big feature was the brewers lorries. In earlier times, before motorised lorries, the area was serviced by horse-drawn drays. That whole back basement area still had a distinct atmosphere of the upstairs-downstairs regime. The drays, and later the lorries, would arrive with the replacement bottles of beer, wines and spirits.

Smartly dressed, I reported for duty on my first day. I passed a couple of uniformed doormen, who, not having a clue to my identity, saluted me. Upon enquiring the nature of my visit they turned a shade puce when I said I had come to start as the assistant handyman. Wasted salutes and no tip to boot. They probably thought that I was an effing student.

I was welcomed by Jim Scotland. He seemed a very nice man, very efficient and happy to see me. His wife stood with him. I remember her as a very charming, stylish lady but a bit more formal than Jim. Mr Scotland introduced me to the chief handy-man, George. Although he was probably about fifty years my senior, he was insistent that I leave it to just George. Jim left me with George who was instructed to tell me my duties. After giving me a long brown cotton coat to protect my clothing George outlined my job description. My first task in the morning was to let the draymen in. I thought it odd that, in a number of deliveries, some cases were short of a few, well actually quite a lot of, bottles particularly in the weeks after I first met these jolly delivery men.

George showed me the standing order jobs which all took place in the morning and explained that the afternoon would take care of itself. The first job was to open the doors of the booze cellar and let the draymen in to leave their delivery and take away the empties.

The draymen would explain to me, the naïve, glaikit twit, that they had been obliged to remove a number of broken bottles and would be reporting back to their head office this very sad but unavoidable loss; sign here son. Apparently the rough cobblestoned back lanes shoogled their lorrie about so much that breakages were unavoidable. I was told not to mention it to my boss as they thought it would only upset him. I was assured that they would make up the loss in the next delivery which, of course, was inevitably short, thanks, apparently to these blessed cobblestones!

After I had overseen the delivery and signed, what I now know as the biggest lie sheet in Christendom, I went on to peel the potatoes for the kitchen porters. I didn't actually have to peel the tatties manually. I just had to tip two or three large buckets of Maris Pipers into a big machine. This machine resembled a small cement mixer. The inner walls of the mixer had a very rough sandpaper like texture and upon switching it on, the potatoes were hurled about the rough walls which stripped the tubers of their skins. Once this part of the job was over I took the buckets of skin-stripped tatties up to the lady kitchen porters. They set about them with special knives that removed any stubborn potato eyes which in turn might have offended the members' eyes.

The next routine job was to empty the waste bins that were to be found throughout the entire, huge building. Remember, this building is now half of a huge department store. I had a job not laughing out loud as senior handyman George talked me through the procedure. Unfortunately George had a kind of speech impediment and he couldn't say empty. He said it with a silent t; so, it was my job to go through all the rooms with a big bin, no black bags in those days, and **empy** the waste baskets into the big bin.

Once I had garnered all the rubbish I had to take the big bin down to the basement, just off the potato peeling section and fling the contents into the central heating furnace. This worked okay for the first week or so. Then, one morning after seeing off the draymen, I set off to empy the waste baskets. There had been a ladies night the day before and the ladies rooms had a number of very full baskets. I gathered up all the ladies' rubbish together with the usual stuff and headed off down to the furnace in the basement. I opened up the furnace door, flung the contents of the bin into the blazing fire, slammed the heavy iron door shut then sat down for a fag and some contemplation, mostly about why was I smoking as an aspiring athlete and rugby player. I no sooner had the fag lit when there was a loud revolver-like bang. I felt a sharp pain in my chest and looked down. There, sure enough, was a bullet hole in my tunic, with adorning flared singe marks. I collapsed on to a seat, holding my chest where I thought my heart was situated. I waited to go cold like they do in the movies. I shouted to the world at large to get word to my mother. I also prayed for a merciful and quick death but was surprised that my life hitherto, was not flashing before me. Hell I was only fifteen, what had I ever done to anybody? Death never came. I pulled myself together and checked my body out. Yup, there was the bullet hole in my brown coat. I stripped that article of clothing off and, good God, there was a hole in my shirt. Off with the shirt and to my relief there was no hole in my chest but a round, red and very sore mark. Chink, something fell on the ground. It was a round, hot piece of metal. As I looked down, there, together with the "bullet" was an exploded warped can of ladies hair lacquer lying on the ground. For goodness sake! I had chucked a pressurised can into the furnace which had blown up, unhinged the furnace door and spat out the top of the lacquer spray into my chest. I'll not do that again I mused. I decided to get rid of my shirt for the simple reason my mum would never believe the truth or if she did, I wouldn't be allowed back to the Liberal Club again plus, as I discovered, a fiver a week for what I did was pretty good going, not to be stupidly sniffed at.

To return briefly to my first day at the Club. The staff all had a delicious daily lunch which was identical to that which the members came in their droves to enjoy. Good traditional Scottish grub: very, very tasty, but thoroughly bad for you is club food. You know the kind of thing, scotch broth made with full fat lamb stock, followed by steak and kidney suet pudding, tatties smothered in butter and minted peas. Bringing up the rear in customary fashion would be rhubarb crumble and custard, all of which were prepared and cooked by the jolly club cook, who, needless to say, would have found it very difficult to get through the turnstiles at Murrayfield. The porters, doormen and handymen all assembled in the kitchen and had all the courses together dolloped onto plates with metal lids atop. The distance between the kitchen and the staff dining area was too far to enable individual course servings. So, it was a big rush to get to our table and bolt the food down whilst it was still hot. At least that is what I did, forgetting I had about half a century on my colleagues.

Mmmmmmmm, it was scrumptious. Although this delicious food had the likelihood of cooling down before it was scoffed, my colleagues were anxious to ask and discuss with me what they obviously thought were a few pertinent questions.

Porter: 'How much are they paying you son?'

'£5.00 a week,' said I tucking in to my soup.

£5.00 a week was quite a lot of money in 1963 and it was possibly close to what these much older guys were earning. In simple layman's terms it was getting on for sixty pints of beer. Gasps and sharp intakes of air were taken by all around the table, apart from me.

'Do you do the gee gees?', said a doorman, still in his heavy great coat style livery, minus the fancy hat. He looked like an Italian prisoner of war who had never gone home. He was also almost as incomprehensible . Thankfully I knew what a gee gee was which saved me the humiliation of asking 'What are Gee, Gees?'

I explained, savouring my steak and kidney pie, that, whilst I didn't do the gee gees myself, I knew for certain that my grannie did, or at least she watched gee gee racing on the telly like the Queen mother did. There were differences though between the Queen Mum and my grannie, I explained to my slack mouthed newly found colleagues. My mum's mum didn't drink gin nor did she have a colostomy bag. My colleagues just stared at each other in wonderment.

Just as I was about to sink my teeth into my pudding, George, my line manager as he would be so described nowadays, came away with what I guess was meant to be a pivotal statement but, at the time, was a bit of a puzzle to me. He said, as though prophetically,

'Just wait till the darkies get a haud oh yay !' An early sixties form of racism I suppose, which sailed right over my young head.

The next morning, Jim Scotland came downstairs to the dark chambers which were the main working places for George and me. He was quite excited and explained that, because the club was getting busier and busier each day, which undoubtedly it was, he had decided to take on an additional permanent handy man. Apparently he couldn't resist a particular candidate because he had such beautiful hand writing. Neither George nor I could see what the devil good penmanship had to do with "empying" buckets and peeling potatoes. Hiring and firing was not our department and so we waited to see what our calligrapher was all about. Next day the scribe pitched up and was introduced to me and George. The man was of very slight build, shook a lot and was late of the British Railways ticketing clerical staff, Waverley Branch. I guess George didn't really want to know about the guy and decided his career as a handyman should be stopped at the starting gate. This was no doubt the reason why I was assigned to "train" the poor wee man.

Education for my new colleague started right away. I just told him to watch me, it was hardly rocket science I thought. We went through the whole routine, draymen, tatties then bucket empying. I actually found myself saying "empy" to the poor wee man who I could see had also, by this stage in the tutorial, figured out that his beautiful hand writing was going to be of very little use to him in his new job. I could also see that he thought that I too had a speech impediment. After about twenty minutes we rendezvoused at the furnace. I explained to him at this point the fright that I got the morning before. I guess I was probably a bit too colourful and com-prehensive with the description of events. Our new man was aghast and started shaking again. I said however, that I would make sure that what had happened furnacewise would never happen again. I checked through what I thought were all the buckets and asked my new work mate to open the furnace door and chuck all the contents of the various containers into the fiery furnace. We sat down for a minute and, whilst I smoked and he abstained, I noticed that he was keeping a very close eye on the furnace door which again, all of a sudden, blasted open and this time missed me and shot the new man fair and square in the chest.

"It is rocket science!" I thought to myself.

After the moment in which my colleague checked that he was still alive, he took off like Jesse Owens and that was the last I, or anybody else in the employment of the Liberal Club, saw of him.

On a Saturday night and sometimes a Friday night too I took on the role of a cocktail barman. There was a very nice lounge on one of the many levels in the building and it served perfectly as a kind of cabaret venue. The view out on to Princes Street and the Castle was superb. Regularly the weekends were taken up by the members, their wives and private guests only. They were entertained by a talented pianist called Price McRae who I knew as an elder in my Kirk. Whilst Price was tinkling out the numbers on the ivories, a gentleman by the name of A B Ross was playing snooker in an adjoining room with three other club members. A. B Ross, otherwise known, I believe, as Sweetie Ross, was retired but had been the head of his family confectionary business, Ross's, funnily enough. Mr Ross and his snooker pals drank only single malt Scotch but each player had his own favourite. Jim Scotland knew the round and every time a bell rang in the bar, triggered by Mr Ross in the snooker room, Jim poured out four different malts. He carefully put them on a tray and told me that malt A went to Mr Sweetie Ross, malt B to Mr T. Alisker, malt C to Mr Glen Farclas and malt D to Mr Speyed McMoggie.

'For the love of Pete, do not, under any circumstances, get them mixed up because they will be able to tell, they will you know,' warned Jim. Ha! I thought, that will be right. The first time I took the drinks in very nervously, giving Mr Ross his one first. I knew who he was, he had been pointed out to me earlier that night. I then announced the names of the other players which they duly acknowledged, and I gave them their drinks in order. I made sure I memorised who was linked to what malt but the frosty looks I got from these men in my faltering debut told me if I went through the routine in that manner again, it would go down as well as someone breaking wind in the Club lift after one of those fabulous lunches.

The bell in the bar rang quite frequently and after about three or four times I thought that, just for fun, I would switch the drinks around. Surely, after that number of drinks, and they were large club measures, nobody on this earth could tell the difference. Being just a young lad, I didn't know that there are big variations between island malts and those from say, Speyside. I had hardly returned to the bar, which was only four strides away, when the bell rang loudly and continuously. Given that I had just taken in a round of malts, Jim Scotland knew that something had gone horribly wrong.

'You better get back in there and quick,' he said supportively.

I knocked on the door and heard a very angry sounding A B Ross bellow

'Come!'

In I went and was advised in no uncertain terms that I had cocked up the round and had caused a terrible upset. 'Take these drinks back to the bar and get Mr Scotland to pour four more'

'Yes Mr Ross' I squeaked.

'Oh and before you go young man, how old are you?'

'Fifteen sir' I admitted.

'Good God, are you still at school then?' Sweetie Ross questioned, almost choking.

'Yes sir, I attend George Heriot's'

That seemed to be in my favour. I was warned by Mr Ross that I was too young to be working in a bar but he would turn a blind eye to it, provided I brushed up on my service and kept as low a profile as possible.

'The Club licence could be at stake,' he warned sternly and with a look on his reddish face that suggested that it would be all my fault, 'so just watch it.'

I promised that I would attend to my duties in the proper fashion. Jim Scotland knew darned well what had happened insofar as the drinks were not matched up correctly to the drinkers but, he didn't know I had deliberately screwed up the round. He stood at the bar with a grin on his face and said,

'Here endeth the first lesson laddie!'

The next week I discovered that Mr Ross was a Herioter himself and generations of male Ross's had attended the school. This explained the eleventh hour reprieve the week before.

The reprieve didn't last very long however. Jo Grimmond, the then UK leader of the Liberal party visited the Club a week later to attend a big lunchtime reception in his honour. Leader Grimmond had a favourite pewter beer mug which was duly filled with India Pale Ale and handed to me to take out to him at the top table. Suddenly, there were dozens of newspaper camera flashes which accompanied the photographing of me handing the beer over to Jo Grimmond. That was bad enough but, when I got home that evening, my mother announced with great delight that I had been on the 6 o'clock ITN news serving Jo Grimmond a beer. Arrrgh, that was it. A B Ross went mental and forced Jim to sack me from the barman job. I couldn't have had a higher profile if I had tried.

I don't know what authority Mr Ross had so far as the Club constitution went but his word seemed to be law. Authority was not new to A B Ross as I later found out. In the early fifties Sweetie Ross was the vice president of George Heriot's School (FP) Rugby Club. The club wanted to sew numbers on the backs of the players' jerseys and have the laundering of the jerseys paid for by the Club. The reasoning behind the numbering of jerseys was sound: spectators and sports writers alike would be able to follow the game more easily. A B Ross was agin this as a point of principle. He thought that it smacked of professionalism and when, for once, he didn't get his way, he resigned his vice presidency.

Times have certainly moved on. If Sweetie Ross could see the average club kit nowadays he would have apoplexy.

So far as my time in the Liberal Club is concerned it probably was not the best preparation for my proper job in the Bank. Unlike the Liberal Club there were not that many laughs in a day but there were moments that have stuck in my mind. One incident, in particular, was costly both to my self-esteem and quite literally my pocket. Work was supposed to start at 9 am and the bank opened at 9.30 am for public business. At 3pm we closed to the public and got on with balancing the day's books and other tasks that we had not finished throughout the day. In actual fact we were expected to be in the office by around 8.30 am but we could leave the bank in the afternoon just as soon as everything was cleared up. If the office had an efficient assistant manager, or second man as he was then called, we could get away home very quickly. The second man at Haymarket branch, a really nice man by the name of George Strachan, was very, very efficient and we always got away by 3.30pm. This enabled me to get home by bus at 4pm, and in the summer, George Strachan to be on the first tee at The Royal Burgess before then because he had a car. So, we were not exactly pushed. There were however drawbacks. For instance, we had a late night on a Friday and working on Saturday mornings was also part of our contract. On Saturdays the male staff were allowed to come to work dressed in a sports jacket or blazer if we liked. Big deal. The joint stock banks operated a wee bit differently. They closed for lunch and did not have a late night.

This meant that most of the ordinary working men and women had deposit accounts with the Edinburgh Savings Bank because we were open at the times that suited them, the customer.

Saturdays, as a rugby player, were often a big problem to me. If I was due to play away the team bus would probably leave Edinburgh around 12.30 pm. The bank closed on a Saturday at 12 noon but of course tills had to be balanced and other bits and pieces filed away and so on. Bearing in mind that Mr Baxter appeared to me to be a bit of an ogre, asking to get away in time to catch the bus was always a nerve-wracking experience. To be fair the boss did have other staff to consider and so letting me leave before them on a fortnightly basis was tricky for him also. Looking back on it all now, Mr Baxter probably wasn't the bogeyman that I thought he was. After a bit of bowing and scraping the Guv always let me away, but only just in time. The gathering place for Heriot teams playing away was always The Usher Hall in Lothian Road. It was a fair old distance on foot but that was the least expensive way for me to catch up with my team mates. I had to run like hell all the way up Morrison Street which was the hypotenuse of Shandwick Place and Lothian Road. By the time I got to the Usher Hall memories of the run from the school bus to the Old Red Pavilion to play Hastie's Balmoral rugby were vivid.

Anyway to return to the costly experience I had.

Most people smoked in the sixties. Bank staff were allowed to smoke in the main office before opening for the public and later in the day after we said goodbye to the last depositor. Mr Baxter enjoyed a small cigar in these periods and the rest of the smokers got on with their Players or whatever. I plucked up courage one morning to take some cigarettes into the office. It was like radar kicking in; the second I took a fag out of its packet Mr Baxter started to stare at me in that unnerving way that he had about him. He said that he hoped that I would use an ash tray and not rest my cigarette on the Bank's woodwork and singe it. I lit up nervously and realised I was still getting the laser stare. Shaking the match to extinguish the flame I noticed there wasn't an ash tray to hand. Fearful of burning Baxter's precious woodwork I put the spent match back in its box which I returned to my suit jacket pocket. One eye on my work, the other on my fag and a third that I had developed since joining the bank, on Baxter, I inhaled nervously hoping I had the James Dean style casual look about me that I had been practising in an effort to look less of a clot. ShaaaaawahWooooossssssshhhShahahhh, like the Liberal Club furnace, my jacket pocket exploded. In a second I was a living incendiary device. The bomb within my pocket was filling the office air with a horrible stink of sulphur and burning Hector Powe suit wool. The blasted match had not been extinguished so igniting the whole boxful of the things. I was still getting the withering Baxter stare and the tut-tutting as I beat out the flames. The rest of the staff were in choked hysterics. Both me and Baxter were now convinced beyond all reasonable doubt that I was, no question, a clot. I had some explaining to do to my mother when I got home that evening.

Looking back on my early days in the bank and Haymarket branch in particular I think that Mr Baxter, in a way, had taken a bit of a shine to me for whatever reason. He and his second in command took me and an office friend of mine out once on a summer evening to the Royal Burgess for a game of golf. Baxter wasn't a bad player as it turned out and was quite complimentary to me on my performance. Unlike my Dad, however, the boss took me into the club house for a drink after our round. Asking me if I would like a pint of export I replied in the positive whereupon another member standing at the bar, and a bit worse for wear, announced loudly,

'That's the stuff my boy, that'll put muscle on your shit!'

An otherwise civilised posh end of Edinburgh experience was shattered.

After I had put in six months at Haymarket I was told one Friday to report to a small branch of the Bank somewhere in the Lothians on the following Monday. Apparently Haymarket Branch was a relief office for when any staff at the West Lothian town were absent through sickness or holidays. On the Monday morning I reported to my new temporary manager after a bus run out from the terminus in Edinburgh's St Andrew's Square. The manager there was called Wullie I Don't Give a Fig. I can't remember his real name so in the tradition of name calling in this book I have given him a made up handle. I have a feeling that due to the astonishing goings on at that branch my brain really is trying to block out many aspects of the experience.

Wullie I Don't Give A Fig welcomed me to the branch and introduced me to Magret. Her name was actually Margaret as she explained later with a tutt and a toss of her head when I addressed her as Magret. Wullie was a bit slack in his pronunciation as it turned out. Anyway Magret was a local lass; the depositors loved her and indeed relied upon her. So that was it : a full staff complement was three. I was astonished at the tiny contingent when, after our morning coffee, Wullie boasted to me that, although it seemed to be a wee branch, we had on deposit, in that small country town, more than all the other Scottish banks in the community put together. This statistic was astonishing because in addition to the Savings Bank the wee town sported branches of the Bank of Scotland. The British Linen Bank, The National Commercial Bank of Scotland, the Clydesdale and North of Scotland Bank and the Royal Bank of Scotland. At first I thought that Wullie was really shooting a line but I soon found out why his claim was probably quite legitimate.

On the dot of 9.30 am we opened for business. Wullie manned the only till and he gratefully took in a number of deposits. Then a poor wee wifie nervously handed over a withdrawal form. This was akin to striking a vampire through the heart with a wooden stake so far as our Wullie was concerned.

'What on earth do you need £30.00 for Mrs Scared to Death?' snapped Mr I Don't Give A Fig.

'I want to buy a fridge from the Co-op across the road.' Said the bank robber, at least that is how Wullie would have described her .

'Dinny be daft Mrs Scared to Death, what do you want to waste your money on one of those new-fangled things for when you, your mother and her mother before her has managed fine with the larder on the kitchen windowsill for all these years'

Mrs Scared to Death had heard exactly what I guessed she predicted she would hear and mumbled something along the lines of,

'Oh aye, right enough,' as if she had had a temporary bout of dementia and off she went screwing up her withdrawal form. There were many unsuccessful attempts to part Wullie and his money that morning. Each traitor was sent off with a flea in their ear.

Wullie eventually excused himself at lunch time having successfully fought off a number of attempted brass necked heists on his bank and handed the till over to me. The hitherto disappointed locals all knew I was a rookie and came back with refreshed withdrawal slips, demanding their money which I gave them knowing I was a dead man walking.

Sure enough I got a grilling about all the withdrawals but I had to stick to my moral ground. I explained to my temporary boss that the people who had made withdrawals were perfectly within their rights to do so. This of course did not cut any ice with Wullie and he never took another lunch break so long as I was around, bringing in sandwiches instead. Wullie was a kind boss to Magret and as soon as he felt things were hunky dory in the afternoon, he sent Magret "awa hame". He and I finished up the paperwork.

Before we finally signed off and left, Wullie's last duty was to lock the safe. Before he slammed the door shut, to my utter amazement, he would stick his backside into the safe as far as it would go and break wind very loudly at the same time.

'Anyone that tries to rob this bank will be very, very, sorry.'

What poor Magret thought of that in the mornings when she opened the safe I will never know.

There were many ways that Wullie tried to put off depositors from making withdrawals. I think the most spectacular was the porkie pies he told people on the phone. Many depositors who lived in the Lothians and its surrounds, commuted to Edinburgh and so, coming into the bank during the working day was probably awkward for them. The bank at that time did not have a current account facility so cash withdrawals were the only way of settling bills, handing over housekeeping etc. Quite often poor souls would phone up the bank from the City and ask if their salary had been posted to their account. The first time I picked up such a call I asked the caller to hold whilst I checked. I went over to the box with all the credit slips in it and started to look for the appropriate payment.

Wullie shouted, 'What are you doin?'

'Looking for a salary slip Mr I Don't Give A Fig.'

It was normal practice at Haymarket and seen there as being customer friendly. Before I got any further, Wullie grabbed the phone off me and started to rustle the morning paper as if he were raking through the relevant filing box. He gleefully announced to the probably skint fellow on the other end of the line,

'No I canny find it here, sorry, come in nearer the end of the week' It was a Monday, poor bugger.

Wullie turned to me and explained the position as he saw it,

'These folk should realise that we canny give that kinda confidential information out over the phone.'

All the man wanted to know was whether his salary was in or not, there was absolutely no question of breaking confidentiality but Wullie's precious deposits were intact so far as that caller was concerned, for a few days anyway.

Knowing I had no personal transport Wullie offered me a lift into Edinburgh at the end of my first day and every day thereafter so I must have performed other duties in a manner that was satisfactory to him. As we were leaving the car park he wound down his window and shouted,

'Hello Sandy, how are ye?'

I didn't hear a reply, in fact I couldn't see anybody around apart from a Golden Retriever.

'Ye see that, I even ken the dugs around here,' Wullie announced proudly.

A couple of weeks later I returned to Haymarket branch, and a year or so after that I was transferred to Blackhall branch and thence to Corstorphine. In total I worked for the Bank for three years . It took me all that time to admit to myself and to my parents that banking was not for me. I moved on to Scottish Save and Prosper and a year or so after that to a major Scottish life assurance company.

Wullie, for reasons that I can have a good guess at, was highly thought of by the Head office officials of the Edinburgh Savings Bank who, shortly after my time at his office, promoted him to manage one of the larger City branches.

CHAPTER 9

George Heriot's School (FP) Rugby Club Beckons

It was August 1966 when I received a letter from John Ross, the captain of Heriot's Former Pupils Rugby Club inviting me, as a recent school leaver, to come along to pre-season training and join the FP Rugby Club. This was to be the beginning of the first of my two distinct chapters at Goldenacre. The other was to open up in 1996; but, of course, more of that later.

I was absolutely thrilled, along with about two dozen other new FPs, to receive this missive.

It was quite easy for the FPs in those days to automatically pick up enough new blood, not necessarily good blood (remember we are talking about people like me) but certainly new, each season from school. It is simply a fact that things changed a lot for the FP rugby club after the school went co-ed and girls started to take places that boys would otherwise have had.

Goldenacre playing fields looked just perfect as I ran out with dozens of my fellow rookies for our first FP training session on a September Saturday afternoon. Head groundsman, Alec Gillies, had ensured, as usual, that Heriot pupils and former pupils would have immaculately groomed and beautifully green pitches to play their rugby on. The scene however was set for a personal physical shock to rival the big boys athletics jolt I had received only a month or two earlier at the much more austere setting of "New Meadowbank".

School sports masters were used to their pupils returning from their summer break being reasonably naturally fit, but former pupils on a seasonal break return were mostly out of condition. As it turned out for me, I was already in a demanding fitness regime with coach Sinclair at Octavians, so, I figured that my first FP training session would be a piece of cake. Aye right!! I was okay with any running exercises but when it came to the demands of press and sit ups, I was useless compared to the older hands. Sitting now, as I write forty five years on, with a sore neck, sore elbows and a stiff back I reflect on these pre- season sessions. I know now that probably very few of my current muscular and skeletal pains were caused by the game of rugby itself. No, the twinges of pain, agony and anguish come mostly from so called fitness and warm up exercises in the weeks before, and indeed, during each rugby season I participated in between1966 and 1983. Perhaps the odd motorbike accident after age fifty didn't really help either!

My understanding of where post-rugby aches really come from developed many years later when I formed a keep fit club in Stonehaven for men over the age of thirty- five. Many of the par-ticipants were ex rugby players and footballers. Rosemary, my wife, used to call it the keep fat club! I will cover the detail of that forma-tion later but suffice to say that after a few weeks of the Keep Fit Club a local physiotherapist became alarmed at the number of men from the club that were attending her clinic. I also made an appoint-ment to see her as I had a very sore back. The physio asked me if she could attend one of our meetings to see what was going on. Come along she did to the very next gathering. She was astonished at what was going on. I don't think there was a single warm-up exercise that she approved of. Some of the routine, in particular a neck movement, and, the way we executed sit-ups was apparently so bad that she reckoned we would all be doing a lot of damage to ourselves. For many of us this was bad news indeed. We had been performing all of these exercises off and on for about twenty years. George Heriot's School (FP) Rugby Club in the sixties was no different.

Apart from the usual boring upper body work out and running, Heriot's had a unique exercise. Back in the mid-twenties the FPs built a stand at the 1stXV pitch that has a capacity for just over eighteen-hundred spectators. It must have been quite something in those days for a rugby club to have such a magnificent stadium. It still is a remarkable construction. Apart from, perhaps, the Stewart's Melville's equivalent it must be the biggest amateur club stand in Scotland.

A good fitness trainer will mix up his diet of physical jerks to keep a session interesting; Heriot's pre-season trainers always, at some time in the programme, took their squads off to the aforementioned stand and sent them running up and down its steps. That was quite a fat burner which also demanded some light foot work on the descents, the steps being relatively shallow.

The session, once over, was nothing like my athletics training experiences. Track event training saw us all off to bed or some other such puritan act. Not so rugby at Heriot's. No, a thirst had been built up which just had to be quenched in the very best of rugby traditions. Unbelievably, Heriot's FP which, at the time I joined, was past its seventy-fifth anniversary and did not have its own club house. Astonishing when you think of some of the facilities that are available now which are mandatory for any self-respecting club no matter what league they participate in.

The cricket club, however, had a very nice little bar situated in the Red Pavilion. The cricketers were only too happy to allow the rugby club to drink in their clubhouse. I loved that wee bar which was like The Tardis in Dr Who. Somehow, umpteen Heriot teams and their opposition crammed themselves into its confines and had a thoroughly great time after games. Heriot's Rugby Club built the first of two stages of their own clubhouse in 1967.

There was something about the relaxing atmosphere after a rugby match pre the modern league competitions. If one's team won, it was job done, three cheers for the opposition, handshakes all round, well played and congratulations and hard luck. If we lost, well, the opposition went through the winners script and we responded accordingly as the sporting vanquished.

As a young FP I thought that the whole thing was just simply wonderful. Being a member of a club that had a 1st XV in what was then known as the unofficial Championship was a very big deal no matter what team I was in. Every team in the Club came together after a match along with the opposition and we all had a great time. I was just simply amazed that I could be standing of a Saturday afternoon shoulder to shoulder with many a Scottish Internationalist enjoying a beer or three. My favourite experience in the cricket club bar was after a Heriot's v Hawick match. The great Hughie McLeod was propping for the Greens as Hawick are known by the respectful. Mr McLeod and his team mates all gathered in the wee cricket bar with the players from the various Heriot teams playing that day. Drinking, chatting, a darts games commenced. I was fascinated by it all, but, my curiosity turned fairly quickly into anxiety as I watched a Hughie McLeod propelled dart dip short of the target and head right through the welt of my shoe just missing my wee toe.

It is true what they say about youth being wasted on the young. I look back on those days and think to myself, "If only I had fully appreciated that I had been in the exalted company of the likes of big, big world class players like Hughie McLeod, Sandy Carmichael, Colin Blaikie, Jim Telfer, Alex Hastie, Jock Turner and many, many more." There were dozens more at that time. Every clubhouse up and down the land sported some of them on one Saturday or another. Professional rugby put an end to all of that. I guess the Scottish star players in our Nation's pro clubs do not receive quite the same adoration that our Internationalists of yester year had heaped upon them. The top Scottish players of pre 1995, which is the year the game went professional, were true amateurs with normal off the pitch lives the same as fellows like me who had much more humble playing careers. Their International status was therefore all the more commendable as they had to combine earning a living in a profession or trade with the rigours of playing for their country as well as for their club. During a meeting at Murrayfield around 2004 to, which officials of all the clubs in the Edinburgh District were invited, some players from the Edinburgh Pro side were on the stage telling us what life as a full time rugby player was all about. It didn't really sound all that wonderful I have to say and I leant over to ask Jock Millican, Heriot's RC president and a past capped player, if he would have liked to have had the chance to play pro rugby. Admittedly Jock had a fulfilling business career but he was emphatic:

'I much preferred to have a more rounded life where rugby was not my job, it was my after work relaxation.' By the way, anybody who saw Jock play for his club or Scotland would never have imagined that rugby was a relaxation for Jock!!

Yesteryear for Heriot's is quite a story. When I was but a very young lad at Heriot's school I remember my English teacher, Gibby Galloway telling my class that between the two World Wars Heriot's FP Rugby Club could expect anything up to ten thousand to twelve thousand spectators at some of their matches. These figures may seem a shade exaggerated but the turnstile meters couldn't lie. One can only imagine the headache the treasurer had counting all the gate money and banking it. That headache would be welcomed nowadays as current amateur club rugby gates have sunk to all-time lows. Ironically, the actual game of rugby is no longer the core business of an "amateur" rugby club. Sponsors and advertisers are desperately sought after by club committees all over the land to fund the day to day running of what is now a sport laden down with ridiculous costs, much of which, even at so called amateur level, is players expenses.

Although Heriot's, along with all the premier league clubs have nothing like the supportive crowds that existed back in the thirties, forties, fifties and the early sixties, there were still gates in the thousands in the seventies and early eighties, and that status obtained up to the days of professionalism. I well remember a Heriot's v Stewart's Melville match in the early eighties which had hype in both The Scotsman and The Edinburgh Evening News for the whole week prior to the kick-off and a subsequent paying crowd of well over two and a half thousand. You could have cut the atmosphere that day with a knife. Dougie Morgan, The Stewart's Melville scrum-half, also of Scotland and the Lions, kicked three penalties very early on in the game. Andy Irvine replied with three penalties, but, with a few seconds left of the allotted eighty playing minutes, Dougie Morgan settled things with a drop goal.

It's really too long ago to suggest that the past was best as small crowds of around three to four thousand, on average, gather at Murrayfield to watch professional Edinburgh play whomsoever in a league which, in its early stages, was sponsored by Magners, the Irish cider people. The glory amateur days, as they might be called, have long gone I think.

My first year with the FP's was spent mainly in the 3rd XV and occasionally the 2nd XV. My brother-in-law, Derek McCracken, who had by this time retired from 1st XV rugby often played in the same teams as I did. He was a great encouragement to me. It's nice to look back on those days; days when we fielded up to seven sides. Now in 2013 it's difficult to get three sides out.

I thought that a great deal was expected of me and other guys of my age. The senior game was obviously much harder physically than school rugby and not nearly so carefree. There was no escaping criticism from one's team mates and there were endless amounts of it. I think the more experienced playing members felt that they had a duty to keep up the high standards of excellence the club had achieved over the years, so, in their eagerness to keep everyone up to scratch, young upstarts such as me were kept firmly in their place.

My second season saw me regularly in the 2nd XV but in terms of enjoyment it was probably not so good as my first season. In fact, after only a few games in my second season I decided to give rugby a rest and concentrate on athletics training. Fraser McRitchie, my school pal, joined me and we trained very hard that winter on weights, road running and other fitness regimes meted out by the Octavians coach George Sinclair. I returned to the FP rugby club the following season. Fraser went off to London to join the Metropolitan Police. He played a couple of seasons for their 1st XV which was a class act at that time.

My status at Goldenacre didn't really improve and some of my pals who had left school at the same time as me were playing regularly in the second fifteen and sometimes in the first fifteen. One such friend was Jimmy Burnett. Jimmy was playing for the seconds one Saturday against, I think, Edinburgh University whilst I was turning out for the third team up at Meggetland against a Boroughmuir side. I don't remember anything about my game but I do remember that day very well because it was the day that Jimmy broke his neck. I believe that Jimmy was trying to shake off an opposing forward who had jumped on his back and somehow propelled himself forward on a sort of arc shape. Jimmy landed on his head and broke his neck. There are a lot more nightmarish details but suffice to say poor Jimmy ended up in the neurological ward of The Western General Hospital which was not that far from Goldenacre. Jimmy was a good friend of mine, particularly in our last year at School when we were fellow prefects. His injury had quite a sobering effect on everybody in the club and it must have been cause for great anguish for Jimmy's family. My pal was operated on and thankfully the outcome was a great success. After that, many of Jimmy's hospital visitors, if not all of us, pleaded with him to pack rugby in. There was no way Jimmy was going to do that. After persuading Heriot's FPRC that his neck had been made stronger he played many times for the 1st XV and even went on to gain four caps for Scotland in 1980.

Before the league structure came into Scottish club rugby in the season of 1973/74 clubs such as Heriot's had a "friendlies" fixture list that was as good as embedded in the tradition of the club. This meant that less so-called fashionable clubs could not get a shot at Heriot's FP 1st XV. It was left up to the 2nd XV to play these fellows and boy did we have a number of battles on our hands. Broughton, based at Wardie in the Granton area just around the corner from Goldenacre, was a very good example of a club that was keen to show the Heriot's committee the folly of their ways. Any time I played them it was a hard slog from the kick off to the whistle for full time. During my last game against Broughton, a kind of general mêlée broke out towards the end of the match. I found out afterwards it was one of our guys that started proceedings. I was foolish enough to walk towards what can only be described as a mass punch up. A large Broughton forward grabbed me by the arm and was, I thought, about to punch me in the face. Just as I was struggling to free myself from his vice like grip and run away (I was never really one for fisticuffs with guys bigger than me !) the referee spotted us. He had not seen the whole event and decided that it was I who had started this little splinter group fight. The main bout was petering out at this point and so the ref focused his whole attention on me and the Broughton giant. After blowing his whistle so loudly that I think three trains pulled out of Waverley station two miles away, he signalled to me that he wanted a word. My Broughton sparring partner retreated with a grin as the ref told me that if I repeated my actions I would be sent off. Now this was bad enough as I had never been spoken to like that by any referee at any time in my career but, to crown matters, my Dad was standing on the touchline witnessing it all. Neither of us ever spoke of the incident!

Looking back on it all now I realise that I was probably very thin skinned at that time in my life but it was hard to take criticism that was dished out in what I thought was an extremely negative way. A FP player really had to be hard or making a fool of one's self was all too easy. I remember one evening after training I complained to a selector about being dropped a team. He just looked at me, patted me on the head and said, 'There there sonny, away home and get your mummy to make your tea for you and run your bath!' Humiliation.

I realised it was my throwing in at the lineout that was weak. As I walked home from training I recalled with cringing embarrassment that my forwards had been fairly ill tempered with me at lineouts. One of our locks actually shouted at me after a bad throw in.

'Dougie Bruce, you must be the worst thrower in of a ball in the whole wide world of rugby union!'

On the plus side at least it had nothing to do with my speed or ball handling, so I vowed to practice my lineout throwing in. Wingers threw the ball in to the lineout then. To be honest I never did get it up to a reasonable standard, but, as luck would have it, the selectors saw my role more as a centre and so I lost that albatross.

Heriot's Rugby club was, if you like, my only transition between innocent carefree school life and the real life outside. I missed out on the extra transitional bridge that university was for many of my friends. At least I was earning a salary, if one could call it that!

Rugby in those days actually had a cost for players - a share of the coach costs for away games, our own laundry (unless a member of the 1st XV) and a match fee to cover the après game jugs of beer for the opposition. Subscriptions for players were also mandatory, a concept which the modern "amateur" player has great difficulty in grasping. It's ironic that when the bigger clubs in Scotland did not have the same need as nowadays for the huge revenue they got from gate receipts, it poured in at every home game. Now, when players apparently need so much for no charge, the gate money just isn't there, at least not in anything like the large amounts needed. The money to keep the very fragile amateur club game alive and kicking has to be found from so called corporate sponsors. These sponsors are very often simply generous rugby loving donors. It is doubtful that much business for them will be generated in return. It may be difficult for many sponsors to be able to put a figure to any return they may notionally make. Some local businesses such as financial advisors or solicitors may well be able to figure out what the debit and credit sides of their sponsorship are but that may be less clear for large companies such as engineers or firms in the construction industry.

For the administrators of the club game there is little fun anymore, rather it is a weekly worry and heartache, the players generally being oblivious to the problems. To be fair, even in the William Webb Ellis days young players never really cared about anything other than playing, except perhaps the odd well-earned beer or two in the bar after the game.

Turning out for Heriot's second fifteen meant that I had the privilege of playing alongside some 1stXV players who were coming back after longish term injuries. On one such occasion I found myself in the distinguished company of Colin Blaikie. Colin was the sixth of our eight famous International full backs at Heriot's. Playing with a class act like Blaikie, I felt that my form took a leap forward. I was still on the wing at the time of this game which was played against Watsonians seconds. They were just recovering from pressure from us, had touched down in their in goal area for a twenty-five drop out. The 'Sonian kicker had decided to kick long and in my direction . I seemed to be under the ball for ages before it came down, the 'Sonian pack thundering after it and me. I was concentrating hard on catching the ball when I heard this voice from what seemed miles away from me shout,

'Dougie, quick, pass it to me'

It was Colin Blaikie and I just did as I was commanded and, as if I was passing down a long spout, I got that ball to Colin who was almost in the centre of the pitch and BOOF he blasted a drop kick from about half way right through the middle of the posts. 'Sonians were not at all chuffed at that double act!!

Heriot's second fifteen could be quite entertaining and not just for their playing skills. Once, when I was on holiday in the capital from my job down in Nottingham, I went to watch the seconds playing Edinburgh Accies seconds. I was standing on the touchline with some committee men and some Accies supporters. Heriot's right winger was one of my school 1st XV fifteen captains, Bruce Welton, sadly no longer with us . At one point he was hammering up the right flank attacking the Accies defences when a successful, if poorly executed, tackle was put in by the opposition left winger. Bruce managed to off load the ball to his outside centre before crashing awkwardly to the ground. Play continued. Bruce a bit dazed, clambered to his feet after what had been a very hard tackle. The tackler was hurt more than Bruce, however, and was still lying on the ground when Bruce misjudged his footing and accidentally stood on the Accie. OOOOyahhhh! exclaimed the Accie as the studs sank in. Bruce seemed to be oblivious to the consequences of his footwork. An Accie supporter had been watching Bruce closely and was to take umbridge at Bruce's next move. It was clearly the last straw for the man.

With an air of well-polished haughtiness, our winger made to re-join play whilst clearing out his right nostril. He did this by evacuating the contents of said nostril using the posh technique he learned during a stint at London Scottish in their 1ˢᵗ XV. It was a masterful combination of the closing of his left nostril using his left index finger, middle two fingers bent and pinkie facing upwards, a deep inhalation through the right nostril and then a thundering expiration made all the more spectacular by using the following winds, his mainly.

The Accie supporter was standing right beside me and was looking a shade disturbed. Further, as I gave him a worried stare it looked like he had bought all that he was wearing from a very specialised shop. He was a tall, very stiff backed, square-jawed guy wearing an enormous, heavily belted coat which had large epaulets and a stiffened upturned collar. The whole ensemble was topped off with a large wide brimmed homburg style hat. His hands were gloved with what looked suspiciously like motorbike riders' gauntlets. Anyway our weird looking co-spectator was clearly unhappy with Bruce's laissez-faire attitude. Astonishingly, he ran onto the pitch in a statuesque fashion and kicked Bruce right up the bum with his right foot which was shod in a size twelve suede boot. Clenching his fists he shouted,

'Take that you dirty bounder!'

Two of the Heriot committee men had to run on to the park to stop the hush puppy kid from having another go at the, now very surprised, and sore-arsed Bruce Welton who, by then, had more than his nose cleaned out.

I have nothing but admiration for committee men, having been one myself for many more years than I care to count, but they, nay we, often make clots of ourselves in the course of our office. Once, when running the line for Mackie, I was standing behind the goals when the opposition kicked a penalty. The ball missed to the right of my post and I stupidly but instinctively caught it. The situation was dumb enough but one of the Mackie players topped it all by shouting irrelevantly:

'Quick Dougie, touch it down!'

Actually, I have done many dumb things as a committee man, full stop. I say this now as I hope it will stand me in good stead when all the folks and the relatives of the individuals that I have poked a bit of fun at in this book come looking for me.

Many years ago a junior team committee man by the name of Ian "Muff" Moffat was pretty good at daft mistakes. Muff had a warped sense of humour which made him a wee bit of a figure of fun with some members but those that knew their rugby would agree that Ian, or Muff as he was nicknamed, was one of the best assessors of players and analysers of games around. He was also a very quick-witted fellow and one had to watch and not find oneself at the wrong end of his humour. Anyway, Muff was asked by the general committee to gather a team together to play a midweek evening game at the far end of the East Lothian coast against a Dunbar side. It must have been a pain in the neck for Muff as that sort of fixture is a difficult one to raise a team for and especially so as he was given very short notice to do it. From the players' point of view it was also a pain because, allowing for the time that the game would take, showering and socialising with the Dunbar lads après match, it would mean a late return to their beds before rising for another day's work. Getting away from work to catch the team bus was a bit of a scunner also. Muff complained all the way down the road to Dunbar, at least an hour away at that time of day, that he had such a job getting fifteen guys together. There is an additional difficulty with midweek games that are not just around the corner: there is usually no time for a warm up or a team talk. This fixture was to be no different. We changed quickly and ran out immediately to the pitch. The Dunbar fellows had finished a good warm up. They were raring to go and, as we Herioters started to take our positions ready for the kick off, Fraser McRitchie, our left wing trotted over to me on the other flank and said :

'Have you counted the number of guys in our team?'

'No, why?' I replied.

'Well if you do I think you will find we have sixteen on the park'

Good heavens he was right. The air turned a very deep blue as Fraser vented his wrath upon Muff. Fraser made it easy for our sheepish committee man to decide who should come off the park. Our extra man, Fraser, was already walking towards the dressing rooms mumbling things like "does that stupid @@!!?? have any idea how hard it was for us to get away from work this evening etc. etc.!"

Worse was to follow for me. Having changed my regular position of wing three-quarter to centre I was enjoying my games of rugby much more than I had been in the first two seasons with the FPs. Remember I explained earlier that wingers used to have to throw the ball into the lineout and I was just simply awful at that skill. Well for this game in Dunbar, as a further help to Muff, I stupidly agreed to play on the right wing. I wasn't getting on too badly with the throwing in so far as the first half was concerned but for some reason I was displeasing my forwards in the second half. I just couldn't get any accuracy into my throwing in. During a breakdown of play caused by a minor injury to a Dunbar player our pack leader came over to have a stern word with me. He asked me if I understood the lineout signals and I said that I did.

'Ok well what are they ?'

'Well' I said 'If the scrum-half taps his left shoulder with his right hand you want the ball at the back of the line; if he taps his right shoulder with his left hand he wants it in the middle and if he taps his chest with either hand it has to go to the front.'

I could see this rather burly forward turning puce with rage but it was not with me that he was angry, rather it was our scrum-half. At a lineout it was his job to pass on the coded instructions to the wings by a sort of conspiratorial hunching of his back and deft touching of his body as previously described. These signals had to be spotted by me right away lest the opposition catch on to the secret. The forwards in their half time huddle had decided to change the codes. Our number 9 was present at this gathering and it had been left to him to come and tell me about the code changes but he forgot to do so. By complete coincidence the left winger had hit the mark correctly in the second half because like me he was useless at throwing in and, for once in my life, I was hitting accurately what I thought was the target. I think our pack leader left the other winger to wallow in his ignorance and I managed to adapt quite well to the changes.

I think we won that game but, whatever the result, I was just glad to get off what was a very windy pitch, get dressed, have a pie and a couple of beers and then return to the capital. I watched Muff very carefully counting sixteen blokes back on the bus.

Dunbar was the cause of another committee man's embarrassment a few years earlier. In the depths of the winter of 1964 Jack Humphreys, who was the chairman of the junior team committee took a side along the coast. Jack was a lovely guy who would have given the shirt off his back to the club. The playing fields at Dunbar rugby club are a shade exposed and on this occasion after twenty minutes or so the teams found themselves playing in a howling gale and a snow storm. It is reckoned that poor Jack was standing on his own peering into the swirling sheets of snow cheering on his beloved Heriot's for over ten minutes before he realised the ref had abandoned the game and everyone was back in the warmth of the dressing rooms wondering where Jack had got to because he had the valuables.

Looking back on my FP rugby club days I think I had much more fun out of the game as a player than the players of today. Perhaps it's different the further down the leagues one goes . Iain Milne and Andy Irvine both told me at the heights of their International careers that they expected their rugby to be sixty percent social and forty percent serious hard work. I don't think Iain will mind me saying that that ratio was probably about right for him but I have an awful funny feeling that it may have been at least the other way around for Andy, if not a completely different proportion!

Heriot's FP Rugby club, although a serious Scottish club in that our 1st XV was always there or there about in the old, unofficial, and later the official, championships there was a very light hearted side to it. That light hearted side applied to both the senior teams in the club and the junior sides. Nowadays training nights throughout the week are taken very seriously. No après fun in the clubhouse after the hard work; it's straight home and work or college the next day, bright-eyed and bushy-tailed. In my playing days at Goldenacre a Tuesday or a Thursday evening after training was spent with my team mates having a few pints, a game of darts and a blether about whatever. Many retired players used to come along also and enjoy a cosy social evening with their pals. Friendships that, in many cases, started at the age of ten, were still going seventy or eighty years later. A rugby club was often the centrepiece of many a bloke's social life, not to mention that of his wife's, fiancé's or girlfriend's, whether they liked it or not!

Whilst Goldenacre was a social focal point for former pupils of George Heriot's School the Scottish Rugby Union, ever vigilant in making sure the spirit of amateurism was not tainted, asked clubs to post notices up on the dressing room doors about the professional code i.e. Rugby League. I cannot remember the exact wording of these notices but it was along the lines of,

"If any club member is approached by a representative of the Rugby League either personally, in writing or even on the phone with regard to recruitment to said league, such an approach must be reported to his club and then the SRU. Failure to do so could jeopardise the amateur status of the member."

Stern warning indeed. Up until 1995 amateur players throughout the world were not "supposed" to benefit financially in any way from the game of Rugby Union. The writing of a book for financial gain before or after retirement from playing at any level would render such an author a professional and end his association with the Union. This would mean complete exile from his club and I suppose any other Union code club house in the land.

Heriot's had a famous member transfer from union to League rugby, namely Roy Kinnear. Roy Kinnear was a member of the highly successful 1920's team and had three caps in the international season of 1926. He was also the father of Roy Kinnear junior, famous TV and film actor. Kinnear snr had a long career with Wigan Rugby League Club. Heriot's committee making sure that they were dealing with the situation properly felt that they had to write to Roy Kinnear and ask him for his resignation which was duly received.

Bizarrely, and one wonders where the following would have sat with the defenders of rugby union amateurism, many a training night at Heriot's rugby club in the late sixties and early seventies could have been likened to a scene from the market in the television series *Only Fools and Horses*. Some of the more entrepreneurial members would turn up to sell, variously: umbrellas, car tyres, shirts and bulk boxes of condoms! Surprisingly, and unlike the wares Del boy would sell in his East London market, the products

were of very good quality, though in the case of the condoms at least one "member" complained that the ones that he got were too small!!

When playing away games a reinforced bladder was an essential part of a rugby player's anatomy. In my early days of FP rugby I was always keen to get back to Edinburgh after a game. The main reason was non understanding girlfriends and, to be honest, spare cash was a bit of a hurdle too. Not that that had anything to do with my bladder. Most of the married guys were never in a hurry to leave the opposition bar and they were in control of the schedule being older, allegedly wiser and, frankly in the majority. Also their courting days were over and a thick skin had been acquired, not to mention deafness. Anyway, no matter how long we stayed in an away clubhouse, industrial quantities of beer were drunk. The same quantities were consumed at home games but a return team bus trip was not then in the equation. There was no such thing in my younger days as a toilet on any of the coaches Heriot's hired and so a nightmare would begin about thirty minutes out of, say, Anniesland in the west end of Glasgow. The driver would eventually stop to let us off when it was discreet to do so but all that did was stimulate the bladder and away we went again another twenty or twenty five minutes further along the old, and usually very cold, A8. Coming away from a Border's club the roads had much more cover for urinating hordes and there were a number of country hostelries along the way, which, if the driver was a good lad would stop at and let us pee and drink yet more beer. It was as if none of us understood nor cared how our bodies functioned.

On one return trip from Glasgow Accies some of the older lads who knew the route and landmarks like the back of their hands got the bus driver to stop at a big roadside chip shop. It made a change from drinking and we could also pee legally. However the service was awful and I would have been quite happy to return to the bus and continue the journey with plans of thinking about anything other than peeing. This mental diversion exercise was to play an important part in my later life and I will leave it up to the readers imagination as to just what that might be!

Suddenly, things picked up behind the counter and the fish suppers were flowing. It wasn't until it was my turn to order that I realised what had happened: some of the older guys in the team had persuaded the chip shop owner to let them get to the firing point so facilitating a clearance of the Heriot's 2nd XV. The "assistants" had donned aprons and in some cases chefs hats, the origin of which I never discovered.

I mentioned earlier that most of the younger lads had dates awaiting them back in the capital; what use we were to them after an away game I will never know. It could therefore be quite tricky keeping a hold of a "bird."

For a wee while I had a girlfriend who hailed from Edinburgh's north- east side which was a reasonable distance from my house. So, if I was to be picking her up in my father's car I had to be careful about my beer consumption. I met her through my employment at the bank and I quickly discovered that she was one half of a pair of absolutely identical and pretty twins. My old school buddie, John Mackie, was not dating at that time and, given that my twin was a tad shy I asked him if he would like an introduction to her sister. John was game and so the match was made. It was an absolutely hilarious and bizarre experience dating these girls. They were not only identical physically but, to confuse matters even more, they both wore exactly the same clothes, applied the same facial make up and sported identical bling. John and I were never really sure if we had the right girl on our arms.

The guys at Goldenacre could hardly contain their mirth at John and me as we strolled into Heriot's clubhouse of a Saturday evening with these clones. John and I had some fun out of it ourselves as I hope the girls did. Their dad was a nice fellow and also very shy. He was the chairman of a local car club. I have no idea what he did for a living, the poor soul trusted John and me but he needn't have worried about us hot blooded Herioter's - his daughters took care of that themselves!

One very rainy Saturday night I went to pick up John prior to collecting the girls and I was taken aback when he answered his door. He was sporting a bespoke tailored Harris Tweed suit. I had never seen anything quite like it. It was one thing going out with identically dressed, identically featured twins who looked like caricatures of themselves, it was quite another making up a foursome with a guy that looked like a Perthshire estate owner. I think what had happened was this: John must have been coming up to a birthday which was probably his twenty-first and his mum had decided to give him a tailor-made suit. She picked out the tailor but left John to choose the material. Big mistake. I didn't say anything to John at the door or indeed ever about the style of the suit, until now that is. Firstly I was just plain speechless and then I just couldn't think of anything to say that would have been mistaken for a compliment.

Off we went to pick up our lassies and John must have got the same glaikit look from the girls' mum that he got from me when she answered the door. In we went for our customary lengthy wait for the twins. John and I usually sat quietly waiting for the girls or had a stilted chat between ourselves about the day's rugby. Daddy was always by the fireside reading The Edinburgh Evening News. As usual he said very little apart from a few polite welcoming words before settling back to his wee world of Saturday night peace and quiet. He was to be rudely awakened on this particular night. The family had a large dog which I will call Charlie. He was usually very docile, much like his owners but on this occasion, he was strangely aroused as we took our seats. Aroused wasn't in it. Charlie made a beeline for John's right leg. Locking his front paws on to the leg,

Charlie started to make mad passionate love to it. Later that evening John and I reckoned that Charlie was attracted to the Harris Tweed suit material which, we were sure, used to be marinated, for want of a better word, in sheep's' urine before being dried, or whatever, and then sold to the tailoring fraternity or at the very least to John's tailor. The rain that had fallen on the suit that night must have acted as a catalyst on the material releasing the musty scent of sheep pee. I don't know whether that is true or not but Charlie had been just good friends with John for several weeks by this time and the dog had not shown before just how much he loved him. Poor John began by politely asking Charlie to stop. Charlie, being a hot blooded male, in time honoured fashion assumed that "no" meant "yes" and carried on regardless. The girls' Dad, no doubt hugely embarrassed, pretended that nothing was going on whilst John tried to physically remove the beast from his leg as quietly and as decently as possible. But, there was no budging Charlie. He was just plain gone. The twin's Dad by this time was very embarrassed. I could tell because he was now trying to read an upside down newspaper. No matter what John did, the hound was going to get satisfaction.

Luckily, if you could put it that way, the deed was over and done with reasonably quickly and whilst Charlie went off to have a wee rest, John excused himself and headed for the bathroom to clean up. I can't remember if the girls remarked on John's suit but I do remember he never, ever wore it again, at least not in my presence and I would imagine nowhere near Charlie.

The last occasion on which John and I went out together with the twins was to a Heriot Club Ball. The Heriot Club is the former pupils' association of George Heriot's school, and is the parent club of all the other FP clubs such as the FP Rugby Club. Most of the Rugby Club and their ladies attended the annual event which was always held on Boxing Day in the Assembly Rooms on George Street, Edinburgh.

It was a huge bash and yet another opportunity in the holiday window to stuff one's face with turkey. Because so many people supported the ball, dining was catered for in two sittings. Dress was black tie for the guys and ball gowns for the gals. Spiffing don't you know.

This particular ball was another chance for the rugby club guys to have a laugh at the expense of Bruce and Mackie but it was a new experience for the non-rugby chaps. Well it was a conversation piece I suppose and a gift to me and John to reply to catty comments with astonishingly witty repartee like "Shut your face ya fat/skinny/bald/hairy / bastard!" Thankfully the meal took quite a chunk out of the evening as old fashioned dancing didn't seem to be something the twins could do very well. I struggled a bit also because I couldn't turn when I got to either end of the floor. This was due to the fact that I was taught how to do the waltz (old fashioned and modern) and the quickstep by my uncle Alec in our narrowish hallway at home. We went up one way, stopped at the end, changed stance, then danced back down again. This, by the way, was not to music but to Uncle Alec counting out one two three, one two three etc. etc.

The evening being officially over, we returned the girls safely to the bosom of their family and oversexed dog. After the usual peck on the cheeks for the twins, John and I returned to the car for the journey back to our homes. John stayed almost on the same road as me but further west. Ferry Road, upon which my house was situated, is a very busy thoroughfare and it only really dawned on us then the implications of me drinking and driving. We figured that, although I had had very little to drink and my consumption had been over a few hours, discretion would be the better part of valour. This meant driving John back mostly along Inverleith Place which is a very wide and quiet road and parallel to Ferry Road. Well, we were almost at the end of the Place when the car broke down. I couldn't believe it. There we were, now very early on 27th December in the freezing cold with only dinner suits on. We had no coats and I just couldn't get the car to go. My transport in those days was a Morris Oxford Countryman, a big estate tank in other words. The model was old enough to have a hand crank start as a backup to an electric start. I was in the middle of turning the engine over and getting nowhere fast when a Bobbie in a Panda car turned up. Oh dear! The young constable got out of the Panda and tried to have a conversation with two chaps in dinner suits who spoke to him whilst variously turning their faces away from him and holding their hands over their mouths. This surely must have made us look even more suspicious.

'What's the matter with the car sir?'

Sir! I thought to myself, imagine a policeman calling me Sir. I explained, whilst facing away from the officer and covering my mouth, that the car just conked out and I couldn't get it started again. We must have looked terribly suspicious and I was waiting for a more extensive grilling - where have you been, where are you going, why are you in dinner suits and why won't you look at me when I am talking to you? But, no, the officer explained that he knew the model and it had an electric fuel pump which was notorious for conking out. He knew how to sort it. Alarmingly at this point he took out his truncheon and asked me to open the tailgate. My God what's he going to do I wondered? Then he directed me to a flap on the floor of the car which, he said, if I lifted, would reveal the fuel pump. He seemed to be really warming to this roadside assistance part of his shift. A firm dunt on the pump with his weapon of defence he reckoned would do the trick.

'Okay' I said. THUMP went the truncheon.

'Now see if she will start sir.'

I climbed into the driver's seat and turned the ignition. The engine roared. John got in, the Bobbie wished us a safe journey home and off we went. Now that was good community policing John and I concluded.

Heriot's Rugby Club, like every other rugby club anywhere in the world, has its characters. Many of them in my time were larger than life and gave a richness to the club with their stories of the game and their experiences in general life. Sometimes they were just simply guys who could not help but give the members something to laugh at, either intentionally or otherwise. John Mackie and I, with our twin birds, were no exception to the latter.

Heriot's has had a tradition of playing fast and open rugby since day one- to have survived for what is now one hundred and twenty years and remain one of Scotland's top clubs is testimony to that but the administrators of the club have also, throughout its history, been top drawer. One has only to read Club historian Duggie Middleton's wonderful centenary book to see just how well the club has been run and how ambitious it has been and still is. I have already alluded to the fact that young players are always so busy just getting on with the game and training that they usually have no idea who is at the helm of the club. I was no exception. So busy was I having fun at Goldenacre I sailed through four presidents in my playing period and at that stage of my time at Heriot's I had hardly any idea who they were or what their contribution to the club as president had been, never mind their overall contribution since leaving school.

My first real understanding of Heriot's RC presidents was when I later became an employee of the club and sat on the club committee as part of my duties. The President at that time was Graham Fraser of whom more later on.

Things are not quite complete so far as my early days as an FP rugby player. A near folly of this period, 1966-70, was when the Apartheid Springboks came to the UK in 1969. A few weeks before this controversial tour took place the Edinburgh rugby clubs were asked by the SRU to supply temporary ground and stand stewards for the International at Murrayfield which was to be played on the 6th December 1969. The sweetener was free admission to the match and some tea afterwards. I volunteered and eagerly awaited the Springboks. On the Wednesday before the Test match the Springboks played up in Aberdeen against the North and Midlands district side. There was huge crowd trouble when the many anti-apartheid protestors stormed the stadium. I saw a televised report of proceedings and decided that stewarding on the following Saturday was not for me. I have to confess that my change of heart at that time in my life was not for altruistic reasons; I just didn't fancy the physical confrontation. I went along to the match as a spectator and witnessed Ian Sidney Gibson Smith become the seventh Herioter to fill the position of Scotland's full back. He kicked a penalty and scored a great try when he came blasting into the line. Scotland won 6 points to 3. The Springboks having kicked an early penalty through their stand-off, Visagie. I was glad that I went to the match, however, as it brought home to me just how fervent the anti-apartheid protestors were. The violence in the crowd was terrible and it registered with me that there was a serious racial problem in South Africa if it took ordinary UK people to confront the authorities the way they did that day. I had been blissfully unaware of how bad things were for the non-white South Africans. The majority of Edinburgh citizens had no clue about racial prejudice and still don't compared to the residents of many of our cities throughout the UK. I was to see what that was all about when I left Heriot's and my home town a few months later. Looking back on that Springboks game, and of course one always has very clear vision after an event, it's a match that I believe should not have taken place.

Here's the story of another match that should not have taken place: The New Year's celebrations following that fateful Springboks test

123

match included Hawick's traditional New Year's day afternoon match against Heriot's 1st XV .We poor buggers in the 2nd XV, played Hawick Trades in the morning. The Trades, now sadly disbanded, was a junior team in the famous border town. What masochist ever thought that morning fixture was a good idea I will never know but our committee thought it was a grand match, so much so that when both were added to the numbers watching the game they swelled the crowd to four. Hawick Trades had sent their two committee men along also!

Just getting to Hawick on the morning of New Year's day was a nightmare. At some ungodly hour most of the team gathered at The Usher Hall as per usual for an away game but others had arranged with the committee men to be picked up en route. It seemed to take ages as we gathered people up from behind walls where they were being sick and wakened guys who were sound asleep in odd positions on pavements but who looked, at first, as though they were dead.

I had stayed awake and alcohol free from about 8.30 am on the 31st December right through till the evening of the 1st January. My form of Ramadan seemed to me, as we picked up one hung-over player after another, a waste of time so far as my team's chances were to be concerned. In time we got to a baltic Hawick and a frozen pitch. The playing surface was like concrete and worse, vehicles had been driven over the pitch when it was muddy. The muddy tyre impressions were now like a scattering of lumber-jacks' hand saws. It was a suicide mission for both teams if the game was to go ahead. To go ahead it was, said our committee man.

'You are, of course, joking!' said our captain

No they were not joking.

Well like The ANZACS at Gallipoli we did as we were bidden and prepared for suicide. Whilst changing into our battle gear our captain noticed that we were a man short.

Our skipper advised the committee of the shortfall. He was told by our officials that The Trades were three short and we were to sacrifice a man in order that he could play for the opposition. That then, would make the sides even. Given that none of us wanted to play for Heriot's never mind The Trades he was told by our skipper to go and take a run and you know what at a rolling doughnut. Unmoved by our captain's exclamation we were ushered towards the pitch, or rather, ice rink.

'I say hold on chaps !'

A burly chap with a low centre of gravity ran towards two shivering teams and the four committee men.

'I say chaps, I think I can solve your player shortage difficulties!'

I recognised this guy from a Heriot's School games day a few years before. He ran in the Former Pupil's 100 yards sprint. He finished a very poor last as I recalled but seemed to be in his element by just taking part. I thought that he was quite old then to be participating in any kind of sport and here he was, prepared, those few years later, to lay down his life for Heriot's.

Finally some good sense returned to our committee.

They knew the bloke, a Heriot's FP, Walter Davidson. Apparently he turned up at Hawick every New Year for many years and nearly always got a game - for one side or t'other. His main claim to fame was that he continued playing rugby long after his sons had packed up! Walter was, I believe, a senior engineer with one of the railway companies down in Yorkshire somewhere. Although the man ticked all the usual boxes he was, in the opinion of the Heriot committee, far too old to be playing rugby. I guess he was around the wrong side of fifty. He was not to be allowed to play for us. Undaunted our mad volunteer produced a membership card of the Hawick Trades RFC. Their committee welcomed him into their ranks, we kept our fourteen men and that part of the equation was squared off.

The game was of course, a complete farce. Because the ground was so hard nobody on either side was particularly keen to tackle and we Herioter's were definitely cagey about laying a potentially lethal finger on the portly geriatric volunteer who, as a result of our reservations, was their man of the match. He even took their goal kicks, though I don't think there were that many.

My stand out recollection of the game was when, as an outside centre, during an attack, I made to pass the ball to my winger: he was not in position, in fact he was way behind play holding on to one of the uprights of our goal posts being horribly sick!

Eventually we got back into the changing rooms colder, sadder and wiser men and a lot earlier than normally would have been the case. After quick showers and a bite to eat we climbed aboard our bus which sped us off to Mansfield Park where, with, I guess, about seven thousand others, we were to witness the years old traditional Hawick v Heriot's New Year's Day rugby match.

Who said that life is fair? It isn't and especially it isn't, down in Hawick on the 1st of January. After the straw clad Mansfield Park was cleared by dozens of volunteers to reveal a lovely springy green grassy pitch the two fifteens ran out to do battle. Note the words springy and fifteens. Key words they are. There was none of this permafrosted pitch or shortage of players scenario at Mansfield Park as per our 2nd XV debacle. So we had the makings of a good hard game of rugby in the true meaning of the word.

That was the first and last time that I played in Hawick on a New Year's day or any other day for that matter. The New Year fixtures have long since disappeared. The advent of the League Championships put paid to a number of traditional encounters for all clubs . The modern amateur player I guess would be horrified at the prospect of playing on the 1st of January .

CHAPTER 10

I Get Married and Join New Clubs in Nottingham

It was September 1969 a few months before that Hawick nightmare when I realised a dream. I was selected to play for the Heriot's 1st XV who were about to leave for their annual pre-season tour to Lancashire taking in fixtures with Fylde and New Brighton. My selection was, in an instant, a shattered dream. I had only just come through an interview successfully with a life assurance company. I knew that if I passed the medical examination I would soon be off to the Nottingham office of the Standard Life. For me, passing such an examination was a given in those dim and distant days. A game for my club's 1st XV was tantalizingly within my grasp but the trip would have interfered with my medical examination appointment. My father, a cautious fellow, advised me not to try and rearrange the timing of my medical appointment and Rosemary, my fiancé, was anxious for me not to jeopardise our future. To be fair I was just as anxious so I weighed up the pros and cons and decided to make myself unavailable for the rugby tour. I thought then that that was my last chance to play for Heriot's 1st XV. I have no regrets though about that decision. I had no idea what my employers would actually have said had I broached the subject. On reflection, they would probably have been quite happy about it but hindsight is always 20/20. Well it was only a couple of games of rugby and the life that Rosemary and I were about to make together with the support of my new Company was much more important.

I got through the medical with flying colours and was formally offered a position of trainee inspector with Standard Life down in Nottingham with a start date of fifteenth November 1970 just before the company year end. So, I had time for a few more games at my beloved Heriot's before I set off south of the border.

It was quite a big deal for me to head off to Nottingham on that early November Sunday. Off I went in my Dad's car via the A68 and the borders of Scotland. Five hours later I was being greeted by my new boss, Gordon Bell and his wife Theresa, on the doorstep of their house in Woolaton, a very posh part of Nottingham. Incidentally, what do you think of Citroen 2 CVs of the 1960s vintage. I was behind one on the M1 in the latter stages of my Edinburgh to Nottingham journey. We were driving along battling against a very strong easterly gale. Spectacularly, with its lightweight tinny body leaning over at 3 o'clock and its wheels stable at the 6 o'clock position the 2 CV occasionally reached speeds above the upper limit. Are the French not just wonderful?

I knew that Gordon, or Mr Bell to me, was a former pupil of Heriot's but did not at that time appreciate how important a 1st XV and sevens player he had been for my former pupils rugby club. I also found out later that Gordon was a trialist for Scotland before he moved down to England. Anyway we had some tea, then Gordon took me to a bar for a number of beers - whilst enjoying them I was apprised of what would be expected of me in the early months. Once Gordon felt that I had had enough information and beer to be going on with, he took me to the hotel where I would stay for a few nights whilst I found digs. Given I hardly had two brass pennies to rub together I realised that first night I would have to find a place, a cheap place and quick.

My first day at my new office and career is now mostly a blur but I do remember being grilled by all of the staff about my background- was I married? Was I a Eriot, note Eriot not Erioter, and was I Scottish? The Heriot one disturbed me and I found out that day that the sub office manager based in Derby was also a Herioter. It became obvious to me very quickly that my new colleagues figured that the Heriot organisation was a sort of secret club and "them Eriots ad it made, dook." Everybody was called dook (duck as in Aylesbury) in Notts.

When I answered the question, was I Scottish, in the affirmative a collective bowing of the heads and "Thought so" was murmured. One fellow volunteered that he thought so because I looked Scottish! After the general wonderment at discovering another Scotsman in their camp and a Eriot to boot, everybody settled down to their work. I was to be guided in the basics of life assurance by a clerk called Peter Raistrick and later a senior inspector called Mike Thatcher would take me under his wing and show me the rudiments of working with, what we now call financial advisors. Mike would also train me in selling basic life assurance policies. Peter Raistrick was to rise to pretty high office in the company; as I type he enjoys a well-earned Head Office position.

Whilst anxious to find a rugby club and a priest who would educate me in the ways of the catholic church, I really had to find digs. The priest part on my list was as a result of a promise I had made to Rosemary's parents that I would take instruction from a catholic cleric on the Roman faith.

I quickly found a bedsit in the West Bridgeford area on the Loughborough Road and joined Nott's Rugby Football Club, now known as Nottingham Rugby Club. The Priest quest took a little longer.

My first weekend away from home, I was told, would be hard as I would probably be a bit homesick. I was missing my girl more than anything else but I knew that that would be remedied in early course. I enjoyed my work a lot and the staff were very nice, so no problems there. I had agreed to turn up to rugby training with Nott's in an area of Nottingham called Beeston in my second week so my first weekend would be spent entirely on my own and in a bedsit. Bedsits can be soul destroying if you let them be, so my first Saturday away from home saw me setting off to Leicester Tigers ground at Welford Road, Leicester.

The East Midlands were playing the touring Fijian side of 1970. Of course I wakened up early on the Saturday morning and set off almost immediately. Although the journey looked reasonably long on the map, it was only a quick hop down the M1 from Nottingham, so a lot of time filling had to be done once I reached Leicester. I spotted a multi-storey car park which I thought was near Welford Road and parked the car. Noting the floor level, I left the car park for a wander around. After a while I spotted a steakhouse and figured it was time for lunch. I scoffed a huge sirloin steak with chips, mushrooms and water cress. I had never tasted water cress before and, after eating it, I wasn't that impressed. There was still time to kill, so I went for a wander. Violent tummy rumbling indicated to me that something I had eaten had not agreed with me and so it came to pass that I had only rented my lunch. In a sort of rugby scrum allegory, my lunch was in the tunnel and out quickly via channel one, confusingly otherwise known as a number two!!!! Here is where the misery of being on one's own, away from home for the first time, begins. To cut a long and disgusting story short I failed to get to a toilet in time. I'll leave the rest of that part to your imagination.

Luckily not too much damage had been done as I discovered in the WC of a nearby pub. I cleaned myself up and, discarded my underpants, I won't say where but I often wonder if anyone ever came across them. I wished I was back home in Edinburgh, what was I doing here in the middle of England? I felt obliged to buy a half pint in the pub and asked directions to the ground. As I walked out on to the street I felt a chill up my backside. This was caused by a combination of three factors: 1. Nae underpants, 2. Nae overcoat and 3. It was November, baltic anyway.

I was glad to get to the ground and buy a ticket for a seat in the stand. The place was packed and that kept a bit of the cold away. I was wishing I was wearing my kilt, at least I would have had a legitimate excuse for the way I was now clad or rather for the way I was not clad. Once the game began I forgot about my wee problems which is what they become when they get so cold!! The game itself was excellent. The Fijians in those days ran with the ball even more so than they do now. The Islander's lineouts were amazing; the ball would sometimes be thrown to the middle and a huge second row man would jump up and, turning at the same time as he caught the ball, he would then hurl it to the outside centre who, having lain deep anticipating everything beautifully, was at full tilt when he caught it. They scored a couple of times from that ploy.

The East Midlanders were, however, more street wise than the Fijians and were better kickers of the ball both from hand and from placed kicks. Thus the more traditional players won the day. It was marvellous entertainment and really did help me get through that first weekend away. More misery was to follow the underpants "hiccup" though, and, very quickly after the match. I returned to the multi-storey car park and made for the floor my car was supposed to be on. No sign. Oh dear, first weekend away and my Dad's car is stolen. That was bad enough but the car was my transport back to Nottingham and my method of returning home to Edinburgh if, and when, I felt I had had enough of living away from home. That feeling was, at that very moment, coming on strongly. I began muttering things to myself like,

"What was I thinking, coming down here, I must be off my head. My arse is freezing. If I get knocked down and get taken to a hospital at least I won't have dirty underpants because I don't **have** any frigging underpants"

I went up and down the car park and, when I finally decided that the faithful Hillman Minx had gone, I made for the attendant's office. I told the guy what had happened - not about the underpants - the missing car and he laughed very loudly and said,

'Ay oop Jock, this park is made up oh three spiralled driveways and there are two more entrances, praps yeve got the wrong un!'

I was so overjoyed at the possibility my car was still in the car park I forgot that the attendant had called me Jock. I used to detest when I got called Jock and very, very angry when I was referred to as "Aggis". I wonder what an Englishman would think if he found himself in a Scottish car park feeling cold, miserable, underpantless and was called "faggot". A faggot is a poor man's haggis. It's a mysterious dollop of ground pigs offal held together with breadcrumbs and God knows what. It's a name that has other dubious connotations. They seemed to like the notionally edible faggot a lot in Nottingham, especially with chips and a curry sauce. My car was, of course, safe and sound but not in the second spiral I tried but, sods law, it was in the third.

Back in the car, bum now warming on the plastic seat of my Hillman it was onward to Robin Hood land. I got into Nottingham just in time for some fish and chips, well cod and chips, call to Rosemary and thence to a cinema just off the city centre to see a film starring Robert Mitchum. It was about how the Americans won the war again for us all, this time upon the invasion of Italy. Still, I liked Robert Mitchum's movies and, well, it would shorten the rest of what was supposed to be the worst day I would have away from home.

The movie finished and the time now around 10pm I thought that I would call it a day and head off to my bedsit a.k.a cell, in West Bridgeford. Blow me if my car hadn't gone a.w.o.l again. This time I knew I had left it in a gap site with lots of piled up rubble in it. I found the gap site loaded with rubble but no Hillman Minx. I spotted a cop and told him my tale of woe. Again, peels of laughter as the cop explained to me that there was loads of demolished buildings and resultant rubble in the city centre area and so my search for the right parking place began all over again. I finally spotted the Hillman and retired to my single bed- room with wash basin, Baby Belling cooker and a wardrobe. Oh dear, dreary Sunday was looming. Then I remembered I had been invited by a fellow trainee inspector, Jim Marshall, to have lunch with him and his parents that Sabbath.

So that was my first weekend over and all seemed to be well. Back to work, relief from loneliness and the start of my training at Beeston with Nott's Rugby Club.

The second week in my new surroundings went very quickly. It was still, however a fairly lonely experience. I phoned Rosemary every evening and we kept up with each other's news from a call box on the Loughborough Road very close to my bed sit. Each sixpenny bit that I put in to the box (we were still on old money at the time) was gobbled up fairly quickly by the STD box. Then, as if by miracle, one night I put in a sixpence and it would have lasted the whole night I think if it were not for a fellow chapping on the door of the call box demanding to know if I had verbal diarrhoea and would I let others have a chance to use the phone. For some reason that particular phone box didn't need to have more than one coin pumped into it after, I think it was, 6.30pm. I can tell you that quirky machine saved me an absolute fortune as we both seemed to have so much to say to each other every night.

Cash was tight and although the rent for my wee room would be considered buttons by today's standards it was commensurate with my salary which was around 25% less than my previous annual earnings. I saw my drop in salary as an investment in the future. I intended to make a success of my new career and, if I did, I knew my income would improve dramatically - the additional benefits that were offered were very generous indeed. These included a non-contributory pension (which incidentally I am enjoying as I type) and a staff house purchase scheme. The future looked good for Rosemary and me.

On the Tuesday evening of my second week I reported to Nott's rugby ground at Beeston. I presented myself to the first person that I saw and he took me to the dressing rooms and introduced me to some of the players. I was told what would happen at training by one of the senior players and at the same time warned that I would not be able to play until I had a tetanus injection or could prove I was suitably protected. Apparently there had been a dog show at the ground in the off season period and some of the pitches had become infected. They knew this because one of the Nott's 1st XV players had been injured by boot studs and the resultant gash in his leg had become badly poisoned. Having had a number of open wounds playing for Heriot's I was up to date with my tetanus injections and so I was cleared right away to play the next Saturday, if selected. A committee man appeared in the dressing rooms and took my details down on some form or other and seemed impressed that I had come down from Heriot's FP . After the admin formalities I ran out to join the training session. I noted that amongst the players present was Dusty Hare. He was not to reach the heady heights of the England team until 1974 but he had played in the Fiji match at which I so spectacularly attended the week before, minus underwear. I don't think he noticed though: he never mentioned it.

The session was run by a Welsh coach called Dai Roberts. He was quite a hard man and quickly discovered that in addition to a Scot joining the Nott's ranks, a Welsh lad appeared that night also. Well Dai gave the Welsh lad a very hard time of it and I think it would be fair to say he picked mercilessly on our man from the valleys. Odd, I mused, that it should have been that way, given both the coach and the new recruit were fellow Welshmen. I thought that if anybody was going to get it, it would have been me, a north of the border Celt. As it turned out I did get some of that medicine a few weeks later, indeed worse, but not from the coach.

The next training night on the following Thursday was more or less a repeat of the previous one but the little, bullied Welsh lad wasn't there. Couldn't blame him really; I don't think I ever saw him again. My memory of Dai is dim after that. I know that he did go off to Canada to be their National rugby coach- perhaps it was round about that time.

The teams were posted for the weekend on Thursdays after the training session. I checked the notice to see if I had been picked. I was to start with the 4th XV on the right wing. As I was scanning the teams a dapper chappie dressed in an immaculate double breasted blazer, collar and tie came over to chat with me. He was a committee man but also played for the 4ths. I can't remember his name now but I will call him Mike. During our wee chat Mike told me that the club had a disco every Saturday night, each team took it in turns to manage the function and tidy up the bar area. It was to be the turn of the 4th XV that weekend. Well I wasn't doing anything so that would wind up a Saturday night pretty well.

I cannot remember who we were playing that Saturday but the dressing room chat before we went out was the usual up and at em strategy and tactics free rubbishy 4th XV stuff. The first real indication that there was some sort of tactical plan was when we got to the pitch. The captain, a second row man, ran over to me to explain that it was a tradition of the team to put the ball through all the backs' hands from the first set piece we won to the relevant wing. We lined up to await the kick off and the ball sailed straight to a handless individual who promptly knocked the ball on, straight into a pair of equally uncoordinated opposition hands. Second knock-on by the opposition. But, we were the first culprits so it was scrum down their ball.

Our backs, preparing for a bit of tackle practice, had to quickly realign deeper as our front row unexpectedly took one against the head and, zoom! our scrum half rattled the ball out to his stand-off and he and my centres passed the ball on down the line to me as per the club's tradition. So, within seconds of my first Nott's appearance I had the ball in my hands and I was off for the line. I had a pretty clear run at it thanks to the quick ball our scrum gave us. Their full back forced me away from the posts and I had to be content with a touch down midway between the outer upright and the touch line. Not bad, I thought. I was only in my first Nott's 4ths game for about three minutes and I had scored a glorious try. I was walking back to join my team mates, head bowed and with a solemnity appropriate for the situation.

'Thanks a bunch you prat,' said my captain sarcastically.

'Why didn't you touch down as soon as you got over the line?'

I had, I suppose, delayed touching the ball down but I was looking for a better place to rest the ball in order to give our kicker an even chance at the conversion. I explained that to the skipper but he countered that the in goal area on the pitch was tiny and I had in fact touched down on a completely different pitch. One of my team mates insisted that not only had I cost the team a try and a potential conversion totalling five points in those days, I had additionally been adjudged offside by some blind referee who was officiating on the other pitch! After that I always had a good look at the in goal areas of any strange pitch before kick-off.

I have no idea what the outcome of that match was and I can't remember if I got another shot at scoring a try but I do remember the so-called disco managing.

'Here Doug take this brush and sweep up the bar floor, there's a good fellow,' said Mike.

'Someone will come along shortly with a shovel and between the pair of you, you can have a bash at sprucing up the old place, all right?'

That was 1970 and it's now 2013 and I am still waiting for the shovel guy.

Once Mike was happy that the clubhouse would pass an inspection from somebody important, it was time for tea. Off we went to a nearby chipper. I was a wee bit apprehensive about this because I was still trying to digest the faggot or whatever funny looking thing it was I'd had after the game. I didn't really have enough readies for the beers I had planned to drink and also pay for a fish supper or as they simply and imaginatively call it, fish and chips. We elected to sit in after we ordered our meals. Everyone to a man wanted cod and chips. I didn't really want cod but as the best white fish accompaniment to chips in the sea is haddock and such a fish is a total stranger to the English chippers I was stuck with a piece of tasteless cotton wool cod. Eventually our food appeared. At this juncture my earlier faggot had been digested and had slithered on to congesting an artery so, I was now starving. The cod piece, if you will pardon the description, did actually look quite inviting. Wiping his lips with somebody else's napkin, Mike asked,

'Anybody want a pickled onion ?' I didn't really but all the rest put their paws up. I was sitting nearest the counter and so Mike said,

'Would you do the honours old chap?'

'Oh, ok,' and off I went. The counter was by this time very busy and it was a foot shuffling eternity before I got to the head of the queue.

'X pickled onions please.'

A disgusting looking jar of the vinegary bulbs was found and x number of them were placed on a bacteria friendly one time waxed, cardboard plate. That will be so many shillings and pence dook!

'Oh, ok,' I rummaged in my pockets and found some change and paid up what for me was simply a ransom. This left me with very little to spend in the bar when we got back to the clubhouse. As I turned to walk back with the very smelly onions I could see my so called team mates were having a bit of a snigger. Yes of course, it was at my expense. Ha ha what a jolly jape: my tea had been eaten by some aliens from another planet. Hilarious, I thought as I ate somebody's pickled onion. The lesson here is:

If you go to a counter to buy side portions of absolutely anything for absolutely anybody, especially any asinine rugby club team mates, don't leave your meal on the table and expect it to be there when you come back. It's now specifically Law 168 in the Laws of Rugby Union as issued by the IRB in Dublin.

My list of important things to do was gradually being ticked off. I now had cheap accommodation, if a bitty sparse, and my rugby needs were settled. Next up was the question of seeing a priest and learning the ways of the Roman Catholic Church. It seemed strange to me that Rosemary was not allowed to get me up to speed on that herself but a promise was a promise.

After a few good games in the lower echelons, mainly at centre, for the 4ths then the 3rds, I was promoted to the 2nd XV which had the grand name of Nott's Corsairs. Clubs in England seemed to do that - give their lower teams fancy names. The first game I had for the Corsairs was against a Liverpool side. Never mind who it was because they were a funny lot.

We were not long into the game when I noticed that the Liverpuddlians were paying an awful lot of attention to our scrum-half. By half time our number 9 was well and truly beaten up. During the break I had a worried word with him about it and I realised as we spoke that he was a Scot. He told me not to concern myself with his welfare, he was a big boy. He came out for the second half unperturbed because most Midlands rugby at this level and lower was always, in my opinion, just dirty, plain and simple, an acceptable, nay necessary part of the game it seemed. Whatever the traditions relating to the physical side of the game it did seem to me that our scrum-half was receiving extra special treatment. At one point I shouted over to our forwards to give our wee number 9 some protection. My shouting triggered an alertness in the opposition backs and I heard,

'There's another one of the Jock bastards!'

It's just as well I wasn't described as a "aggis bastard" because I was angry enough by then. The opposition defence on me was a "take no prisoners policy" and it was pretty evident as I staggered off the pitch at full time looking like a survivor of a hand grenade attack. My jersey was simply in tatters and I was sporting so many cuts and bruises that I could also have been mistaken for a whole traffic accident.

Around this time I was missing my Rosemary terribly and so I decided to go home one weekend. Gordon Bell very kindly let me go immediately after lunch time on the Friday and I set off in the Hillman feeling pretty pleased with myself and looking forward to seeing my gorgeous girl.

Rosemary worked on Saturday mornings so I used that time to have coffee with my sister and brother in law, Margery and Derek McCracken. Traditionally they met a bunch of their friends every Saturday morning in a coffee shop in Castle Street just south of Princes Street in Edinburgh. Included in the party on this occasion was a fellow called Tom McClung. Tom is an Edinburgh Academicals Football Club member and was capped as an Edinburgh Academical for Scotland at stand-off in the mid-fifties. I was, of course, excited to meet this famous Scotland player and really pleased to be seated next to him on my right.

I could not and still cannot help myself when I am in the company of any international athlete, imagining what it has taken them to gain International honours. I just have to ask them questions about their sporting careers. Tom was no exception and he found himself at the end of a barrage of probably silly enquiries such as "What's it like to play for Scotland?" and "Do you know Kenny Scotland?" "What did it feel like when you pulled on your Scotland jersey for the first time?" "Did you score any tries?" and so on and so forth. As I no doubt blethered on I thought to myself,

"This coffee house is awfully grand !"

Both Tom and I were sitting in enormous, leather upholstered, high backed, very solid oak framed chairs . They were almost like thrones. The arms sloped downwards and under the table. My chair had, idiosyncratically, a big round knobbly bit on the hand end of the right arm rest but not on the left one. As I gabbled on and on to my hero, I found myself nervously and sweatily grasping the knobbly bit and, sort of caressing it. Tom seemed distracted so I thought at this point I might fling in to the conversation the fact that I was currently playing for Nott's Rugby Club's second XV. I was taken aback when Tom reacted in what seemed to everyone an uncharacteristic way, judging by the alarm in their faces. Up until then Tom had been pretty quiet and a hesitant participant in my question and answer interlude, but then, rather abruptly, he came out with what could have been taken either as a statement of fact or possibly a question. 'You play rugby?' He crescendo'd with a disgusted look on his reddened face.

Squeaking 'Y e s s' as I looked down and saw something awful. Oh God no! My heart sank, my brow went into a cold sweat and I wished the ground would swallow me up. I was in a nightmare. I wanted to be sick. The knobbly bit that I thought was a funny sort of carving on the end of the right arm of my chair was, in fact, Tom McClung's left knee. I had been inadvertently petting it for God knows how long and God knows what he thought of me. I never went back.

Rosemary and I had a lovely time together during that brief but significant weekend. I didn't bother telling her about the experience I had put Tom McClung through. Sadly it was soon Sunday afternoon and time for me to head back to the land of Robin Hood and his merry men.

Nott's RFC didn't take kindly to me taking a weekend off and, quite rightly, I suppose, they dropped me back to the 4ths. I figured that I would be up and down to Edinburgh again at Christmas and between Christmas and the end of the rugby season, so my time with Nott's was going to be interrupted somewhat. By this time I was pretty well focused on buying a house and marrying my sweetheart.

To be honest I couldn't really be bothered with the hassle that I knew I would get from and give to Nott's over the potential tooing and fro-ing and so I decided that I would forget rugby after Christmas and concentrate on my future marriage and my career.

In the course of idle conversation I told the fellow who was responsible for my sales training that I was going to pack in playing for Notts. He asked why and I told him that continuing with Nott's, certainly for the remainder of that season, would not be fair to them or to me because of the trips back and forth to Edinburgh. That chance conversation was to come back and bite me later.

Christmas was soon upon me and off I went again to Edinburgh to spend some time with Rosemary and our families and friends. My, by now on the job training, was going well and I was on schedule for a position as an Inspector by my birthday on the 16th May 1971. Our wedding day had been set for the 9th June 1971. Realising how much we both missed each other, Rosemary and I on one of our sixpenny phone calls, decided that she should come down to Nottingham with me when I returned from the Festive celebrations.

I was all for it but it was a bit complicated.

Remember this was 1970 and unmarried couples did not live together as they do now, especially when the girl half has a Bishop for an uncle. Rosemary's Dad's brother, Joseph McGee was the Roman Catholic Bishop of Galloway based in Ayr.

To enable Rosemary to come down to Nottingham and reside there honourably I had to find her digs. I advertised in the local Nottingham Post and the best response I got was from a Mrs Bouffant who lived in a big house quite near my bed-sit. She was an eccentric sort of widow woman but, she was a genuine soul I guessed. Her house was in a very respectable part of West Bridgeford (Jim Baxter of Scotland and Rangers fame lived in that area when he played for Nottingham Forest).

The drive down to Nottingham on the 3rd January 1971 was hairy. Everything was going ok until we got to what was and possibly still is an infamous part of the M1 which approaches Nottingham. There it was fog: palpable, dense, damp and chewy fog. Rosemary and I had never seen the likes of it before. It was also the freezing type of fog. We managed just to make out a motorway exit that was appropriately illuminated and looked like it was heading towards Nottingham city. Inevitably we encountered a roundabout. The only way we knew what was what was by sticking our heads out the windows and trying to x-ray view any kind of sign. In those situations people really don't care where they end up just so long as they do end up somewhere and in one piece. So how do they ensure that? They follow someone very closely and hope he knows what he is doing and that he has a definite destination. We could hear the odd crump as some poor wretch got hit by someone behind him who didn't know someone was in front of him. Swearing, muffled by the fog, could be discerned but as to the source one could not accurately tell. Luckily all crashes were at about four miles an hour so not much lasting damage was done unless, of course, one's car was a British Leyland model! We went round that roundabout about five times before I was reasonably certain that I had found an exit. When I saw the exit I entered it and continued for about five hundred yards and, just as suddenly as the fog arrived, it just as suddenly lifted. Rosemary looked back and said,

'My God there are about twenty cars behind us.' They were all by now tooting their horns in appreciation . I felt like Ward Bond from the fifties TV series *"Wagon Train"* and, like him, I had gone a long way to settling a territory!!

I got Rosemary to her digs. Mrs Bouffant made her feel very welcome and took us to a sitting room where she introduced us to Dixon, a fellow paying guest, who was a police constable. Coronation Street was on the telly. Dixon was sitting on a sofa beside a teetering side table which was supporting a capacious tea pot. You know the kind of vessel, you see them in all church halls and community centres. They normally need two very fit people to lift them up to pour. While Rosemary was being given the grand tour of Mrs Bouffant's detached house, Dixon offered me a pailful of a treacle brown liquid from the pot and then engaged me in banal conversation. Firstly he explained that the TV was permanently on the ITV channel because Mrs Bouffant thought that so long as the BBC was never switched on she wouldn't have to pay for a licence. Secondly he seemed to feel he had to anticipate a question from me which he thought would be "Why are you living in digs?" I couldn't have cared less really but he went on anyway.

'Ti reason I am living in these ere digs is cos me yoonger broother as a dialysis machine int room we used ti share before is kidneys went dahn on im.'

One thing I have forgotten to explain is that Rosemary needed a job to complete this phase of the transition to life in Nottingham for the soon-to-be-wed Bruces. Theresa Bell, the wife of my boss, had set up an interview at a branch of an international salon called Robert Selligman in the city centre of Nottingham. Selligman's was an American company and operated as a "store within a store". The store they were operating in was one of the Debenham chain.

Rosemary's interview was the next day. I suppose it never crossed our minds that she wouldn't get the job. My girl was a very talented hairstylist and had the qualifications and the confidence to prove it. Get the job she did and at more money than in Edinburgh, more also than I was earning at that time.

So that was us both settled into our jobs and our accommodation. Next step really had to be the Roman Catholic teach in.

Gordon Bell had kept the Catholic question in mind and, because Rosemary and I were now ensconced in Nottingham, he suggested that we both attended some bazaar or other in the Cathedral Church of St Barnabas. Priests would be in attendance and they would sort something out for me.

Rosemary and I got to the church Bazaar and were soon introduced by Theresa Bell to a young, actually a very young, cleric who had agreed to meet with me, us, for the purpose of drumming into me the way the Catholic Church affected Rosemary.

Rosemary proclaimed sotto voce, 'My God, that father Youngpriest is just so good looking, what's he doing being a priest?'

I have to admit the guy was smooth and probably only slightly older than me and, yes, he was better looking than me, mind you, who isn't? It was therefore a huge embarrassment to me to have to call him "Father". Actually I was never comfortable calling any priest father, but this young guy was a father too far!

The diaries were out, well in my case, the back of a fag packet was out.

The first instructional meeting was to be in a pub. I can't remember which one but it wasn't far from the big church that held that bazaar.

Dressed completely inappropriately Rosemary and I turned up at the designated pub in plenty of time. No sign of Father Youngpriest but the place was heaving with workmen originating from many nations throughout the globe. They were of all shapes and sizes wearing similar donkey jackets but with varying construction company names on their backs. I easily recognised Polish and Irish accents and the rest were of other East European extraction, West Indian and, of course, Nottinghamshire. The Irish were the biggest contingent.

Peering through the dense and smelly fag smoke I picked out a small table with some chairs around it. Actually I found the table with an ease that surprised me - normally such an evening find in a Nottingham pub would be like discovering gold. I bought Rosemary her customary Bacardi and coke and I ordered up a pint of best bitter. Having finished our drinks and realising the priest was now about twenty minutes late we were coming to the conclusion it was time to go when our holy man arrived. He was dressed for rain and also a draft as he had a University scarf around his neck. Choosing to keep his bad weather apparel on he asked us if we would like a drink to which we replied in the affirmative. Before we could say what our preference was Father Youngpriest was off to the bar. He returned a few minutes later with three pints of bitter. Rosemary was aghast as she had never in her life a.) been bought any sort of drink by a priest. b.) drunk alcohol with a priest and, most importantly, c.) She had never tasted beer before, never mind the muck that they were serving in this place ! Being very respectful of priests my girl drank her beer without saying a word.

After the usual small talk: what have you been doing since we last met? are you enjoying living in Nottingham? And so on, we got down to what I thought was going to be a wee lecture on the Roman faith. I couldn't have been more wrong. We discussed rugby, football, cricket and just about anything to do with sport and nothing to do with religion. Rosemary, after listening to her table companions rabbit on, got a word in and explained that she knew very little about the foregoing apart from going to Hibs matches with her Dad. She had no idea what it was all about and did it just to keep him company, but did know something about hockey, tennis and swimming. She explained to us that she didn't like hockey very much because she always seemed to get whacked on the shins by errant hockey sticks and had long since given it up as a bad job. She was just about to launch into a story about tennis and a weekend she had at a mixed tournament in Grantown-on-Spey, when suddenly and mercifully, a big telly up on the wall at the far end of the pub came on. It was, of all things, a boxing match between Mohammed Ali and Joe Frazier. Just as the two mountainous men were about to start knocking blazes out of each other I noticed the disappointment on Father Youngpriest's face as all the workmen I described previously moved right into the centre of the pub floor and indeed anywhere that they could get a good view of the telly. The TV in the pub was as big as could be bought in those days but nothing to match the boxes you can buy nowadays. It dawned on me why we were supposed to be immersing ourselves in religion in this particular venue. Father Youngpriest was wanting to see the fight. So, I asked him if he would like to postpone the chat meantime. He said he would if we didn't mind, I said we didn't. He made to get up. I asked him what he was doing and he said he was going to ask the fellows who were in great numbers, and who were blocking our view to move aside so we could see.

'You must be joking' I whispered. I could visualise what was going to happen and what was going to be said to our so called religious teacher.

'It's ok Father I'll speak to them.'

I looked at Rosemary for what I thought would probably be the last time, told her that my BUPA policy was up to date as was my life assurance and made to plead with the masses. Fr Youngpriest pulled me back and courageously set off on the mission himself.

'I say, I wonder of you fellows would mind standing aside so that my friends and I can have a view of the boxing match on the television?'

Collectively the motley crew cried out highly obscenely in various accents, for example the Irish:

'Well youse can go and f...k off you little gobsh..e'

'Who the f...k do youse think youse are now?'

'Whose yer feckin man?'

Rosemary and I were black affronted and, just as the men seemed to be working up to becoming very, very ugly (in every aspect of the adjective) the young priest stood his ground; and, flicking his university scarf away from his about to be strangled neck, he revealed his dog collar. It was like Moses parting the Red Sea.

'Make way for di faahther, make way for di faahther!' The Irishmen ordered. In a trice everyone, bar us three, was pressed hard up against the side walls of the pub and we had the perfect view of the pugilism. Ali won, I got more drinks in, this time with a Bacardi and coke and the next of the trilogy of religious meetings was organised for some weeks away.

In the meantime I had packed in rugby with Nott's and therefore was at a loose end with regard to Saturdays because Rosemary was at work in the salon until about 6 pm. Occasionally I took to watching football of all things. A few guys from the office took turns to drive over to the Baseball ground to watch Derby County. Why not watch Nottingham Forest I hear you say? That was a no-brainer: I'll explain. I went along to watch Forest play Manchester United one Saturday afternoon. There were three good reasons for doing that: Denis Law, Bobby Charlton and George Best. The famous trio were in the Man United team that day and although I know very, very little about the beautiful game, I did appreciate that such an opportunity had to be seized with both hands. I had no idea just how bad football violence was in those days. If I had there is no way I would have been seen within three miles of the Forest ground.

Having watched the famous three demolish Forest I found myself in a departing crowd that was uncontrollable. It is all the more amazing that the crowd were not to be calmed given the huge police presence. There were mounted police, huge dogs that looked more like lions - their handlers looked even meaner - and the bridge over the Trent had police cars, I think either Triumph 2000s or the Rover equivalent, parked on both pavements at an angle of about forty-five degrees, bonnets facing towards the city centre, ready to race on to the road after the nutters. In their hundreds the Forest fans, at least I assume that that was who they were, chased the Manchester United fans all the way back to the main railway station. I heard later that they boarded the trains and settled their differences with the Manchester supporters in the carriages' compartments. Whilst all that carnage was going on I was, along with two pals from the office, stuck in a bottlenecked heaving crowd trying to get out of the ground. My friends and I saw a poor fellow, a dad I guess, being grabbed away from a young boy by a bunch of thugs. They pulled him aside from the crowd and then a group of their mates queued up to have a run at the guy and kick his head in. Before I could say or do anything about this atrocity my office chums warned me against getting involved as I would just be the next victim. It was a sickening experience. That was the only game I attended at Trent Bridge.

If football had to be watched then it was to be done in Derby. There was a huge number of Scots supporters who followed Brian Clough's men. The railway locomotive construction yards and Rolls Royce factories in the Derby area employed a number of my fellow countrymen and there was at least a couple in the Derby team at that time: John O' Hare and Archie Gemmill were stars in the side and they also played for Scotland.

Whilst my sporting favours were to be given for the time being to football at Derby County, my religious instruction resumed. The next meeting with Father Youngpriest was to take place in what I guessed would be a block of church flats next to the cathedral.

Rosemary and I arrived at the appointed time. I rang the door-bell and whilst we waited for someone from within we agreed with each other that at least this time, not only would there be no boxing to intrude on our wee symposium, there would most certainly be no alcohol consumption. We were fifty percent right i.e. no boxing!

A fellow, akin to a butler, eventually came to the door and said plummily,

'You must be Mr Bruce and Miss McGee!' Nodding politely, we were ushered in to a hallway and then taken upstairs to a large empty lounge. We were told to take a seat in a huge leather settee and that refreshments would follow. Follow they did, a tray of little canapés, three wine glasses and an ice bucket containing a bottle of Mateus Rose` wine. All were carried in by another fellow who poured some wine into the glasses. Soon Fr Youngpriest made an appearance and this time we got down to some religion, but not much. Nothing was discussed that I could honestly say had anything to do with helping me understand what specifically was different from my church and its beliefs as compared to Rosemary's church and its beliefs. Anyway the wine was good and there was plenty of it, so much so that the butler fellow suggested we take the bottles away and use them to make lamp bases for our new house which we had just bought. Such a practice with Mateus Rose` bottles was commonplace at that time. Before we left in search of a taxi our third and final meeting was arranged again for a date a few weeks away. Rosemary asked our instructor if he could meet us at our new house which we were "doing up at that time". She wanted the young priest to bless the house. He readily agreed and asked for directions. Rosemary started to explain that after the straight run out of town in a northerly direction there was a series of left and right turns when he would reach the village of Ravenshead where we were going to live. Our man couldn't be bothered trying to note it all down and said, 'Oh never mind all that, just give me the name of the pub nearest to your house, I'll find that easily enough.'

Rosemary and I continued to progress at our respective jobs and it was about this time that the comment I made to my colleague, Mike Thatcher, about me packing in Nott's RFC came back to bite my backside. Mike suggested that perhaps I had really given up the game because I was not likely to get a first team place, especially if I could not commit to Nott's every weekend. I hadn't really thought about the situation in that way, although my performances in the games I had with the Corsairs were pretty good even if I say it myself. I just didn't want to commit to any club at that time because of my occasional unavailability. I told Mike what I thought was an honest self-appraisal and he just smiled.

'Look' he said with a sales pitch demeanour, 'how would you like a regular 1ST XV place but with a junior club?' I was about to interject with the commitment problem when he went on hurriedly, 'Don't worry about the commitment thing because the club I have in mind will understand your situation ; believe me, they will understand!'

'Ok what's the story?' I asked.

'Well one of our top connections here in Nottingham is a member of the committee of Old Nottinghamians and they are always on the lookout for new blood.'

'Go on' I said suspiciously.

'I have already taken the liberty of telling the fellow concerned that you would be interested,' said my colleague confidently.

'Oh have you now ?'

'Yes and I have told him that we will go round and see him at his offices today, in fact, now!"

Thus compromised, I was going to find it very hard to say no to this "offer" because I had to work with this important connection on a daily basis. One other nagging problem was the fact that my future wife was not at all keen on me playing rugby because her dad, who she adored, had told her it was a dangerous game and not the sort of sport a married man should be participating in. Well it troubled me that Rosemary was so worried about my health, but, I felt sure that she, along with every other girl who was associated with, engaged to or, indeed, married to a rugby guy would come around to the idea that rugby was an essential part of her "bloke"; a part of his soul even. I also realised that in the meantime her concerns were going to cause all sorts of problems.

Before I knew it I had been taken round to the Nottinghamian committee man and had agreed to play for the rugby club of the former pupils of Nottingham High School. I presumed it was an open club.

Just as I thought, my Rosemary was not at ease with what I had done. I tried to appease her by suggesting I wash my own kit and see if I could play for the club without attending training nights so I could drive us both home when Rosemary finished work, given we only had one car. All I could do for the club was to make myself available on Saturdays. Home games would be easy enough, away fixtures were difficult, but I managed. My new club seemed to be happy with my peculiar behaviour so long as I was around of a Saturday at kick off time.

Nottinghamian's ground is situated at Adbolton Lane near The National Watersports Centre at Holme Pierrepoint. Both the situation of the club i.e. near water and the name Nottinghamians seemed to suggest to me that the famous book *"The Art of Coarse Rugby"* had used my new club as the basis of the mythical Rottinghamians. That amazingly coarse and hopefully fictitious club was the basis of the accounts on rugby by Michael Green. The Nottinghamian casual style of rugby and the standard at that time was another dead giveaway to my mind, yet it was great fun to be a part of.

Whilst I played for Nottinghamians the captain was a fellow Scot by the name of Ian Lidster. Ian was a laid back kind of a bloke who did know his rugby but, I guess, like me, he was not able for whatever reason to play for a more senior club. He may also have been press ganged into joining this particular club for exactly the same reasons as me. Ian as I recall worked for a general insurance group and no doubt did a great deal of business with the same committee man that encouraged me to join Nottinghamians. As I remember it, quite a lot of Nottinghamians were insurance men.

There was rarely any chat with these chaps about business, partly I suppose, because it just wasn't done and also because I was strictly a life assurance man and they were general insurance officials only. We wouldn't have known what the other was talking about!

Rosemary and I had the beginnings of our third chat with Fr Youngpriest in The Little John Inn near our newly acquired home. We were really chuffed with our three bed semi which was located in a lovely leafy cul-de-sac in Ravenshead. Ravenshead lies about ten miles north of Nottingham. The plan was, you will remember, to meet first with our religious instructor in the pub and then make our way to the house where we would complete our trilogy of meetings and then have the house blessed by the priest. Rosemary and I were in the inn made famous by the second in command of the men in Lincoln green about fifteen minutes before our catholic mentor. We had a drink on board by the time he made his appearance. Father Youngpriest didn't even bother asking us if we would like a drink as he approached the door end of the bar. He acknowledged us with a nod and a smile as he spoke to the barman, then, a loaded drinks tray in hand, he joined us. This time it was three glasses of Newcastle Brown ale. I have no idea why he changed from draft bitter but change he did. Just one of the many mysteries attached to this emissary of the Pope. Off we went down a catholic learning trip refreshing ourselves on the way with another Newcie for the men and an orange juice for Rosemary. She opted to drive the car when we returned to the house leaving me to the alcoholic accompaniment of the Father, who seemed to be happy to drive his car up to the house. We drove off from the pub in convoy stopping first at a "beer off" as they call offlicenced premises in Nott's Thinking of the Father I though it might be a nice touch to buy a carry out of Newcastle Brown ales to go alongside the Bacardi and Coke I had previously bought for my fiancé.

The second part of our teach in was similar to all the previous religious education, namely fairly liquid but with the added features of the tour of our house and the grand finale, the blessing of our house. Some years later when Rosemary and I entertained a bevy of Scottish Bishops in our Stonehaven cottage this alcohol fuelled blessing of our Nott's abode came to our minds. Our kids were quite wee and the Bishop of Dundee, a kindly gentle man but a man who looked like a heavyweight boxer dressed up as a cleric, blessed our wee lassies whilst sitting them on his knees. He was in the middle of the blessing when he remembered he still had a fired up Capstan full strength cigarette in his blessing hand. This was remarked on by the Bishop of Galloway, Rosemary's uncle, and the said weed was extinguished hurriedly. I hastily add that the gracious bishop had consumed only a cup of tea.

The third and last meeting with Father Youngpriest was over and as we bade him farewell a worried Rosemary suggested that it might be a good idea, given the Newcie Browns that he had consumed, if he abandoned the company car, as he so named his transport, and let her drive him home. The young cleric said that everything would be just fine; he would flick his scarf away from his jacket collar to reveal his holy collar to any enquiring constable that he was a man of God and on an errand of mercy. That didn't wash with my girl and she insisted on doing the sensible thing. The young Father took no further persuasion and off they went, safely, to Nottingham.

Not too long after the last meeting with our tutor priest, Rosemary and I travelled north to Edinburgh to be married by her Uncle Joseph, the Bishop. I have a sneaking suspicion that "The Bishop" would have been amused at the unorthodox methods Father Youngpriest adopted to educate me in the ways of his church. I also suspect that Father Youngpriest knew from the word go I had a pretty good idea what Rosemary's faith was all about and there was really nothing that he could teach me. I think he just enjoyed the company of a young couple who he could see were starting what was to be a very happy marriage.

My rugby at Nottinghamians continued in a fashion which was akin to the surreal. On the one hand there were team mates who had an understandable connection with insurance and indeed every-day commerce but, out of the blue, a bunch of what I remember as trainee vicars turned up at the club. I have no idea where they studied or otherwise practiced their vocation but they were, generally speaking, not bad rugby players. I often think about these fellows and reflect on the fact that I didn't really find it at all odd that I was playing rugby with men of the cloth who had to put up with, a great deal of bad language, spitting, farting, belching, drinking, smoking and dubious observation of the laws of the game of rugby football.

I sometimes found the coarseness (dirty play) of junior rugby difficult to deal with. It seemed to me that Nottinghamians, whether they liked it or not, were in it up to their necks. By that I don't mean that Nottinghamians were in any way a dirty club, far from it, but they played in a league which seemed to expect and indeed condone filthy play. It just seemed to me such a stupid defiling of the pure game of rugby. It wasn't considered a match for many of the lads we played against unless physical superiority up front, and at any cost, was seen and taken on as a challenge. In fact, it was the whole point of the Saturday afternoon for many.

Whilst with Nottinghamians I often found myself in peculiar situations that I believe could only happen in junior rugby. On one occasion I was due to play somewhere in Lincolnshire and was picked up by a fellow in a very old "Herbie" lookalike Volkswagon Beetle, backfiring as it coasted toward me at the meeting place. There was room left only for me as three trainee vicars took up the other passenger spaces. I say spaces because there were no back seats in this particular Hitler's dream wagon. There weren't even any carpets but there was a spare wheel for the vicars to tussle with.

Arriving stiff as boards, we really needed a warm up but, of course and as usual, there was no time for limb and back stretching after the panic change into our playing kit. There was even less time than normal on this particular occasion as one of my team mates started a period of team procrastination. With a hand angled over his mouth he stage whispered,

'Ere lads coom over ere an take a look through the coats at this.'

We were in one of those communal style changing rooms where the teams were separated by a long tubular metal framework which had clothes hooks bolted on to it. As usual we had arrived before the home team. It's another one of those IRB laws of the game of Rugby Union but appertaining specifically to junior rugby: Law 989 para 6: "The nearer a team is to a stadium the greater is the need to be last to arrive."

Anyway, there we were at the coats and jackets on the hooks stage when we heard the sotto voce invitation to take a look. Positioning our heads at various levels like a longitudinal many-headed Buddha we peered through a partition between the two longest coats like some nosy neighbour does with the lace curtains. For God's sake, there was the sole member of the opposing team still wearing his shirt, tie and socks but minus his trousers and underpants. No doubt we each felt like some perverted voyeur but it was impossible not to stare in wonderment at the length of this guy's dick. It was humungous. I would prefer not to put an actual measurement to it just in case many readers think it was a normal sized willie and I am the odd one out but, take it from me, and judging by the envious looks on my team mates, that thing had to be bigger than any of the dicks belonging to the Nottinghamians that were staring at it that afternoon. We never did get to see if he had a jock strap big enough to cope because the rest of his team came in at our collective gasp of, "In the name of the wee man" or in this case "In the name of the big man!" as we about turned. I have a feeling, looking back on it now, that Big Willie's team mates traditionally arrived after he had put his whatsit out of harm's way as they, themselves, must have been suffering from a loss of self-esteem and confidence brought on by said Big Willie's willie. One thing we all reckoned was, that however late he got home after a rugby Saturday there would be no complaints from Big Willie's girl!

Funnily enough most of my memories of Nottinghamians were of away games. I can't explain why that should be but it's a fact. I have to say that pretty well every away game was quite a trek and I was not really used to that as a Herioter. The away games down to the Borders of Scotland were a mile or two away but as nothing compared to some of Nottinghamian treks. The M1 helped a bit to get journeys over and done with. One such M1 route took us way south to the ground of the mighty Leicester Tigers!

No, I didn't play against the Tigers but, I did have a game at stand-off against one of their junior XVs.

For such a minor wee game of rugby football I was surprised at the size of the crowd that had gathered to watch this far from exhibition game. My memory of the match draws a blank on the final score but I do recall that the Leicester umpteenth's standoff was a fellow called Roger McDonald. He was, as it turned out, a Heriot FP and better known to me as a middle distance runner for Victoria Park Athletic club in Glasgow. The Leicester supporters were seriously vociferous and typically rugger types. You know the sort : they shout inane instructions to their team that are either stating the bleeding obvious or are just plain daft. Here is but a small sample from this game.

"Shove Leicester umpteenths, shove," at every scrum. Pointless to pull you would think.

"Jump Leicester," at every line out. What a novel idea!

"Tackle Leicester." Was the plea whenever we Nottinghamians ran with the ball, which wasn't too often in this game as I recall.

The call to tackle is one of those desperately annoying commands that are shouted, whatever the circumstances, at a defence, any defence in any game anywhere in the world, never mind our Leicester friends. It is simply beyond the pale however when, say, an attacking scrum in any game you care to think of is fully expecting to win the ball and all their backs including the blind side winger have lined up in an almost sprint start position on the open side. They are imagining priceless overlaps and a try under the posts after slick passing of the ball down the line. This of course is the very occasion when an underdog scrum finds that extra something which its supporters have been exhorting them to discover and they go and heel the ball against the head. Usually it's not a heel at all, rather the other hooker has accidentally toe bashed the ball forward and straight through the other side of the scrum. Anyway the scrum-half goes blind and puts away the blind side winger who hitherto has done didley squat. Typically this fellow is a ringer home on his holidays and is no ball player but he can do evens for the hundred yards with a Blue from his University to prove it. Off he goes for a certain try and the attacking backs are not only caught badly on the back foot they are also now frantically transforming themselves into defensive backs. Whilst their plan B is being put into futile action they are treated to,

"Oh for f**k's sake the idiots have lost the bloody scrum," pause to draw some more breath, "for God's sake tackle him you stupid pathetic bastards, the laws say you can you know!" the sarcasm is often followed by something along the lines of "He's probably a University ponce." They got some of it right, unfortunately it wasn't very technical.

The so-called ponce rubs the whole thing in by celebrating the try he still has to score fifteen yards off the line. But, score he does, and backwards trudge the favourites to stand under the posts and watch the conversion sail over the crossbar.

Another oft heard touchline remark, "For the love of God, he's (some sloth of a forward) dropped the bloody ball again, the stupid prat." There is always a fellow in any team of junior or coarse rugby who simply cannot be trusted to catch a rugby ball, even if it has been carefully placed in his hands. This fellow should by now be well known to his team mates and his team supporters on the touchline. So it's no bloody use shouting and swearing at him because that, if it were possible, can only make him worse.

"No, no, for God's sake no, don't give it to HIM, he will only drop it." This is a player who has a huge repertoire of anti-skills in his anti-skills portfolio. He is only in the side to add bulk to the pack. Again he can be found in any team around the 5th XV level and that's because the 6ths don't want him. Leicester Umpteenths of course had such a chap. He got quite a lot of attention from a bloke in the crowd who was also constantly berating the referee. He was a long haired hippy student sort of guy wearing an RAF great coat. It's unlikely he was one but we will call him an Erk. After a series of unpleasantries aimed at the arbiter the whistle blew for a stoppage of play. The ref shouted in the direction of our hippy critic.

'I say you there, yes you, you in the RAF coat. Leave the ground immediately!'

'What for Ref?' the idiot queried.

'Well let's see now,' began the ref.

159

'Oh yes, we can start with what about the effing knock on Mr. McGoo?'

Then there was, 'Are you going on their team bus next effing Saturday ya 5th columnist creep!'

'Oh and that was hotly pursued by your accusation that I was the president of Nottinghamians Rugby Football Club.'

A fellow, seemingly a weel kent face, with a bit of a stammer, started what was probably meant to be a brief statement and which was met with great patience by the crowd. He took ages over what he had to say 'Hey Ri, Ri, Ri, Ref you ffff ffff fff, ffforgot, the the, the one whi, whi, whi, whennnn hi, he shi, shi, shhhhouted hi, how mmmmmooch are they pi, pi, pi, paying you?'

Having had their winter shortened by the aforementioned stalwart, the crowd on the touchline were now anxious to jog the ref's memory regarding other of the long haired chappies unkind remarks; but, as they excitedly chimed in, the match official putting his index finger to his mouth in a shoooshing sort of way thanked them very much for their evidence but claimed that he could manage the situation without any further ado from the crowd.

Turning to the man in the dock, so to speak, the referee passed sentence.

'You are a pain in the neck, you are ruining everybody's afternoon and I want you out of my sight before I restart this very good and sporting game of rugger!'

A number of spectators whose sympathies seemed to lie with the referee started to laugh and point at the heckler. This of course didn't really help and the disturber of the peace began to assume an air of extreme annoyance manifesting itself in a volley of oaths more akin to the language associated with stoker matelots in the Royal Navy rather than the more genteel expressions one has come to expect from RAF personnel. The last straw for the abused official was when his parentage came into question. It was at this point the ref demanded that the loutish spectator march, nay run, out of the ground. The referee's mood change from calm to almost frothing at the mouth startled everybody, not least the miscreant. It was Jekyll and Hyde all over again. As if hypnotised, the Erk, with bowed head, aimed for the exit. I guess the gate for our now humiliated and unwanted spectator was at least a couple of hundred yards distant. After a few steps he turned round with a look of appeal on his face and saw the referee, arm stiffly outstretched and index finger pointing to the gate and still with a face like thunder. The ref then, as if signaling a match decision to the crowd, waved his arm at the hapless twit in a shooing off fashion.

'Out, get out and not until I have seen you close yonder gate behind you will I restart this game!' he bellowed.

'Yes, fook off you stupid RAF bastard!' A particularly noisy and coarse spectator exclaimed.

'Wi well d done rrrrref, he's a known Ki, Ki, Ki, Ki, Ki, clot !' claimed our speech impeded friend injecting, as he stammered, a worry in the others about exactly what he was going to say.

More clapping and jeering; this was fun I began to think; just what coarse rugby is all about. It also had the benefit of giving the players much needed rest!

It seemed like an eternity before our spoilsport eventually did as he was bidden by the ref and reached the gate. The barrier slammed shut and simultaneously the whistle blew for the restart of the game. As I previously mentioned the score has escaped my memory forever but the après match fun remains stamped indelibly on my brain. After showering and changing, we Nottinghamians made our way to the bar. The opposition and their followers were already there and welcomed us as I have never been welcomed after any game of rugby. The hospitality, mostly of the liquid variety, was on an industrial scale and as a bonus, the traditional visiting team's meal was unusually delicious and very welcome.

Sadly, like all good things, this Leicester-style fun had to come to an end and so we trooped of to the car park and returned, with great consideration for our bladders, to the HQ of Robin Hood via all manner of back roads. The M1 you will appreciate is not conducive to pee stops!

One of the weirdest games I have ever played was against the Boots the Chemists XV at West Bridgeford, practically in the heart of the city of Nottingham. The pitch we played on was almost immediately behind the main stand of the Nottingham Forest Football Club ground. To the best of my memory there was only one spectator, namely my father who had come down with my mother for a long weekend; yet, the roars that we seemed to be getting and at times when nothing was happening were deafening and came as if from around thirty-thousand staunch supporters. The noise, of course, was coming from the crowd at the Forest match and, strangely, it seemed to have a motivational effect on our team. So far as the Nottingham Forest effect was concerned the Boots lads, being used to the racket, were quite unmoved. I have absolutely no recall of the final score; I remember we won and the surreal episode is stamped indelibly on my mind and my inner ear.

The last away game that I played for Nottinghamians was against The Nottingham High School 1st XV. I remember the school grounds and the school itself were very grand. I think we won but other than that it was not a particularly memorable day. I only found out fairly recently that the school produced a number of prominent MPs, including Ed Balls, currently Shadow Chancellor; Kenneth Clarke QC, Lord Chancellor, Secretary of State for Justice ; Edward Davey, Minister in the Dept. for Business, Innovation and Skills; Geoff Hoon former Leader of the House of Commons and Piers Merchant, former MP, who resigned in disgrace.

During the winter of 1972 my dearest Rosemary and I were thrilled to find out that we were expecting our first child. My father took seriously ill around this time and whilst Rosemary and I looked forward very much to the birth of our first baby, due in May 1973, we had also the deep concern about my dad constantly on our minds. Sadly my poor Dad died on the 24th May in Edinburgh's Western General Hospital, only a few hours after Kirsten was born on the 23rd May in the Edinburgh Royal Infirmary. Ironically Kirsten should have been born in The Western General but when Rosemary attended a clinic at that hospital in the early days of her pregnancy the examining doctor seemed unhappy about Rosemary having her baby there and not in a hospital in Nottinghamshire. So he told her basically to get lost. However, undaunted, my determined little lady got her way so far as having our first child in Scotland was concerned and The Simpsons Memorial Maternity Pavilion staff delivered her of a bonnie wee baby girl, Kirsten Scott Bruce .

I had decided to hang up my boots for what I thought would be the last time in early 1973. Later that year I was transferred by my employers to their Aberdeen office. We moved to the North East of Scotland in December 1973.

Me, Rosemary and "The Bishop" on our wedding day 9th June 1971

164

CHAPTER 11

On My Own in Aberdeen

I had gone up to Aberdeen in mid-November of that year and when Rosemary and our by then six-month old Kirsten joined me we moved into our new home in the Kincardineshire fishing town of Stonehaven, about eighteen miles south of the Granite City.

It was a tricky time as there was an oil embargo by the Organisation of Arab Petroleum Exporting Countries. It was sparked off by the USA supplying the Israeli military during the Yom Kippur war. All of that seemed so irrelevant in my life but caused ordinary folks like me a great deal of trouble when it came to filling up their petrol tanks.

I was glad to be back in Scotland. Nottingham was very good to me and my family but I never really felt as though I could settle there. Rosemary however was happy with everything about our exile but could see that I was not, so, as was typically unselfish of her, she happily agreed to return to our homeland.

Whilst I was trying to establish myself in my new area and with all the people I hoped to do business with, Rosemary got on with selling our house down in Nottinghamshire. During the first few weeks of my Aberdeen honeymoon, Torry Loon, a fellow inspector, had expressed concern over my hair, maintaining that it was far too long for the tastes and fashion of Aberdeen business folk. For my own good, he suggested, a trim was in order. My colleague was a much older fellow and was of a different generation to me. I should have smelled a rat.

I was not all that keen for a trim as Rosemary, being a hairdresser, had looked after my coiffure ever since we started dating and I knew that she would not be happy about anybody else touching a single hair on my head. Anyway, seduced by my determined colleague I set off for the barber that he recommended.

In my humble opinion and with great respect, Aberdeen in the early seventies, despite the oil boom, was a bit behind the rest of the major cities of the UK so far as fashion trends, shops and entertainment were concerned. The backwardness of the capital of the North East of Caledonia was to be found in many areas not least of which was men's hair styles and indeed hairstylists! I couldn't dwell on my early feelings for the city under the Northern Lights; I had to go through with this blasted haircut.

I walked into what looked like a ladies hairdressing salon which of course should not have been a surprise because that was indeed what it was. The clue was the banks of old fashioned hairdryers encasing a number of hairnetted "Aiberdeen" ladies. Upon enquiring as to where the barbers department was I was told by a helpful and highly animated middle aged woman "doonastairs, look, ken." I saw the directional index finger sign which she was pointing to with a pair of what looked like garden shears! Down I went and lo, I found a very large room with a long row of barbers chairs.

There was one barbers' chair standing empty but, worryingly, there was still a number of gents sitting on seats that adorned three quarters of the perimeter of the room. A very tall fellow possessed of a hairstyle resembling the Big Bopper's and with a funny accent that I did not recognise as Aberdonian came rushing towards me flapping a towel. He ushered me to the empty seat. Conscious that I may be accused of jumping the queue I protested mildly whilst waving my arms at the remaining waiting gents,

'But what about all of these gentlemen that are waiting?'

'No, No it izz Ohkay, they do nut mind!' Came the reply in a very deep and husky sounding voice.

So down I sat, the towel being wrapped around my neck.

'Zhhiort buck and zides, Yez'

'Well actually' ---- snip, snip, snip.

Too late he was off. The clipping was punctuated with barber humming tunes that were not familiar to me. The task for which he seemed to be expecting payment, now finished and, of course, the singing terminated, out came the rearview mirror. I could hardly look at the barren desert at the back of my head for gawping at the obverse disaster.

I was shorn and speechless. To add insult to injury the sheep shearer had the cheek to say to me that I was going bald and could he interest me in a toupee.

'No much wonder I am going bald, you've left enough hair on the floor to make a dozen rugs ya scissor happy scalper.'

'Sverray good haircut, your mama vood be werray prowid.'

No wonder none of the waiting gents were rushing to sit in that guy's chair.

I returned to the office and my colleague, the one responsible for sending me to Tomahawk. Torry laughed like a hyena when I walked into our room.

'Sid the Polak was it?'

The man who had just assaulted my precious hair was indeed called Sid.

My colleague told me that Sid was a Polish soldier stationed in Scotland during the 2nd World War and stayed on at the cessation of hostilities.

I begged to correct my fellow worker. So far as I was concerned Sid had changed sides that day as hostilities had definitely not ceased so far as I was concerned.

My hair was cut so short that, a week later, I was stunned when, not recognising me, Rosemary with little Kirsten in her arms walked right past me on platform 1 of Edinburgh's Waverley Station. I was waiting for them to complete leg two of their three legged journey to Stonehaven. Leg three took our wee Bruce family to the Mearns town and the next phase of our lives but with no rugby included in the plans.

CHAPTER 12

In Which I Join Ken Scotland's Old Club and Help Found Mackie FP

Settling into our new home the phone rang one evening. Rosemary answered and seemed pleased to hear from whoever it was judging by her excited tone.

'Oh, hello Andy, great to hear from you Andy that would be lovely Andy, yes we will see you then Andy, Bye Andy!'

'That would be Andy then!' I said.

'Oh, yes, it's wonderful, an old friend of Bernard, my brother, called Andy McFarlane, lives just north of Aberdeen and he and his wife Maura have asked us out to lunch next Sunday!'

Keeping our date, Rosemary, Kirsten and I set off for the Macfarlane's farm at Loch Hills near Dyce. It was a glorious December day and despite the actual time of year we were full of the joys of Spring. This day was to write a story in our lives with quite a twist in its tail.

We were welcomed by Andy and his lovely wife Maura and immediately given a stiff drink to warm the cockles of our hearts.

I was glad that Rosemary had agreed to that drink as I think it possibly softened her up for what I had a feeling was about to come.

After our drink and a wee wander around parts of the farm, we sat down to a generous and delicious lunch. Andy as a Herioter had played both school and FP rugby before taking on the farm in Dyce. This move to the Aberdeen area prompted Andy to join Aberdeenshire Rugby Club. At the time of this story Andy was still playing for Shire. Not too many years before Andy's arrival at Shire, Kenny Scotland graced their team and also the North and Midlands. During the après lunch chat Andy asked me if I played senior rugby. No negative reaction from Rosemary, which did surprise me.

'Oh no I said, I gave that up when I moved up here.'

'Oh, so you have played up until recently?' Andy queried.

'Yes but not to a great standard,' I humbly, but accurately, stated.

I don't know if this said more about me or Shire but Andy replied, 'Oh that's okay Shire are glad of any new player. What position would you like to play in?' Note the farmer's skilful use of the closed question!

I expected Rosemary to make it clear to everybody round the table exactly what she thought about me playing rugby but I guess because she knew Andy as a friend of her big brother and she liked all his pals (I think she quite liked Bernard too!) she was relaxed about the whole matter. So it came to pass that I would attend the next training session of Aberdeenshire Rugby Club. First though I had to buy an Aberdeenshire jersey. It turned out that such apparel was as rare as hens' teeth. Not one sports shop had any left in stock and so it looked like I was going to either have to play in my bare chest or borrow one from somewhere; stealing one belonging to a clubmate was not an option I figured.

I happened to mention my dilemma to my brother-in-law, Derek McCracken and he suggested that since Kenny Scotland had played for Shire he may perhaps have an old jersey that I could borrow. Kenny did indeed have a jersey for me but it wasn't a Shire issue, rather it was a Canterbury RFC jersey that Kenny had acquired from a Canterbury player when the Lions played them in the famous 1959 tour of Australia and New Zealand. Canterbury's livery was identical to Shire's at that time. What an amazing thing to happen to me. I just managed to squeeze into the jersey and away I went, a very happy man I can tell you.

When I joined Shire their HQ was within the grounds of Aberdeenshire Cricket Club at Mannofield. They also shared the cricketer's club house which reminded me a wee bit of Raeburn place, home of Edinburgh Accies. After my first training session a coach took us into one of the back rooms of the building to have a chalk and talk meeting. I hated that sort of thing ; for me it turned rugby into an academic subject and that was anathema to me. If I recall correctly, this coach was a PT teacher at a West Aberdeenshire academy. He seemed to know his rugby, in theory anyway, and the wee "class" wasn't too bad: I probably switched off early on anyway which would have taken the drudge out of things for me. Later in the bar the coach, who was obviously a prop by trade, asked me who I had played for, what I did, did I like Aberdeen and so on. He told me a bit about his training as a gym teacher. As part of his course he had to learn to ski and did so on some mountain or other somewhere in the French Alps. Never having skiied before that trip he was desperate to get up as high in the mountain as he could to achieve some speedy thrill. Up he climbed as high as he dared and set off downwards parallel to the packed ski lift. He began to accelerate alarmingly towards a row of trees that were directly in his path. Because he had only learned the very basics of skiing at this stage he had no idea how to swerve or, indeed, stop. Realising he was done for he thought, "Oh well f..c. it," and he stuck his shoulder out with the intention of showing his first and what would be his last tree a thing or two. Boooofffff! He hit the first tree and went straight through it, bark, wood and lichen flew everywhere. The eyes of the people in the ski lifts were now transfixed as they viewed, with some considerable awe, this mighty superman who, with the same steely determination, battered through the next tree and the next and the next and the next before the friction of hitting trees caused him to halt. Scraping bits of tree, parasitic Ivy and the likes off his face he stared at the trail of devastation he had left behind him. It gradually dawned upon him that he had just hammered through a line of trees that had probably been dead for scores of years so were absolutely hollow and rotten.

My first game for Shire was for their 3rd XV. We played on a pitch in a vast Aberdeen Town Council park in the Hazelhead area of the city. There were countless football pitches in this park and I think there was only the one rugby pitch or maybe two. Our opponents were from Stirling University. It was a dull miserable wet day, the rain coming down like stair rods. I have only two memories of that game. The first was at the point of the opposition's kick off. I had been picked to play at outside centre and was standing at my post thinking to myself,

"What the hell am I doing here?"

I hadn't played for absolutely months by this time and had not done any training in that time either, apart from the previous Tuesday and Thursday night. Some time into the second half I began to wonder where Rosemary had got to. We had driven in together and I left her to go off in the car whilst I changed and went to play the game, the idea being that she would come back and watch me play for the very first time . I was beginning to settle with the explanation that she had stayed away meantime as the weather was so bad. Then suddenly, I heard a familiar voice:

'Excuse me, hello, excuse me, hello do you know Douglas Bruce?'

It was Rosemary. She was trying to attract the attention of our full back who was almost as big a stranger to her as he was to me. Our number 15 was trying to focus on a high ball that was succumbing to gravity and heading towards him on the perpendicular trajectory. At the same time the Stirling forwards were approaching him horizontally. Our man would have caught the ball and cleared it but he was distracted by my wife and was flattened by the snarling Stirling forwards.

Ouch! The defender was well and truly buried.

The poor guy eventually emerged from the heap of men. The play was broken down completely as the ball had squirted out of the tangle of players and into touch. Rosemary was still trying to extract clues regarding my whereabouts from the battered but slowly recovering full back.

'Hello, sorry to bother you but do you know Douglas Bruce? He is playing a game of rugby for Aberdeenshire somewhere near here.'

The fellow of course hadn't a clue who I was. Typical of a third fifteen he had not been introduced to me at that stage. Whilst the ball was being recovered and everybody was taking their places for the lineout I managed to shout over to Rosemary to let her know that at least I was alive and well, which was more than could be said for our number 15. But of course I couldn't speak to her just at that time.

Whilst the ensuing lineout was forming the full back quickly introduced himself to Rosemary and told her how to find the Shire Clubhouse. He further explained that we would all catch up after the game and have a wee chat.

It turned out that Rosemary had not taken proper bearings after she left me earlier on that afternoon and when she came back to Hazelhead, she later confessed, she had sat in the car for ages watching a distant football match before realising that not only was it not my game she was watching it wasn't even a rugby match.

After the game we headed for the changing rooms. During the course of showering and changing amidst legions of footballers I had a chance to become properly acquainted with my team mates not least of whom was the full back, a fellow called Peter Mitchell. Peter was and still is a good friend of Andy Mcfarlane and now of the Bruces.

Once Rosemary had got over the embarrassment of causing Peter to get hammered by the Stirling pack, we settled down to an evening which could only be described as a one man comedy cabaret act by our newly found full back friend. Peter Mitchell is today one of the funniest after dinner speakers in Scotland but at the time of our first encounter he was little known out with the Shire circles. Rosemary and I were having a ball that is until a wee bit of a bombshell struck at the very heart of our, up until then, unbridled fun. The wife of the club secretary was circulating amongst the happy throng; she spotted me and Rosemary.

'Oh you must be Mrs Bruce !' ventured the secretary's wife.

'Yes I am and by the way it's Rosemary!'

I had a bad feeling about this encounter. Rosemary was always very good when meeting people for the first time but I was to see her good nature seriously tested during this wee introductory meeting.

'So nice to meet you Rosemary, and so glad your husband is joining the club. I am Mrs Rugbywidow, my husband is the club secretary and I do my best to help him as much as I can.'

Oh no, I knew what was coming next.

Come it came.

'I hope that we can count on you joining the ladies' tea group and can we put you down for heating the pies and what not next Saturday?'

'Well no actually you can't. I am not too knocked out that my husband is playing rugby on Saturdays and I am even less knocked out that I have to abandon my Saturday to rugby as well.' Silence: Rosemary continued, "in any event I have an eight month old daughter to consider!'

Oooops!

Luckily the secretary's wife realised that not every wife was as keen as she was or felt that she had to be.

'Well ok then, I understand,' said Mrs Rugbywidow and she floated off to speak to others.

All was to change greatly with my Rosie as time went on.

After I played a couple more games in junior sides I was promoted to the 1st XV but, as I feared, I really did not have time to train with Shire during the week because I had a great deal of late night working to do. When I did have time in the evenings I wanted to spend it with the family. I was going to have to pack it all in the next season or demote myself to a lower team and not train in Aberdeen with the club.

As it happened my family were to have me all the time for a few weeks because I collected a bad injury in a game for the Shire 1st XV at their old ground at The Aberdeenshire cricket club. In the opinion of my opposite centre I late tackled him and he told me he would get me before the afternoon was out. This he did quite spectacularly. After an early tackle he sat on my right shoulder as I was trying to get up, my left shoulder was grounded at the time and the upshot was I popped all my rib cartilages. The pain was absolutely excruciating for days despite the horse pills I was prescribed.

After missing a week or so of work I returned with difficulty as I found steering my car awkward and pulling on the handbrake was a whole new experience in pain. My office colleague, Torry Loon, you know the barber referee, opined that my employers would not be very happy about me missing work due to a rugby injury, and, if it was to happen again they may ban me from playing rugby. Of course, this was all made up in his head. Torry didn't really like rugby and all the snobby school boy types that, in his head, play the game. So far as he was concerned, being from an earlier generation, we were all "poofs", us rugger buggers. It has to be said that rugby was not, at that time, a game that was played by very many clubs in the city of Aberdeen or indeed the county of Aberdeenshire. Association football as is usual in most of Scotland ruled the roost at the expense of most other sports including rugby. Up until very recently the two top clubs in Aberdeen were Gordonians and Aberdeen Grammar. Kenny Scotland had to join Aberdeenshire when his employment took him to the North East, Shire being an open club, were blessed to have this icon of Scottish and British rugby join them. Kenny had his last cap for Scotland in 1965 whilst a Shire player. Stand-off was where Shire preferred to play the famous full back ninety times between 1965 and 1969. Kenny also played twenty-three times for the North and Midlands and eleven times for The North. Much has changed in rugby throughout the world since the early seventies and the North East of Scotland is no exception. All clubs, old and new, are now open in that region and only Aberdeen Grammar is in the top flight. It must be hard for the likes of Grammar to maintain that place given their geographical position more than anything else. Borders clubs suffer also from the attraction that central belt clubs have for young players these days.

I continued to settle into my new area as a salesman. Many of the agents that I was to try and do business with were what were called Nationals. These agents would normally have their HQ's in London or some other large English city and have branch offices in many other UK cities and towns. Aberdeen had its fair share and amongst them was one that, to my surprise, and great pleasure employed Ian

McRae of Gordonians and Scotland. Ian was known throughout the North East of Scotland rugby world as Spivvy McRae. Unfortunately Spivvy and his boss Leslie Moffat, another Heriot FP, dealt only in general Insurance. They had nothing to do with life assurance and pensions which is what I was trying to sell. That position changed as Spiv's employers eventually included personal and company financial advice in their list of services. However whilst there remained that gap I had great pleasure in meeting Spivvy from time to time taking the chance to talk to him about his International career. Ian got the nickname Spiv at primary school in Bucksburn. He lived in a neighbourhood called Sclattie Park near the Clover Leaf pub (where there used to be strippers!!) and says simply,

'I seemed to be a bit better turned out than a lot of the other kids and the name stuck when I went to Robert Gordon's College.'

It was suggested to him several times at the height of his rugby career that he would get more caps if he were to move to Edinburgh or Glasgow but his answer was always no. He felt that if he was good enough to be picked from time to time to represent his country from Gordonians, who he loved, then he should be good enough for his country at any time so long as he was showing form. Ian McRae made his debut for Scotland in 1967 against England but he had to wait another two years before he got another cap. This time it was against France and Scotland won 6-3. Ian made history as Rugby Union's first ever replacement. Gordon Connell of London Scottish, and Trinity Academicals was injured very early on in the game and Ian came on to take part in a very famous victory. Jo Maso of France kicked a drop goal to draw even after a Scotland penalty and Jim Telfer scored a try (3 points) to seal the victory. That amazing match and Jo Maso were to play a part later on in my time in the Aberdeen area. Spiv had six caps altogether over a span of six years. I had the great privilege of playing against Ian in

The Mackie Academy FP sevens tournament back in 1978. I also played with Ian on a few occasions for a select team organised by Peter Mitchell of the Press and Journal. These games were strictly friendlies organised to hansel a new pitch or possibly a pavilion but Ian always played very competitively in them, as he did in all of his matches.

My second season with Shire just didn't work out. I had to work late most evenings and so attending training regularly was impossible. I couldn't repeat the play-no-train approach of my days with Nottinghamians - the fixtures at Shire were too tough for that so I had to resign my membership.

Rugby, however, as we know from my earlier experiences in Nottingham has a habit of jumping up and biting one when it is least expected.

CHAPTER 13

I Help Form A New Club; Club Dinners; Famous
Visitors; History and Traditions; Community Spirit;
Stockholm Exiles, Heriot's Cavaliers

My time being up with Shire I hung up my rugby boots in the dustbin and settled down to non-rugby weekends.

Rosemary, Kirsten and I had the whole of every weekend to ourselves apart from shopping trips into Aberdeen from Stonehaven. Rosemary could see that spending Saturday afternoons in that way was not my cup of tea.

I have to say I didn't really miss the training aspect of the game, but, I did miss the matches and the après match nonsense. Rugby camaraderie was an amazing and relaxing release from a stressful working week.

Unbeknown to me at the time, work was afoot to start school rugby at the local Academy in Stonehaven. Eventually there were enough FP's with skills in the oval ball game to consider starting an FP rugby club. One of the founder members and a next door neighbour of ours ran about Stonehaven drumming up support through the distribution of leaflets advertising the potential for a rugby club in the town. My dear girl was happy with the prospect of me going off yet again to join a new rugby club. She liked this young man and his family which seemed to count for a great deal. The early meetings to establish a club took place about a month before our second daughter Sarah was born in 1975.

Mackie Academy FPRFC although strongly connected to the Mackie Academy in Stonehaven was formed as an open club. In the opinion of everybody that was involved at the birth of the club it was the best way to begin, but, after a few years a number of members wanted to scrap the connection with the school and rename the club Stonehaven Rugby Club. There was an Extraordinary General Meeting to debate and vote on a proposal to make the change. Both as president at the time and as a member I wasn't for a change because having the school onside and with a built in players' nursery seemed to me the most sensible thing to do, especially because we were in a relatively small community. At that time many of the influential people in the town were former pupils of the school and I thought that we would alienate ourselves. We also, at that time, depended on the school playing fields to play our matches. No point in pissing people off. Presumably those now in charge continue to think along those lines as the club remains Mackie Academy FPRFC.

The first president of Mackie FPRFC was a wonderful fellow called Bob Lewis. Welsh I believe by parentage, but, quintessentially, English. Bob had two sons at Mackie. They were both too young in the early days of the Club to play for the FP's. It must have been quite a family sacrifice for Bob to give up so much of his time to provide Mackie with the firm foundation that it still stands on to this day. The first captain was a Watsonian called Torquil McLeod and the vice captain was a former pupil of the Royal High School of Edinburgh, Brian Thomson. Torquil and Brian were both very good players. Torquil learned his rugby at George Watson's School, a school renowned for its rugby prowess as was Royal High. As a matter of fact I don't remember being in any age group Heriot School team that beat a similarly aged Royal High School team. In his youth Brian played for a SRU colts side, coached by Kenny Scotland.

Brian was good with the younger more raw players; he had a unique way of encouraging and enthusing some lads that were lacking in confidence. I remember playing as a centre for Mackie under the lights at Strathallan watching Brian, our number 8, cause the late Tommy Murray, a statuesque and quiet lock, to get quite worked up. It was marvellously simple: Brian kicked Tommy right up the bum and when a now enraged Tommy turned to belt his kicker, Brian pointed at a Strathallan lock and said 'It was him!' Hilarious.

It was not all plain sailing in the beginning. Some of the playing members were suspicious of a few of the inabootcomers, such as me and John Mackie; they thought that we influenced such important facets of the club as team selection - picking players from inabootcomers ahead of local lads born and bred. This was not of course the case but it took years in some cases for suspicions to subside. I suspect for some it has never gone away. Mackie depended on all-comers as there was simply not enough rugby playing former pupils of Mackie Academy to stock all the teams.

There were two teams right away. From time to time, a 3rd XV ran out; a 4th XV was formed a few times during a difficult period in the early eighties for the North Sea oil and gas industry. Many of the Mackie players worked offshore and were normally unavailable for selection for a month at a time. Given that not all the prospective players worked the same shift and that some lads were on call, putting together teams was a bit of a headache for the selectors and the team secretary. During the downturn in the North Sea operations later in the early eighties, a number of the lads that had been laid off work became available for selection regularly and at the same time. This temporary glitch in the offshore oil and gas industry gave the Club the opportunity to expand its fixture list albeit for a brief period. I had the signal honour of coming out of retirement to captain our very first 4thXV. An away fixture had been arranged with a Garioch side in Inverurie, but when the team assembled at our usual meeting place in Stonehaven's Market Square we only had eleven men available. In true amateur spirit, and believe me it was amateur, we made the journey northwards. Upon arriving at the Garioch ground we discovered that our opponents were only thirteen in number. Garioch also flew the true amateur flag that day and gave us a player. The sides were even. My accustomed positions were either on the wing or at centre but I played at scrum-half that day. We played with seven forwards, a scrum-half a stand-off, one centre and two wings who also assumed, when necessary, the positions of outside centre or full back. Both sides were mostly made up of players who had no idea what they were doing or were far too unfit for the purpose. Attacking was a limited exercise and as for lineouts and scrums, they were a complete lottery with neither side showing any dominance. Mackie were fortunate in that the opposition either did not have the will to tackle or simply didn't know how to. In addition to what was probably the worst example of a game of rugby that afternoon in the whole of the North East of Scotland, the temperature was freezing. Encouraged to come out of retirement, Roy Bruce, one of our props received one of those skelps on his ear that is particularly sore when it is a cold day. The ref stopped the game so that aid could be administered to a very fed up Roy. Our stand-off that day was an Irish fellow called Dave Surplus and, like most Irishman I know, Dave was a bit of a wag. He claimed that he could fix things as he knew a bit about ears. He went over to Roy and, holding his hand up to the sore ear, said,

'Now then Roy, tell me how many fingers you can hear?'

Such is the humour of the Irish and the nonsense that went on in the lower fifteens.

My last game as captain of the 4th XV was against a newly formed club called Turriff, Buchan and Formartine. They don't exist now so far as I know. The skipper of the club came to our dressing room and asked to speak to our captain. I went out into the corridor and asked what was up. He explained that some of his team had hardly ever played rugby before, some indeed never at all and most had only met the previous Thursday at training. It was his fervent hope that we would bear that in mind. I was aghast but could see that there was a desperation in this fellow's tone. I cast my mind back to the day I took that band of eleven lads to Inverurie just to honour a fixture and give some pretty hopeless team mates a game of rugby. I told the Buchan captain that we would play the game in the spirit he hoped for.

On the walk over to the furthest away pitch at the Ury playing fields I had a word with the referee about my opposing captain's difficulty. Actually every time I clapped eyes upon this particular ref I had a job to keep a straight face. The reason for that had nothing to do with rugby. The fellow was English and he had formed a group of Morris dancers who held alfresco gigs all over the place including some performed immediately outside the Marine Hotel which is situated on the Stonehaven harbour front.

I am really sorry but, when I see grown men dressed up in trousers adorned with floral nicky tams (farm worker's gaiters), shoes covered in little bells and waving sticks with pigs bladders attached, I can't help thinking that they look comically odd. They appear especially so when they do that hopping sort of dance. I concede that kilted Scotsmen probably look similarly, shall we say, out of place, especially to the English. However, men in the Highland Regiments wore their kilts in the heat of battle during the Great War, my Grandfather was one. Whilst in no way suggesting that the English soldiers fighting in the "War To End All Wars" were any less brave than their Scottish companions-in-arms, I don't think any Sassenach regiments charged the enemy in florally decorated gaiters whilst brandishing pig's bladders on their Lee Enfield rifles.

Incidentally the World War One kilt of my Dad's Dad is in our attic. He was a very proud Argyll and Southern Highlander and engaged the Germans on the Western Front; not all on his own you understand, well not at the start anyway. When I was but a wee boy of around four my Dad proudly showed me his Dad's battle kilt. It will be a hundred years old in 2014, the anniversary of the start of the First World War. He told me a great deal about the history of his Father's kilt and how brave my Grandpa was in the war etc. etc. I was convinced up until I was around twelve that the holes in the kilt were caused by German bullets. I think it was around the same time my Mum was telling me that there is no Santa Claus, no Tooth Fairy and I was going to be getting a pair of slippers for my Christmas, that she told me the bullet holes were in fact caused by moths! Talk about devastation.

Anyway, concealing my mirth as best I could I told the referee that the opposition were pretty green but keen and when he blew his whistle for an infringement on their part could he please give as full an explanation as to why he had done so. "Okay" he agreed. Well we all got to the pitch and my Morris dancing match official blew his whistle indicating his need for the two skippers to approach him and deal with the coin tossing etc. to enable the kick off to take place. Before we went through the heads or tails stuff the three of us shook hands and as I was doing this with the Buchan captain I couldn't help noticing his spanking new rugby jersey, his equally new and well creased shorts and a very flashy looking pair of side lacing boots. But there was something missing and I couldn't immediately think what until it dawned on me that he wasn't wearing any stockings. Once that had registered and adding it to the Morris dancing ref image in my head, I had a great deal of difficulty taking anything seriously for the rest of the afternoon.

The game finally got started. It wasn't long before we experienced a plethora of Buchan offences, each one of which was dissected by the ref and explained in full to our Northern friends. After about fifteen minutes the occasional Morris Dancing-pig-bladder brandishing ref blew his whistle very loudly and announced with great exasperation:

'This isn't a game of rugby it's more like a f**king tutorial!'

Mackie FP were like every other rugby club when it came to Friday nights. That is the time when the team secretary comes into his own and believe you me he is definitely on his own! All other committee members will not be seen on a Friday for dust. He is entrusted to deal with last minute calls off from all teams. The reasons for a call off are many and are often difficult to hear on the phone thanks to the diverse and loud background noises that are likely to pollute the line clarity - such as people shouting at barmen for drinks rounds. Some examples of excuses are things like flu; the mother in law is dead, or at least I hope she is; my house has burnt down; my wife took my kit to the charity shop; I got done for drunk driving last night and so can't get in to town; I got diarrhoea through a hole in my shoe; my girlfriend is pregnant or at least she will be in twenty minutes, and so on and so forth.

Once the team secretary has been made aware of the individuals that are unable to take the field he has to assume the mantle of a covert scout looking out for players. However, the gaps in the 1st XV are easily filled from the 2nd XV, thereafter the 2nd XV benefits from the ransacking of the 3rds and so on. In recent years the need for a replacement bench has exacerbated the whole nightmare. The problems for the team secretary become a big headache when there simply are not enough registered players left to fill the now collapsing human pyramid.

A team secretary is judged by a few things, not least of which is his wife's patience level on any Friday that her team secretary husband has to break his promise, yet again, to take her out to dinner or whatever. Broken promises of social dates with the wife are usually occasioned by an extraordinary number of calls off coupled with the fact that many playing members, without telling anybody, have a nasty habit of changing address phone numbers and, it has been known, names have been changed on the eve of a match by deed poll. Tedious detective work then follows. If the TS can get through a night like that and have a full turnout the following afternoon he is judged as good. When a team secretary achieves that standard of excellence in his appraisal, various consequences befall him and, of course, his good lady wife. The most devastating of these is the narrowing of his promotion prospects within the committee. He becomes too valuable to the club where he is; his onwards and upwards climb on the administration ladder falters because he has become a victim of his own success. The time a good team secretary really excels is when the list of known players is completely used up and there are still gaps in the bottom team. Ageing, retired players who get wind of this deficit run or, more likely, hobble for the hills. If they can't get out of their house for whatever reason they take their phones off the hook, douse all lights and generally batten down the hatches, ready to repel all boarders. "We have the plague" signs have been seen, from a respectable distance, on players' front doors. When the foregoing happens two sources often available to team secretaries but invisible to the uneducated eye are 1.) Players who would possibly like a game, probably new to the area, but don't know of the club's existence and 2.) Innocents who have never played before but at least have a pulse, are still warm, have not reached state retirement age and look like they may be of the male gender. Both categories of potential position fillers are sniffed out by an excellent TS.

Some team secretaries lacking in intestinal fortitude fling the towel in at the first sign of a difficult Friday night. It is an understandable reaction given the foregoing but the show must go on. After a difficult phone call between a simpering, gibbering wreck of a failed team secretary and his president in which the team secretary himself calls off, or rather surrenders, a reserve secretary is called in. In a junior club's case it is usually the president or captain. It happened to me one eventful Friday night when I was captain of Mackie. Four places were blank in the 2nd XV that were due to play at home against an eager Ellon side. We needed a prop, a centre, a number 8 and a lock. My friend John Mackie who was also the club coach, filled the prop's place, I the centre and so we were left with two positions to fill. I had come home early from work that Friday to keep a doctor's appointment of all things because I thought that I had the flu, so playing rugby was not exactly the most clever thing to be doing. I had called off therefore from the 1sts. During the medical consultation the doc confirmed I had a stomach bug but he also advised me that an Irish fellow, I will call him Mick, had just registered with the practice. Mick told the doc that he was employed in the North Sea oil and gas business and that he had played for one of the big Irish teams in his day and had had a trial for Ireland. I was to be glad of such information later that evening. Mackie's team secretary called me about 8pm that night with the news of his abject failure thus far in the evening. There was to be no talking him into continuing the struggle as his wife, standing right beside him, was shouting things at the poor sod like,

'Don't you dare give in to that blankety blank Dougie Bruce,' and 'It's ok for him in that blankety blank cushy blankety blank captain's blankety blank job the blankety blank blank that he is.'

It was a kind of surreal phone call; the team secretary appeared to be taking on the role of a person interrupting his wife because the thrust of the vocals at his end of the line were mainly coming from her and, oddly, as I now recall, Les Dawson was on the telly at the time hosting "Blankety Blank!"

Two of the four places filled, we still needed a lock and a number eight. I remembered what the doctor had said about the Irishman, Mick. I called him and he told me that Mick, along with some other guys, was renting a big house further up the coast.

John and I rushed out to catch these guys before they went to the pub. It was, after all, a Friday night and for reasons explained previously these guys could have got wind of the fact the only local rugby team was short of hands for the following day. Knocking on the door, John and I could hear a lot of darting about from within the house and people speaking in hushed tones.

'Make yourselves scarce.' 'Quick get rid of it!' 'who the f--- can that be?' were initial phrases I remember closely followed by 'Ringo, you go to the door and get rid of them.'

John and I figured at this juncture that we could be forgiven for thinking that we had found ourselves on the lot of a movie in the Mob genre. We were just about to high tail it when the large front door creaked slowly into action. It seemed to be an automatic door at first because, unusually, it opened up in an outwards direction and there was no apparent door pusher. A few seconds elapsed before the four fingers of the right hand of an inhabitant appeared hooked round the door edge just under head height. It was as if the door acted not only as an invaluable front line of defence in the time honoured fashion of all front doors, it was also holding the pusher of the door upright. Next, the outward momentum of the heavy door caused the fellow who owned the hand to involuntarily accelerate round the door and towards us. Startled by this, John and I stepped quickly backwards as the guy straightened up and came to a halt, right in our faces. 'Whaddayawant ?' in a strong Liverpool accent was slurred at us.

'Does Mick live here ?' I enquired.

'Eee might do, why, ooose askin?'

'Good evening, I am Douglas Bruce, captain of Mackie Academy FP Rugby Football club and this is my colleague and club coach, Mr John Mackie!' At that, and, from the depths of this cavernous dwelling Mick shouted in the musical lilt of a southern Irishman, 'It's okay Ringo, let them in!' Ringo wasn't really his name but he sounded like the famous Beatle, so that's what we will call him.

'In ye come, just go straight through, Mick's in the back sitting room' Ringo directed as he staggered about the hallway.

The voices we had heard earlier seemed to indicate to John and me that there had been a few more people in the house than the two visible inhabitants were suggesting. We both just left things as a bit of a mystery best not to be questioned.

Mick realised immediately I spoke, why John and I had called and said that if we were looking for a player he was our man. This was not the answer we were expecting at all, given what seemed to us to be a bit of a long shot from the beginning. As things then stood it seemed very unlikely that anyone in that house, at least the ones we could see, was capable of standing up never mind playing rugby.

'Actually it's a couple of blokes we need for our 2nd XV and the game is tomorrow afternoon here in Stonehaven,' said John.

'Well that's still ok, cos Ringo can come along too, can't you Ringo me boy?'

'Yer moost be fookin joking ye Irish prick, I've never played roogby in me life.'

'Oh shut yer face ya big 'Nancy', I'll show you what to do' Mick mocked. 'By the way what positions are ye needin filled oop?'

This seemed to Mick to be of interest but not as much as just getting a game. That was the main point. John told him we needed a number 8 and a lock.

'Dats joost grand, cos I can play back row anywhere and we can stick this lump of a scouser in the second row where I can keep an eye on the bastard.'

'Oive just been to the doctor today and Oive got a bit of a chest complaint so oi may not be at me best you understand!'

It was as if Mick was a character straight out of Michael Green's "Art of Coarse Rugby." I think Mick would have played had he contracted pleurisy and double pneumonia. Anyway I don't know what I was marvelling at, I had a tummy bug to cope with. I told them that we would supply as much kit as they needed and we would see them at the ground an hour before kick-off. John drew them a wee map of how to get up to the Mackie playing fields and we left.

As we walked to the car the hushed tones started up all over again:

'It's okay youse can come out again, they've gone!' "mumble, mumble"; 'Of course we know what we are doing,' more mumbling, 'Well you'll just have to go to the frigging shops yourselves.'

The next day dawned and lo, I didn't feel too bad. I wondered how our Irish and Liverpudlian friends were getting on. They seemed fit enough as we joined the rest of the seconds for our game.

We lost, but, both John and I scored a try, Mick was a hero and John did his usual grand job at prop enjoying the huge shove that came through from Ringo who was a very big lad. Shoving in the scrum was about all he was good at but nonetheless he seemed to enjoy his first game of rugby. We were to get more out of Mick as the season went on but that was almost the last we saw of Ringo. Happily the tummy bugs that Mick and I were suffering from on the Friday had gone by Saturday post match.

The very next night, Sunday, we had a players supper in a local hotel. It had been arranged for some weeks and everybody in the club had been looking forward to it. Mick and Ringo were invited along when we were in the bar after the game and they seemed delighted. Mackie FPRFC were, and no doubt still are, noted for their hospitality and friendliness despite some bizarre outcomes.

Luckily it was an Aberdeen local holiday the next day because these sort of evenings have a tendency to get a bit out of hand so far as the beer consumption is concerned. Our president, Bob Lewis, set it all up. We had singing, loads of beer, the consumption of which was copious and made interesting by the occasional and very messy drinking game. Bob had a yard of ale glass and that added more spice to the proceedings. A hearty supper was included in the celebrations so all in all it was quite a night. Mick, our new found back row man, having been brought up in the rugby tradition understood all that had happened over the weekend and took everything in his stride. Ringo, on the other hand was simply mesmerised by his 48-hour experience and was trying to make more out of his weekend than there actually was. He seemed to connect everything up and suddenly he leapt to his feet and announced to all and sundry in his rich Liverpool accent, 'For fooks sake if this is wharappens after we fooking lose, Whadda we get if we fooking win, a fooking trip to the fooking Be-ahamas.'

That players' supper night was one of two regular social functions that Bob Lewis introduced to the club. It would be fair to say that not only did he help introduce rugby to the town of Stonehaven he was responsible for sewing the seeds of great fun that is the spin off from the true amateur game of rugby union. Camaraderie in its purest form. The second and probably the most important social event of the club followed very quickly.

After the players' supper night Bob asked me if I would run the Club's first dinner. I had never done anything like that before but Bob seemed to think I would manage the whole event easily. Well Bob did the hardest bit, he secured the main speaker, Douglas Elliot also known as W.I.D. Elliot. Quite a catch as Dougie Elliot was one of the most famous back row forwards ever to have been capped by Scotland, his first in 1947 and last in 1954. At the time of the dinner his twenty-nine caps as a back row forward still stood as the record number of caps for that position. John Jeffries took the record from him in 1990 when he gained his thirtieth cap against The All Blacks. Quite apart from Dougie Elliot's achievements as a player Bob's reasoning behind choosing to write and ask the famous player to speak at our dinner was because Dougie Elliot was at that time the president of the Edinburgh Academical Football Club, the oldest club in the land and Mackie Academy FPRFC was then the youngest club in Scotland. Only two or three of the attendees of that dinner back in 1977 in The St Leonard's Hotel in Stonehaven had ever seen Douglas Elliot play for his country, indeed probably that same small number were the only ones to have even heard of the man but he was listened to attentively by his, in the main, very young audience. The next day we all had to crawl out of bed and get ready for a match against an Edinburgh Accie's side. It so happened that an Accies junior team was coming north on an Easter tour and when Bob Lewis was making the dinner arrangements with Douglas Elliot a fixture was made between that Accies touring side and Mackie.

We won that match and later we had a great time with the Accies lads in the pub. It occurred to me that if this was to become an annual dinner, the celebrations could be extended to make a weekend of it.

I realised that the young lads playing for our club had probably never experienced a senior club match and therefore the only time they would see a famous Scottish player would be either from the terracing at Murrayfield or on the television. A top player would be inspirational for them; to hear what they had to say at a club dinner would be wonderful. A top player recounting his experiences in test rugby for Scotland and possibly the Lions would be just what the doctor ordered.

Finding top rugby people that would be prepared to come all the way to Stonehaven for at least one overnight stay was a difficult task but I had many friends in the rugby world who could help including Peter Mitchell then rugby correspondent of the Aberdeen Press and Journal. A better connected fellow than Peter so far as Scottish social and sporting events are concerned would be hard to find.

So, it was thanks to Peter Mitchell that our second dinner was graced by Nairn McEwan who was capped twenty times for Scotland as a flanker and was appointed, the year of our second dinner, as "Advisor to the captain of the Scottish XV". Nairn was also the coach for The North and Midlands District side. The SRU, steeped deeply in amateurism just could not bring themselves to appoint someone to a position named coach. Nairn spoke well. Realising we were a very young club finding our feet, he suggested that, since we didn't have any history and traditions, we should start making some. Well we had started the tradition bit by having the supper nights and now the dinners. The history was something intangible or was it? That dinner started a tradition both for Mackie and Heriot's as it turned out.

John Mackie and I had been at a New year party in Edinburgh, 76/77. The hosts were a fellow Herioter and his wife, Dougie and Eleanor Lee. The party was made up almost entirely of school pals and their wives. After a good few beers the bash was going like a bomb and a few of us started to talk about a Heriot XV, albeit unofficial, travelling up to Stonehaven to play Mackie. Sure enough up came a squad of Herioters in March 1978 to play Mackie in a game the day after our second dinner.

The next day dawned and there was a match to be played. As I started to come to. I began thinking about Nairn McEwan's remarks about history and tradition. Well, we had started a bit of a tradition trend with the dinner and the players' supper nights but for the history to follow it may need a bit of a nudge.

One day, during the run up to that first dinner, I called in to John Mackie's architects office to find him sitting doodling at his drawing board. John had been helping me with some of the dinner organisation and he thought that it would be a good idea to make up spoof pen profiles of some of the players in the Club. I looked at some of the examples he had drawn up and they were hilarious. I suggested that we illustrate the profiles with photographs, mounting each one on a gallery at the Hotel on the evening of the dinner. The subjects of the profiles would then be "invited" to buy their little potted history. The proceeds would defray any expenses that the Club incurred such as top table food and drink etc. Everybody had a laugh at each other's expense. John and I made up profiles for dinners after that but we were soon joined by Rod Richmond who added another dimension to the proceedings. Rod was on the same humour wavelength as John and I, so we had a huge amount of fun writing out these ridiculous stories about members of the club. It became a wannabe for guys. They would have felt desperately left out if there was not a profile on them displayed for all to see at the club dinner. In its own way we started up a wee fringe tradition all on its own. I believe it may still be going at the club all these thirty-six years later.

Gradually we were building up a history and some traditions.

Over that second dinner weekend, John Mackie, our wives and I had a lot of fun with our pals from Heriot's. A few days after they had returned to the capital, John and I wrote to them in a light-hearted fashion inviting them to come back to Stonehaven the following year, both for the dinner and another match. I remember John, with tongue in cheek, wrote suggesting that during their first visit their style on the pitch had been cavalier to say the least and we hoped that they would adjust their behaviour accordingly.

The Heriot's lads picked up on the cavalier remark and when they came back the following season they replaced their Heriot match jerseys with plain white ones which had a McEwan's (of brewing fame) cavalier sewn on to the left breast. The Heriot Cavaliers were born and they made an impact on the history and tradition of Mackie Academy FPRFC. The spin- off for Heriot's was that they had a new touring team: The Cavaliers. Conceived originally for a second unofficial Heriot's RC tour to Stonehaven, they flew off to California a year or so later for a very enjoyable tour. Heriot's club history will say that it was the Heriot's California tour that gave birth to the Cavaliers but now you know, reader, that that isn't the case.

The third dinner was graced by Andy Irvine no less and it was a sell-out. A couple of years later Rosemary and I followed Andy round the Royal Deeside Golf club course when he played in a Pro Cel Am tournament. Audrey, Andy's wife, walked with us and we had a fine afternoon in warm sunshine. It was quite a day. When the round was completed and we were waiting for Andy to change, I was bowled over when Douglas Bader who had been playing walked past us closely followed by fellow competitor, Peter Cook. Two more of my heroes.

After a meal with the Irvines and a number of other celebrities, all the players, sponsors and so on, Rosemary and I left the car and got a lift back to Stonehaven with Andy and Audrey on their way to Edinburgh. Rosemary and I were going to be opening a hairdressing salon later that summer and she asked Andy if he would come up and open our new business for us. Andy agreed and up he came. The local newspaper, The Mearns Leader, heard about Andy's role on the day of the opening and the editor came along himself to take photographs for the story, to be printed in that week's paper. The occasion was a great success and Andy got Rosemary off to a flying start.

The Mackie FPRFC dinners were becoming quite a talking point in the North East of Scotland rugby circles. In fact, our club was causing a bit of a stir in the town, a stir of the wrong sort in some circles. After a couple years or so of Mackie FPRFC's existence, I discovered that not everybody in the town approved of the rugby club. I suspect it was because we were like nothing the locals had ever come across before and, no doubt, some of the harmless high jinks that the rugby lads got up to were not going down too well with some of the townsfolk.

The day after the third dinner we all turned out either to play against the Cavaliers or to watch. Actually, as in the previous year, John Mackie and I played for the visitors. The game really should have been cancelled as there was snow lying on the pitch and lots more was descending on us throughout the game. We, the Cavaliers, were hard to defend against because our white jerseys were the perfect camouflage in the conditions.

The game over, it was on with the traditional carryings on in the Hotel and the dance with the women's' hockey club.

The late Jimmy Ross, Heriot former pupil and president of the SRU was our next speaker. A signal honour for such a young and as yet unfashionable club.

Noting that the Heriot Cavaliers were in the crowd and that they may even be staying in the very same hotel as he was, Jimmy caught a train back that night!

That particular visit by the Cavaliers was punctuated heavily by a tour theme. These guys were very, very, funny blokes and they had incredible imaginations. They invented a fictitious deceased character called Duncan Swaingate. The tour was called "The Duncan Swaingate Memorial Tour." Elaborate detail went into making this Swaingate fellow appear to be real. It was almost as comprehensively worked out as the efforts made by British Naval Intelligence to make "The man who never was" appear real to the Germans during the Second World War.

This could never happen again, probably because it did happen once: the Cavaliers inserted a piece in the "In Memorium" columns of the Saturday morning edition of the Aberdeen Press and Journal. It read as follows:

Swaingate, Duncan: We always think of you when on tour.
The Cavaliers.

That Friday's Aberdeen Evening Express carried a full page advert:

Champagne Rugby
The Duncan Swaingate Memorial Tour to Stonehaven
Come and see the Cavaliers play Mackie Academy FPRFC
Ury Playing Fields K.O. 3pm. Entry free

At 3 pm both sides ran out on to the centre of the pitch where the referee was waiting. One of the Cavaliers had briefed the ref and another walked solemnly on to the pitch carrying a huge wreath which he placed on the centre of the halfway line. Facing the crowd from the midst of the two teams the good humoured match official announced to the crowd that there would now be two minute's laughter in memory of the great tourist, Duncan Swaingate. He then started the laughter which of course was amazingly infectious. Before we all knew it everybody was laughing. The cacophony turned from a sort of on command stilted stage laughter effect to real live lung bursting hysterics. It just got louder and louder and the situation got funnier and funnier; like perpetual motion it fed on itself. Then, bang on two minutes, the ref blew his whistle, the laughter stopped, the wreath was carried away to the touchline and the game got under way.

After the match, having showered and changed, we carried the wreath in a solemn procession down to the harbour and cast it into the very cold and choppy North Sea. Then followed the annual dance with the women's hockey club and all the regular tomfoolery. Great fun and very happy memories. The whole ridiculously bizarre and very funny weekend was a new style of rugby fun to the Mackie lads. They liked it and wanted to do it again; they were addicted. I could see all of that and I had no doubt these Mackie lads would soon be emulating the Heriot lads and many more rugby lads like them. Rugby is a special sport and has a unique presence on the sporting front so far as its culture and simple common ground around the world is concerned. In 1982 Fran Cotton, England and the British and Irish Lions, came to the Mackie dinner and he enthralled the lads. There is a rivalry as we all know between Scotland and England with absolutely every sport but the Mackie lads that night were neutral so far as the Auld Enemy was concerned. They were wonderfully entertained and inspired by one of the all-time great England rugby players.

Later that night Fran came back to the Bruce household along with Iain Milne and the pair of them cleaned us out of bacon rolls. Fran and Iain found themselves in a conversation about what rugby was all about with everybody present as an audience. Fran told us that he had travelled all over the world playing our wonderful game and he said in his surprisingly high pitched Lancashire accent,

'If yer not roogbay yer soon fownd owt.' Those of us who had been involved in the game for a number of years knew exactly what this giant of International rugby was on about.

The reply to the toast to the guests on the night of the Fran Cotton dinner was given by the late Ken Dron. Ken although a Stonehaven man was, at the time of the dinner, the rector of Brechin High School. Ken was a well kent man in the Mearns, if you will excuse the pun. He was heavily involved in the Stonehaven community mainly through his association with the local drama group. Ken was also a wonderful after dinner entertainer. He spoke very highly of our club and told me after the formal part of the evening was over that he had had doubts about accepting our invitation to speak at the dinner. He explained that we had a bad name in the more conservative circles in the town and he was so pleased to see that this description of us was not true as he had enjoyed his evening thoroughly and was impressed at how well we had all behaved. He went on to say that he would be going, as usual, to the "club" at lunch time the next day to sing our praises amongst the doubters. The club of course was The Conservative Club.

Although, as the town's only rugby club and just by our very existence with our HQ at the school playing fields we were part of the local community, I resolved, thanks to Ken Dron's remarks, to involve Mackie FPRFC in a more obvious and positive way in the community.

On our quest to be involved in the community we helped the local Pony Club with their competitions, involved ourselves in sponsored walks for local causes and the like. Such involvement was easily seen by the people of Stonehaven but we also helped out in the community in a less obvious way. A few lads that came along and joined us may well have come to no good and may have fallen foul of the law. This was not difficult for lads that were hot blooded, shall we say, in a small town like Stonehaven. I know this because a couple of dads told me that themselves. They were thankful that we had given their sons a healthy pursuit that had brought out the best in them. One of our wilder members, Doug McConnell, benefited from being a Mackie player and eventually Captain. His dad often tells me that rugby kept his son out of serious trouble and indeed pointed him in the right direction in life. Doug has carved out a wonderful career for himself and has done extremely well in his industry. He has a gorgeous wife, beautiful children and enjoys a very happy family life. This ex Mackie FPRFC Captain is immensely proud of how things turned out for him. There are other similar stories about Mackie FP rugby club members never mind the hundreds more that I am sure most rugby clubs could tell us all about.

You can't buy that kind of outcome and it is heart-warming to me and all the guys on Mackie committees and in the teams of players that we have those stories to tell. I am sure many rugby clubs will have similar stories.

Throughout the eighties Mackie gradually became more and more of a fixture in the town of Stonehaven and the local Community Council which sported a number of the leading lights in the town, started to take notice of our growing strength and influence. Their initial, official contact with the Club was when they gave a civic reception for us and The Stockholm Exiles in the Town Hall. The Stockholm Exiles visited us twice in the mid-eighties and we travelled to Sweden three times, once to Malmo and twice to Stockholm. Our visit to Malmo was via a game in Copenhagen in Denmark. The Stonehaven Community councillors welcomed us and presented the Stockholm Exiles with a painting of the town. Drinks and nibbles followed, allowing us to mix socially with the Towns VIP's. For me that was the point at which we could say our Club was part of the furniture so to speak. However waves would come along later to unsettle our steady course and cause a great degree of angst for me in particular and the club in general. Association football and all the baggage that that game has was looming.

Prior to my connection with Mackie I had been associated with rugby clubs that had their own pitches. It was foreign to me to be connected with a club that had to apply, annually, through the local authority for the use of the local school pitches. Worse, the Regional Council based in Aberdeen delegated the processing of such applications to a bunch of people based in the community centre who allegedly concerned themselves with ensuring that no sport using the local authority premises and sports grounds was elitist.

I was telling Rosemary one evening over dinner that the Club was not in control of its destiny thanks to the pitch problem and we would have to own, or rent on a long term basis our own pitch. Rosemary thought that one of her hairdressing clients, Lady Diana Holman, might be able to help. Lady Diana, her Husband, John Holman, and their son Richard Holman-Baird own the Rickarton Estate which is just to the west of Stonehaven. Rosemary thought that these local landowners may have some spare land that might fit the bill. She said that she would ask Lady Diana.

Rosemary took the opportunity to ask about the land during the very next visit Lady Diana made to the salon. To our delight Rosemary's valued client returned home and put the question to her son. He said that there was a field in the Redcloak area of Stonehaven that could be used as a pitch if we were prepared to level and drain it. This we did and a further piece of land adjacent was found for our second fifteen. The Redcloak plot was to be rented at a value which, although extremely reasonable, we couldn't really afford so Richard suggested that we work off the rent. That agreement turned out to be a win/win situation all round. We didn't have to find any money and the estate owners got lots of work done on their land by the Mackie lads. The bonus so far as the Mackie lads and their coaches were concerned was more bonding like the work we did as a team for the Pony Club. Remember the bonding included a well-earned beer or two after the work had been completed. The main jobs that we did were heather burning on the shooting estate, sheep dipping, fence erection and field wall repairs.

Notwithstanding the pleasure the Mackie players derived from their relationship with the Holmans and the Holman–Bairds, it is impossible to estimate the true value of what the Rickarton Estate owners did for Mackie Rugby Club and the community at large. By setting aside some of their land, they enabled rugby to establish itself and grow in the area. I was grateful to Lady Diana and her family for their community spirit and I know that the Club continues to benefit from their generosity.

One of the lads in the club asked his dad, who was a civil engineer, if his company, Hunter Construction, could adapt their modus operandi to building a suitably drained pitch for us . They could and they did. It turned out that Hunters thought that pitch construction would be a useful additional string to their bow and would use Redcloak to advertise their versatility in the construction world.

We would have to find a way of funding such a major project so I got to work on a local councillor, the late Harrison McLean, who was a good friend and who I knew appreciated what we were doing in the community. I hoped that the local District Council would afford us a grant out of the ratepayers contributions.

The local authority came up trumps. We were on our way.

The only difficulty with having our own playing fields was the fact that the Mackie schools pitches also came with changing facilities. We would have nowhere to change unless we built our own pavilion. There was no money for this and finding more free or cheap cash was proving difficult until, one day, we heard that the school was planning to demolish their existing pavilion which was situated in the grounds of the fairly recently built or New Mackie Academy. This intelligence was brought to us by some senior former pupils of the school who, whilst scholars at the original Mackie Academy, had been, along with all their fellow pupils, fundamental in raising the cash to enable the construction of the pavilion. Rumour had it that the headmaster of the school wanted the building to be razed to the ground because some pupils hid behind it when they had a smoke.

I have played rugby at far too many clubs where changing and showering after a match were sheer misery and it wasn't going to happen to anybody playing at Mackie if the committee could help it. Secretary, Rod Richmond took on the task of finding out if there was any way we could stop the demolition of the Ury pavilion and like the great secretary that he was he found a "Third Way". We leased the building from Grampian region through their property department. I mentioned earlier that the school, its grounds and all the buildings on those grounds were the property of Grampian Regional Council and managed by their property department. We had a permanent lease on half of the pavilion and further, Grampian

Region were responsible for its upkeep. On top of all of that the Region's property department renewed the boiler that heated the water for our showers.

Rugby, at my humble level, gave me and Rosemary such a wonderful time. I have, as a consequence of being a member of Mackie FP, a small junior club in the North East of Scotland, met so many famous names in the game. All of them really nice, decent guys and great fun.

Many more celebrated rugby players were to grace the top table of Mackie dinners which were now a fixture in the traditions of the club.

Iain the Bear Milne is a great friend of Mackie, indeed he and his two brothers are honorary members of the club. Iain helped the club in many ways. He conducted many coaching sessions and generally inspired Mackie players during the eighties. He has spoken at our dinners and encouraged his brothers, Kenny and David to do the same. The Bear also helped us lure main speakers to our dinner including Scott Hastings, Sean Lineen, Roy Laidlaw and Bill Cuthbertson.

You will recall my earlier recollection of a hurdles race in which I ran against Gareth Edwards. It occurred to me that Gareth might come to Stonehaven and be our main guest at our annual dinner. I got a contact address and invited Gareth to the dinner. Along with my letter I sent two enlarged copies of the photograph that had been taken of the pair of us in that hurdles race way back in 1966. I asked Gareth if he would autograph one of the photographs and return it to me. Back came the autographed photo with the annotation "Those were the days". Too true. As I sit here typing, there is no way I could get up and run even for a very slow bus as my knees are pretty well shot!! Gareth said that he would call me about the dinner in due course. This he did, and to my astonishment and utter delight, he agreed to come.

It was obvious to me that every one of the Internationalists that came to our dinners were extremely proud of their caps and only too delighted to share some of their precious free time with us. Some went beyond their appearance at our top table: Roy Laidlaw, the 1984 Slam scrum-half spent a couple of hours on the Saturday following the dinner at the Ury playing fields with The Mackie Minis. None of the wee guys involved would have seen Roy play for Scotland but their daddies had, and they were all there to see the famous Scotland and Lions scrum-half.

Bill Cuthbertson actually made two speeches at the dinner he attended. Bill had never made such a speech before and he was, of course, well received but I could see that he was not pleased with his contribution. Doug McConnell our captain had almost finished his reply to Bill's toast to the Club when Bill whispered to me that he would like to say more, would that be okay. It was, and as soon as Doug finished Bill leapt to his feet, this time with no notes. Speaking from the heart he told the lads that if he could get a cap for Scotland, anyone who had the passion and ambition could do the same. He explained that after working very hard at his game he had to wait until he was thirty-one to make his International debut but went on to gain twenty–one caps and become a Grand Slammer in 1984. He was an inspiration to the young audience. The lads were delighted to have Bill at the top table of their dinner and then beside themselves when he played for Mackie the next day against an official Heriot's 3rd XV. Truly one of the nice guys in world rugby.

In 1985 our guest had to call off only about a week before. What were we to do? When lost and needing serious help, turn to Peter Mitchell. Peter sorted it and Jim Aitken, Grand Slam captain of only a year prior to this dinner, agreed to join us for yet another memorable occasion.

The list of famous rugby players that spoke at Mackie dinners grew and grew. It included Douglas Morgan, a captain of Scotland and Sean Lineen. Kenny and David Milne followed in the footsteps of their big brother Iain and sat as principle speakers at the top table of our dinner. Like the Bear, they were both excellent speakers and their stories of International rugby and famous characters such as coach Jim Telfer were met with great appreciation. The ordinary rugby bloke would never normally have a clue what commitment is required of an International player, but the Milnes gave the Mackie lads a very clear picture that the game at the highest level demands great focus. The upside which made it all worthwhile is the huge amount of fun to be had from being a top player and the opportunities for world travel.

Scott Hastings came to our dinner just before the 1993 Lions tour of New Zealand and I remember Iain Milne and Scott having a chat about the tour in our living room. Scott was reasonably confident that he would be picked to go. He was in fact included in the squad and had already played for the Lions in 1989. He would be accompanied by Gavin his brother, Peter Wright of Boroughmuir and Kenny Milne.

Peter Wright spoke at my last Mackie dinner. In 1997 Rosemary and I left Stonehaven to return to Edinburgh and start another chapter of our lives.

I persuaded Peter to come up to Stonehaven early on the day of the dinner and I took him, along with Peter Mitchell, for a round of golf at Stonehaven Golf Club. Rugby in those days was in a bit of turmoil and some clubs that had bigger budgets than others were starting to pay players reasonable sums for them to switch club allegiances. Peter told us during that game of golf that he was headed for Melrose but we were to keep quiet until the official announcements were made. Peter, at that period of the upheaval in rugby union so far as professionalism was concerned, was actually a blacksmith. As

I recall he played golf like a blacksmith; he could hit his drives 300 yards without them ever crossing the front of the tee!!

The concerns of professionalism in rugby union were a million miles away from a junior club like Mackie and so it was of no consequence to us. Peter was welcomed by the lads in the usual manner and a great night was had by all.

Earlier in the series of Mackie dinners, Rod Richmond suggested that we ask Jim Telfer to address our 1983 bash. I thought that that was a great idea, if a bit farfetched. Undaunted, Rod duly sent a letter off to the National coach inviting him to be our principal guest. Much to my astonishment Jim replied in the affirmative.

Telfer has an imposing presence. Many of the books written about him suggest that he may be a bit of a bully. Suffice to say that, sitting beside me in the body of the kirk during that dinner, Iain The Bear Milne, hid behind his menu trying not to catch the eye of his coach. Jim gave us all a very entertaining speech. Telfer spent some time berating professional association football and why he thought paying players was likely to be the death of that sport. Ironic really when you think about how Jim was the architect of the professional game of rugby union in Scotland as we now know it.

The late Adam Robson, another famous Scotland back row player of the late fifties and early sixties spoke at the dinner when he was vice president of the SRU in the season 1982/1983. Adam was a true gentleman and the very next year was to become the President of the Union in the 1984 Grand Slam year. It couldn't have happened to a nicer guy.

I always enjoyed our club dinners at Mackie, not least because I could see that they gave our young playing members such a lot of fun, but we had our own little traditions attached. As well as the pen profiles of our players and some committee men there was a lunch on the day of the dinner for those that helped organise the main event; and, for a period, the company of the wild guys that were the Cavaliers. Conversely I never really enjoyed being a guest of another club at their annual dinner. I think every club has its own dinner culture in which the members of that club are comfortable. As a guest of another club I never found their formats anything like as good as Mackie's but I guess many, if not all, of the club guests we invited to the Mackie dinners may have found themselves in an environment that felt strange to them. I like to think however, that any guest at a Mackie dinner enjoyed listening to all the famous characters that spoke from our top table and of course that we members of Mackie were hospitable towards them.

Of the few dinners I was invited to, either as a member of Mackie, or later in my capacity as secretary and manager at Heriot's Rugby Club only two really stand out in my memory. The first was Aberdeen Wanderers Accies. Their captain invited me as his personal guest and so I wasn't even sitting beside him at the dinner because he had to make a speech from the top table. That was no problem but my difficulty was the time the whole event was taking. Rosemary had kindly agreed to arrange a baby sitter and drive into Aberdeen from Stonehaven pick me up and take me home. The event took place in the Crescent Hotel and was pretty wild. One of the top table speakers was sick all over the table in front of him as he had far too much to drink. Worse, he was yet to speak and, worse still, the curtains in front of the open French windows that led out to the garden of the Hotel started to flap in and out and finally part to reveal a very bad tempered wife. She had been waiting for ages outside in her car for her hubby to exit the dinner. We will call him Wullie. They must have prearranged a likely finish time as had I with Rosemary. Well, Wullie, like me had been uncomfortable for at least forty minutes or so, I guess, when his wife, as if by magic, appeared through the curtains. She had Wullie's coat over her arm and shouted and pointed from about ten yards away,

'Hey you, hame, cmon, hame................... aye you, Wullie Redface.'

Poor Wullie just could not believe what he was seeing and hearing. The whole dinner erupted into mocking laughter as Mrs Redface beckoned her mortified hubby. Off Wullie went with his tail between his legs and as far as I know he never returned to the club again.

My Rosemary sat patiently in the hotel reception and as soon as the final speech finished, I stole away from the table and found my dear girl who whisked me off into the night.

The other dinner that sticks in my memory was a Hawick RFC soirée. I was treated royally by the members that were asked to look after their guests. The meal was excellent, but every now and again during the whole course of the event, someone would stand up and sing a ballad. Don't misunderstand me, the singers were very good, but, they were part of a culture that was completely foreign to me. The Hawick lads loved it all, as they should, it was their dinner. I understand that the singing of ballads is quite a common feature of Borders rugby clubs. That dinner, by the way, featured a top table that included Jim Aitken and John Beattie sr. Jim spoke about how awful it was that the SRU parachuted players in to the National side from foreign parts but he recognised the need for clubs to import players to augment their otherwise weak teams. I just didn't understand why on the one hand the SRU were culpable but teams at club level were not. Make no mistake Heriot's had a few imports in my time as secretary and manager and the same applies to most other so-called fashionable clubs. It's still a mystery to me why some Scottish clubs that have little, or no money, choose to spend most of what they do have to pay players. Why they don't get together and agree to stop pouring money down a very deep drain, I just don't know. Well, actually, yes I do, they want to win championships or at least avoid relegation.

Mackie Academy FP RFC Club Dinner
Jim Calder, Stewart's Melville FP RFC,Scotland and Lions
and Rod Richmond (Secretary Mackie FP RFC)

Mackie Academy FP RFC Club Dinner
Bob Richmond, Mackie Vice President sharing a secret with
Jim Calder whilst Iain "The Bear" Milne, Heriots, Harlequins,
Scotland and Lions advises the cameraman to go away!

Mackie Academy FP RFC Club Dinner
Gareth Edwards, Cardiff, Wales and Lions, "The Bear" and Me

Mackie Academy FP RFC Club Dinner Sean Lineen, Boroughmuir and Scotland,
Rosemary and our daughter Sarah in our living room prior to a club dinner

Mackie Academy FP RFC Club Dinner
Left to right: Bob Richmond, Ian Pace, Iain Milne, Peter Mitchell, Ken
Hutchison, CEO Scottish Sports Council, Rod Richmond and Rosemary

Mackie Academy FP RFC Club Dinner
Iain Milne and Fran Cotton

The Opening of Snippets, Rosemary's hairdressing salon
Andy Irvine opens Rosemary's hairdressing salon. Rosemary looks on
as Andy gives Kirsten a trim and Sarah waits her turn. (Photograph
by kind permission of The Mearns Leader, Stonehaven)

213

CHAPTER 14

New Clubs in the North;
A Madcap Coach, Mackie Minis

In the mid to late seventies a number of new clubs were formed in the North East of Scotland; Mackie FP was the first followed closely by the previously mentioned Inverurie club, Garioch, pronounced "Geeree". John Fraser and Jim Black were founder members of Garioch and were club mates of mine when we played for Aberdeenshire. Granite City was the next in line and was formed out of young, former pupils' of Robert Gordon's School. One of their members told me that he and his club mates had become disenchanted with the selection process at their former pupils club and decided to start up their own XV. They were like a breath of fresh air to the Aberdeen club scene. As well as being very good players they were, to put it mildly, a bit on the wild side but great fun. In the main, their membership was made up of young professionals in the city of Aberdeen. Whilst their club was only in its formative state, they had the air of established rugby tradition about them. Refreshingly, their behaviour was not hindered by stuffy old committee men. Ellon was the third new club to get under-way. Named after the North East dormitory town, they struggled initially to establish themselves, but are now very much on the up and up. Like Mackie and Garioch, Ellon depended upon a number of experienced players who had moved into the area from else-where in the UK. Foreign players also played a big part in all of the new clubs' selection process. The oil industry in the North East of Scotland employed loads of Kiwis and Aussies and they were glad to get games when onshore.

It was probably about the second or third year of Ellon's exis-tence that Mackie found themselves sharing a dressing room with the Ellon seven at the now established Garioch Sevens. I had been foolish enough as a utility back to be persuaded by the club coach, a Welshman by the name of Parry Reynolds, to play at prop. Parry reckoned that positions in sevens were all about horses for courses and, given that I had put on a bit of beef but could still nip smartly about the park, I would be the secret weapon of the Mackie team. Tying my boot laces I pondered over the programme which had Mackie's first appearance listed in the second round. Thank God we had a bye in the first round. That was a bonus, a second round start against a first round knackered bunch. My relief was shat-tered however by an Ellon man who explained that they had been put out of the competition by RAF Kinloss who, it was alleged had a bunch of ringers in their side from bases in the south of England. Guess what? We were due to play the winners of that very tie. My heart sank. Ellon, like so many of the newly formed rugby clubs, had a number of players from out with their area and the inaboot-comers for them, at that time, seemed to be predominantly from the Glasgow area. At least their sevens team seemed that way. Glaswegian blokes are well known for their friendliness in that they are not backwards at coming forward with help and advice. In this case one Weegie Ellon player, in particular, had much intelligence to give us about our military opponents which was about as reliable as the previous allegations that had been made.

'You have tae watch oot for they RAF guys, they come at yae frae oot o the sun,' was one really helpful hint, quickly followed by,

'I think the boy they have oot oan the wing is Douglas Bader which would explain why he's no very guid but its oafy sair when ye tackle him.'

We reckoned our coach, Parry Reynolds, was possibly, what we call in the rugby game, a "Phantom." That is a guy who claims to be much better than he actually is. Phantoms will also suggest that they come from a really well known club which has its HQ hundreds, if not thousands, of miles away in another hemisphere. The chances therefore, in those days of poor communications, of any of his newly acquired club mates actually knowing anything about his previous club, never mind him, were extremely remote. Parry claimed that he had served his time at stand-off just before Phil Bennet at Llanelli !

The Mackie sevens team had been benefiting from Parry's shortened game experiences for a few weeks before the Ellon event but, sadly, the experiences seemed only to cover set penalty moves. I forget who it was but someone asked Parry,

'What if we don't get any penalties?'

'Oh you're bound to, these North East of Scotland sides have very poor discipline and they are terribly unfit,' said our resident Welshman.

He went on to warn us yet again of being properly prepared for the bonanza of penalty opportunities that would present themselves as we worked our way through the ties. To say we thought our coach was limited was putting it very mildly. The actual tie went something like this: Ellon kicked off, I caught the ball and took off at top speed. Forgetting I was a prop and not a back and might be required to shove in a scrum later on, I ran virtually the length of the pitch isolating myself from any hope of back-up before being tackled; the ball was spilled forward in the gut busting defence action, they knocked it on as well and so being the first clumsy idiots we were in a scrum situation - their put in. My earlier sprint was now to be called to account. We lost the scrum of course and with it went the very last drop of my breath and all of this after only about two minutes. Their scrum-half who was a prop turned number 9, booted the ball back up the park with the velocity of a siege gun. It seemed to take me an eternity to get back for the lineout which we lost and from which they scored a try. To say RAF Kinloss then ran riot is an understatement of the greatest magnitude. What, no penalties?

We sacked the coach from sevens duty but he appeared again as a fifteens expert. Scrums for Mackie were much more secure in the "bigger" game as we had a very good choice of front row forwards to give our pack a decent chance. They were not big names in the world of rugby but local heroes Keith Littlejohn, Duncan Richmond, Rod Richmond, Alan Masson and Alan Davidson. All were very strong lads the stalwarts in the darker side of the game. Alan Masson particularly enjoyed a couple of Guinesses before a match.

Even in fifteens rugby, Parry the coach couldn't grasp that Mackie, at that period in its life, needed to take things stage by stage on the park and stick to simple straightforward rugby football. Many of the recruits to the club had only played school rugby and not very much of that. To learn and put into practice some of the Parry tricks of the trade in such formative years was a shortcut to disaster. Our resident Welshman's expendable player theory was one ploy that thankfully never found favour amongst any of the Mackie players and was never executed. The idea behind such a tactic was, at best, stupid and at worst very dangerous. The plan was to select a player that was useless but brutal.

His job was to take out the best opposition player. Our brute would be sent off with no great loss to our team and the opposition would be minus their star. Even supposing this "technique" was applied nowadays, it would of course be counterproductive, given the modern replacement system. Another gem of Parry's was "The Jersey up and over move." It was possibly a forerunner of the Australian "Up the jumper move." The latter is where a pack of forwards in possession has their ball carrier stuff the ball up his jumper and the remainder of the pack scatter. The opposition has no idea who has the ball and is seriously confused by the antics. The practice was banned for not being in the spirit of the game. Our Llanelli man had a different form of "The up the jumper move" This glorious idea was where the team in possession would help their ball carrier on his way to the try line by accidentally-on-purpose pulling their opposite number's jersey up and over his head thus disorientating him and temporarily hindering his potential to defend. Parry did have his good points and he was helpful to the backs at least whilst some of the older heads in the players ranks, such as John Mackie, Brian Thomson and a hitherto unmentioned founder member, Mike Walton, mentored the forwards. Watching the development of Rugby Union in the North East, the sleepy Royal Deeside town of Aboyne realised it had the potential to start up a club drawing from all along the western part of Deeside. Aboyne Rugby Club got cracking and is now firmly in with the bricks. For those of you who take an interest in things financial or who like unusual sports facts, Sir George Mathewson, one time Chairman of The Royal Bank of Scotland, used to play on the wing for Aboyne 2nds when he was in charge of Scottish Enterprise back in the eighties.

What to do with all of these new clubs. How could they fit in to the District Union? Who would give them fixtures? A District league was formed by Gordon Masson and the late lamented Charlie Ritchie of the North District Union and off we all went. Incidentally, both of these gentlemen became Presidents of the SRU. Charlie Ritchie's main claim to fame however was as a hooker who could "heel" his put in with his head. I have played against him and have seen him do it.

Before everything was formalised, Mackie played against established outfits in the Aberdeen area, usually their 2nd or 3rd XV . The last game of the first season was played against the, then newly formed, Garioch Club. It was their first game and their team was made up from players of varying ability. Having just formed, their kit was also pretty diverse. I played opposite a burly centre who wore London Scottish stockings and white shorts which were probably also London Scottish issue. During the short space of time between the teams taking the pitch and the kick-off, most players will suss out their opposite number, give him the once over and decide who is going to get it that day - him or me. I figured that this London Scottish guy was in the area because he was in the oil and gas industry but more than likely he was a number cruncher and strictly office. He therefore was not likely to be chucking huge drill bits about on an oil rig. Indeed it was likely that he was older than me given the very bald head and lack of teeth, and probably not very fit. Nae bother then, he was mine!

After a tawdry afternoon punctuated by what seemed like dozens of late tackles from my Anglo Scottish opponent, I thought I would seek him out afterwards in the bar and ask him what he thought he was mucking about at on the pitch. I searched everywhere but there was no sign of him. Eventually I found the Garioch Captain, and one time team mate of mine from Aberdeenshire,

John Fraser. I asked him if he knew what had happened to the bald, ex-London Scottish centre as he was nowhere to be seen. The Garioch skipper, laughing like a drain, pointed across the bar to a guy who was sitting on a tall stool, set at an angle of forty five degrees wedging his stiffened frame against the wall. He had a fixed stare at ninety degrees to his frame. He was, effectively, a large ornament. To my astonishment he was now sporting a full head of hair and gleaming white teeth. He had an unlit pipe in his mouth which came straight out of his face. His arms flopped out from his shoulders as if he had no control over them, his hands were upturned on his thighs, completely inanimate. It was difficult for me to stop imagining this guy preparing for the game in the dressing room; taking his false teeth out and removing his wig, placing them both securely in his kit bag. With his body now wrecked, the reverse performance after the game of standing in front of the dressing room mirror adjusting his rug in front of his team mates, must have taken some nerve.

What was his excuse for the late tackles? Actually his face turned an off- grey colour when he recognised me striding across the bar towards him. Thinking, presumably, that attack was the best form of defence he immediately proffered an apology for his tardiness in the tackle situation, claiming that he was just so unfit, that, by the time he took aim at me, put his head and shoulders down in the text book position and fired, I had passed the ball. Explaining his position further, he said that he was on a short holiday from London visiting his parents in Inverurie and, along with some others, had got nabbed by the Garioch team secretary the night before in the Gordon Arms. To his now great regret, his London Scottish kit had been left at his folks' house some years before and had come in handy that weekend. His was a familiar story that has been told over the years by many hundreds of guys that should know better. Having hung up their boots at a sensible age they are talked into putting them on again a few years later to make up the numbers in some scratch side. Such behaviour usually leads to at least a week of not being able to walk, open doors, bend down and get up again or turn round properly whilst driving to see if anything is coming.

One of Mackie's very first games led to similar physical reactions in me and John Mackie, my old school pal. We both had a few beers in the Queens Hotel with the lads after the match and left our cars outside. The effects of the beer and the bonhomie relaxed us as we strolled home. The following day, both feeling very stiff, we went to pick our motors up. I had a flat tyre. Normally that sort of thing is just an irritation and reasonably easy to put right. Not so this particular morning. I discovered that the only way to raise my arms to open the car boot to get at the jack and the spare, was to swing them back and forth from behind my back in a sort of pendulum motion starting with small swings leading to bigger ones. I grabbed the well sprung boot clasp on one of my upswings and it opened violently, so I had no choice but to shoot upwards with it. This had the alarming effect of involuntarily straightening my back to the tune of aggravated gasps and some fairly bad language. After I unclipped my fingers releasing myself from the boot, and, whilst falling backwards, I advised John that I thought I would close the boot later, probably Wednesday in fact. Luckily, the position of the kit for changing the wheel didn't involve much bending, and fitting the car jack was a piece of cake compared to all the other stages of this project. The jacking up of the car was also relatively easy - almost therapeutic. I got the car up and the offending wheel free from the ground. Now to get it off the bearing and the spare on. The pantomime that then followed involved all sorts of hip and arm swinging based on my earlier experience with the boot lid. After an eternity and the invention of a number of new Latin American dance steps the new wheel had replaced the old and I was off back to bed.

After I did a stint as captain of the Club my opportunity to pass on the wise counsel of my games master at Heriot's, Donald Hastie, came when I was Vice President of Mackie Academy FPRFC. The office of Vice President of Mackie did not really mean much in that there was no job, as such, to do. One just waited to become the President and I was not prepared to be idle, so John Mackie and I started the Mackie FP Minis: rugby for primary school kids. The Minis played and practiced at the Mineral Well, a public park in Stonehaven. The early days of the Mackie Minis saw huge turnouts. I think this was because many of the dads, who were inabootcomers, had played rugby themselves. There was no primary school rugby in the area so they saw Mini rugby as the way to introduce their sons to the game they loved. These youngsters soon learned and bought into the meaning of fair play and good sportsmanship, as well as learning the rudiments of rugby football. Some of them started to acquire a rugby sense of humour, even at their young age. A good example of a boy who probably enjoyed the social side of mini rugby more than the actual playing of the game was a laddie called Euan Brown. Euan was not a first pick lad but like all of those boys that turned up at the Mineral Well on a Sunday, he got a game. Euan turned up late one Sunday, the usual practice game was already underway. I thought that the best place to put him was at full back. He could do the least damage there. So as not to make Euan feel as though he was just a make weight I shouted to him,

'Hello Euan, you can go to full back in the red side and pretend you are Andy Irvine!'

'Ok I'll do that Mr Bruce, would you like my autograph?'

I thought that lad will go far with a sharp sense of humour like that at such a tender young age. He has gone far as it happens: to Australia as an estate agent in fact.

Two of the early Mackie Academy FP mini intake went on to play for the Scottish Schools XV, though not directly from Mackie but from the sixth year at Stewart's Melville College in Edinburgh. These lads were the sons of Stonehaven GP Dr Graeme McIntosh and his late wife, Liz.

Mackie Academy FP RFC 1st XV Back Row Left to Right:
D Squires, N Hubbard, A Davidson, C Beaton, K Littlejohn, G "Dod" Thomson, D McConnell
Front Row Left to Right:
I Gray, J Sorbie, R Murdoch, D Bruce (President), P Beatt (Captain), R Pittendreigh (Vice Captain), R Richmond (Vice President), A "Buck" Buchanan, Ian Pace

Considering that they were still trying to overcome the effects of their annual dinner the night before, the Mackie Academy F.P.s "seven" pictured above did well to reach the semi-finals of their own annual seven-a-side tournament for the "Bon-Accord" Trophy at Ury on Saturday! They eventually succumbed, however, to Gordonians, by the narrow margin of 16-12.

Mackie Academy FP RFC 1stV11
Back row Left to right
G "Gogs" Henderson, D Bruce, R Pittendreigh, G Coates
Kneeling left to right
D Birse, K Miller, I mitchell

Hunter Mabon, President of the Swedish Rugby Union shares a joke with kilted Peter Mitchell of the Aberdeen Press and Journal

A Mackie XV on Tour in Sweden
Back Row Left to Right
D Bruce, C Salter, G Gordon, R Richmond, R Bruce,
G Henderson, K Littlejohn, C Rankin,
L McIntosh, R Pittendreigh
Kneeling Left to Right
P McGinn, J Lambton, R Smith, C Beaton, D McConnell, G Houlihan

CHAPTER 15

In Which I Become An Administrator; I Meet Jo Maso

Before I became the Mackie captain I was elected to the position of treasurer.

I take my hat off to people who assume that office. It is a reasonably simple task to take in money and to pay it out but to accurately record these transactions in a set of accounts in good time for the Annual General Meeting of a club is quite another matter. Trying to prepare for my first AGM as treasurer I remember sitting in my wee study at home with my pen in my mouth staring at the mess of figures. I thought that the whole horrid task was as bad, if not worse, than one of those primary seven arithmetic problems. You know the sort of thing I mean: you are told that, if a train of 30 carriages long is thundering up the down line at 100 miles an hour and a goods train with a squillion trucks is ambling down the up line at 20 miles an hour, how long will it take to fill the bath in the guard's van?

I always found these arithmetical conundrums impossible just as I did organising a set of accounts. I had to go to the club captain,

Bob Richmond, an accountant, and ask him if he could translate my jottings of ins and outs into something that would be acceptable to our auditors and therefore to our members. It has never ceased to amaze me how quickly these chaps can turn a chaos of meaningless figures into decipherable columns of numerical clarity. It was ironic that Bob had been our treasurer before taking on the mantle of captain and I sought the captaincy if only to get out of being the treasurer. I suppose we were multi-tasked and easily interchangeable!!

The AGM that I presented my audited set of accounts to duly elected me as captain. I was chuffed that this gathering of eager youngsters wanted me to lead them on the pitch. Perhaps, though, they thought I would do less damage to the Club as captain than I was likely to do as custodian of their cash!

My vice-captain Alan Davidson and I started to work immediately on plans for pre-season training.

Alan and I organised and ran the very early lung-busting, hard-work training sessions. Parry Reynolds and John Mackie would be the coaches. One training night we were working at fitness in a public park called the Mineral Well. It was still a time meant for general conditioning and everyone was wearing the footwear for that i.e. trainers. It had been raining earlier in the day and so the grass was wet and slippery. Parry interrupted the session. He took the forwards away which seemed a bit odd given he was the backs coach. We, the backs, decided to play touch rugby and were having a great time. During a restart after a try had been scored we heard this incredibly loud crack. It sounded like a fairly stout tree bough had snapped.

We Brylcream boys looked to where the forwards were training and saw them lying in a huge heap. Parry, much against some very sensible advice from John Mackie, had got the lads to form a scrum and he had put the ball in. It was a daft thing to do wearing trainers..... none of the sixteen lads had boots on. Somebody deep within the scrum skited on the wet grass and the whole thing collapsed. It was obvious to the human components of this heap what had happened, a leg or an arm had snapped but nobody knew whose it was, including, at the time of impact, the owner of said broken limb. Not even a whimper could be heard from within this pile of humanity. The boys started to pick themselves up carefully as if there was a bomb in amongst them. Gradually the hillock of bodies reduced in number, each lad feeling his arms and legs to make sure he wasn't the cripple. Finally one body was left, that of Norman Banski, a hooker. The realisation that it was he who had a badly broken leg triggered the start of the oooooooyaaaaaaahhh aria.

This injury having been incurred in the very early eighties preceded mobile phones. Someone had to run at least half a mile to a public telephone. Instead of calling for an ambulance he called up a local doctor who came along right away in his Austin Maxi. Norman, having bravely borne the awful pain as quietly as he could after the initial banshee wailing, was about to have a completely and hitherto unknown experience in pain. Furthermore, and unbelievably, this pain was to be perpetrated by a doctor of medicine, a man dedicated to healing the sick and to the reduction of pain and suffering of mankind. The Doc asked some of the guys to help him put Norman on to the back seat of his car and he laid a blanket over, the now in shock but brave, Banski.

A contrite Parry Reynolds, the root cause of the whole situation, was standing thanking the Doc, as was I, when the Doc slammed shut the very heavy back door of his Maxi. He had quite forgotten that there was a bloody great arm rest on the inside of the door which, with some thrust, battered the sole of the foot at the end of Banski's busted leg. OOOOOOOOOOOOYAAAAAAAAHAAHH !!!!

Collateral damage.

The hairs stood up on the back of everyone's neck as their blood curdled at the racket Banski was making. In a sort of reflex action Norman grabbed the fabric of the car ceiling and ripped it off. What a night.

Not long after that affair and in more or less the same area of the Mineral Well we had another bad training injury on our hands. This time, ironically, caused by the guys wearing studded boots. Stand-off, Richard Gibson, got caught in the middle of a mêlée on the ground during a wee practice match. He was accidentally studded on his right thigh which was seriously gashed. One could see the brown fat of his thigh. Bandaging his wounds with towels, we rushed him into my car, which was close by, and, along with some helpers, I drove like hell into Aberdeen Royal Infirmary. In those days we trained on Mondays and Wednesdays. This was a Wednesday evening. Richard was wearing a Mackie rugby jersey which is red. As we drove up to the A&E door a policeman ran up to us and directed us to a side door that I had never noticed in my many mercy trips to that hospital. Nurses and porters took Richard from us and said that they would take care of everything and we could get away. Well we couldn't just go as we had to get Richard back to Stonehaven. We were looking for a waiting room when the Policeman who had welcomed us came over to me and said, 'Fit wye are things at Pittodrie the nicht?'

Translated from the Aberdeen he said 'How is Aberdeen Football club getting on in the game that they are playing at Pittodrie stadium tonight?'

I said that I had absolutely no idea and couldn't really have cared less frankly. Our, up until then, cheery cop started to form a puzzled look upon his large face. It dawned on me what all the fuss, extra care and attention which was being heaped upon our Richard was all about. The Bobbie, seeing the similarly coloured jersey Richard was wearing, assumed our man was an Aberdeen football player.

The special treatment that is clearly laid on for the City's fitba team was put into action.

Soon, my first and, as it happened, my last season as Captain of the club came around. It started off fairly well although an old knee injury started to bother me again. I went to see Doctor McIntosh. He referred me to an orthopaedic surgeon who advised the removal of my knee cartilage, the real medical term for which is "meniscus". The lateral and anterior meniscus are two cushions which, basically, stop the knee bones from grinding against themselves, eventually rubbing off the cartilage on the bones leading to very painful arthritis and causing an inability to climb stairs, run or even walk. A person minus his meniscus cushions should keep up his physiotherapy by, amongst other things, exercising his quad muscles to stave off the evil end. I, of course, failed to keep up regular physiotherapy. I carried on playing rugby for a while, riding my bike and took up half marathon running as well as playing as much golf and squash as possible. The inevitable happened: I gradually suffered the consequences and turned into a hobbling wreck.

On the 27th June 2011 I was blessed with a new knee joint after years of pain. They won't give you a new knee until you are old enough. In my case sixty-three. After three to four months of intense physio and pain I was like a new man.

Anyway around half way through my season as Club captain I had the meniscus operation and that was supposed to be that so far as my playing days as captain were concerned. In those days such an operation on the knee was a much bigger job than it is now. I was off work for about two months.

I did play a few games in the seasons following but administration and assisting in other ways was going to be the way I would contribute my spare time to the running of the club.

I suppose the ultimate office in any amateur rugby club is the Presidency. I first became president of Mackie in season 1983/84. Being president of a junior club like Mackie is a bit more hands on compared to the experience a Premier club president has. It's a huge help however if a junior club committee has a good secretary and treasurer. I had both of these. For a while, a fellow called Eddie Murray held the position of treasurer and then Bob Richmond, who was my vice president, also looked after the money. Eddie was a good all round committee man and possesses a great sense of humour. Eddie is an architect by profession and later in the life of the club he was to become invaluable with regard to planning applications and the like. The secretary in my early days as president was Rod Richmond, whom I have mentioned earlier. An English schoolteacher by profession he was made for the job of secretary.

As the months and years marched on for Mackie, we the club members were to have some amazing experiences which were, I suppose, the stuff of a new club finding its way. A number of tours were undertaken: twice to London, once to Copenhagen, twice to Stockholm and once to Houston Texas. I will leave the details of these tours for another time. Too many people involved are still alive!

Around the mid-eighties I travelled up with some pals from Stonehaven to watch a Mackie XV play an Aberdeen Grammar XV. We arrived about ten minutes after kick-off and I spotted Peter Mitchell of the Aberdeen Press and Journal standing on his own behind our goalposts. I asked him if there had been any scoring and he said that he didn't know but would ask a fellow standing on his own nearby. Back came Peter with an amazing story.

'See that guy I have just spoken to, he is Jo Maso!'

'What????????'

'Yes, I asked the bloke what the score is and he said he wasn't sure because he had only just arrived but zee team in zee white shirts ave just scored a try'

'He sounded French and so I introduced myself in French and he said he was Jo Maso.'

I suggested to Peter that he bring the celebrated Frenchman into our company which he did and a round of introductions ensued.

Word of this encounter moved swiftly around the ground and Jo was invited up to the Aberdeen Grammar club house for a drink. Maso as you will probably know, reader, is the current Manager of the French National side and was, in the sixties, a celebrated centre and stand-off in the French side. So this was quite an occasion for the Grammar Club members. While we were there a number of people descended on Jo to shake his hands and tell him how much they admired his rugby skills. Some of us were quick to get to work on Jo, and by late afternoon, he had agreed to speak at the local Referees' Society dinner and to coach the Mackie Academy FPRFC backs. I don't know how the refs' do went but only a week or so after I met Maso, he came down to a Mackie training night and duly gave the backs a session. The lads said they enjoyed what they were given to do and learned a lot from the world famous three-quarter.

I thanked Jo for taking the time to help out and asked him if he would like to join me for lunch one day and he accepted. We got together the very next week and, as we were chatting about rugby, he suddenly said to me,

'Dooglas, oo do you sink waz zee best French back?' I went through a few that I thought might fit the bill such as Sella, the Boniface brothers, Blanco and of course himself; he shook his head and said,

'No, no, no, no eeet was Quasimodo!' Then he giggled a lot. So our newly found French friend had a sense of humour. He also had a generous streak and insisted on paying for lunch.

Gradually the news that one of the most famous French players of all time was in the North East of Scotland reached all the clubs in the Aberdeen area and some of the fellows in the Golden Oldies, a team for ex-players that just can't give it up, staged a game between themselves and a French side at Hazelhead on the very pitch I'd had my first game for Aberdeenshire. I wasn't playing: I had enough sense. A number of French North Sea oil and gas men turned out for the Froggie side and they invited Maso to play for them. Jo was not by then the player he once was but, in my humble opinion, his performance was okay, not that his team mates nor the opposition were much of a yardstick.

The Aberdeen team did have a couple of pretty slick fellows like Gordonian, Ian "Spivvy" McRae and Ronnie "Bomber" Comber of Aberdeen Grammar FP. After the game everyone repaired to a hotel for a drink, a bite to eat and a yarn or two. It was an education because Spivvy and Jo Maso went over the game that they both played in back in 1969, the one Scotland won in Stad Colombes thanks to a last minute try by Jim Telfer. Every tiny detail was examined, from the early moment that Spivvy ran on as a replacement to the final whistle. Astonishing, given the match had taken place fifteen years previously.

It was after that game that some older blokes, displaying their vast knowledge of the game, remarked on how poorly they thought that Maso the maestro had performed. Maso was not nearly as fast as he had been in his International days, that could be forgiven; it was his general handling skills that had been a disappointment.

Some people were not happy to leave it at that; indeed one of the Mackie players, Raymond Pittendreigh, went so far as to look into

Maso's career at an Aberdeen library. No googling then. He found some rugby books which contained photographs of Maso playing for France. It had to be said, the pictures and the guy we all knew did not match. To be fair a fellow's looks can change quite a lot in a decade and a half but one's imagination would have to stretch quiet a lot to account for the differences in Maso's appearance as highlighted by pictures of the star in the library books.

I mentioned earlier that Phantoms crop up from time to time in rugby clubs but they are usually harmless, bizarre may be, but harmless. I was unhappy about the thought that the Jo Maso we knew and loved might be a phantom and a prize one at that.

If this Frenchman was a phantom then he played a game of very high risk phantomese. Jo asked me one day if I might arrange a meeting between him and Andy Irvine at Goldenacre on the day of an International at Murrayfield, it was not against France, rather, I think it may have been Wales. Jo explained that he had trained with the French team at Goldenacre before a Murrayfield International and had fond memories of it. He then went on to describe Heriot's school playing fields with great accuracy.

I gave Andy Irvine a call to see if he could make it to the Heriot's clubhouse after the match to meet Maso. Andy agreed to the meeting and said that he would love to catch up with the Frenchman whom he had met a few times before. He explained that he would be doing a radio broadcast on the match that day and may be late or even not make it all and could I please make sure that Maso understood that. Andy asked me what Jo Maso was doing in Aberdeen and I told Andy that Jo worked at Dyce airport as a navigation equipment engineer on helicopters which operated in the North Sea oil business. I knew this because he invited me, Rosemary and our girls to visit him at Dyce to look over a chopper and then to have tea and biscuits with some of the aircrew. Andy thought that it was strange that Maso would be involved in that sort of occupation. Anyway the date was made.

In the meantime Jo had given me a stack of tickets for the France v Scotland match in Paris later that month. Some of the tickets were for the Presidential box. I gave some to people in Aberdeen and a few to Mackie and Heriot's members. It is perfectly feasible for ex Internationalists to score tickets like that, I suppose, given their connections, especially a star like Maso.

The day of the meeting between the two big guns arrived and I met with Jo and his girlfriend at Goldenacre and introduced them to a number of the stalwarts of the Heriot's Rugby Club. Many of these Herioters had seen Jo play both in Edinburgh and in Paris. Andy phoned me at the club and apologised explaining that he was detained and would not be able to make it to Goldenacre. Jo was disappointed, had a couple of drinks with me and left to return to Aberdeen.

Towards the end of March 1985 the Mackie dinner took place and we invited Jo to join our top table. The main speaker that year was the 1984 Slam captain, Jim Aitken. He was of course introduced to Jo at the pre- dinner drinks and again at my house for one of Rosemary's famous after- dinner parties. That evening Jo took Rosemary aside and explained that he knew that Rosemary and I loved motoring to France for our summer holidays and would she like to stay in a Gite owned by Philippe Sella. Sella was, at the time of this story, a regular in the French national side and went on to win one hundred and eleven caps for his country; he played his club rugby for Agen in southern France not too far from Beziers. Jo knew Sella well and he would arrange everything for us and would get back to me. The idea of a Gite appealed to us and we waited with anticipation for the call from Jo to say it was all okay. Jo duly called me and gave me the phone number of the Gite. He explained that he had booked us in for three weeks starting from a few days after the kids were on holiday from school.

The potential of Jo being a phantom was gaining momentum in both Stonehaven and Aberdeen. I called Andy Irvine again and told him about my concerns. He asked me to describe Maso's skills on the pitch in the Golden Oldies game referring to the kind of skills that I would know very well from watching the likes of Keith Robertson and Jim Renwick.

'Nope, he never looked like a Renwick, a Robertson or a Rutherford come to think about it,' I reported to Andy.

'I will call up some of my pals in "L'EQUIPE" in Paris and get back to you as soon as possible.'

Late on the next afternoon Andy called and I remember his opening statement like it was a minute ago.

Hardly able to control his mirth he began,

'Well Dougie, there is good news and there is bad news, how do you want it'

Good news first please.'

'Jo Maso is alive and well'

'Oh........and.......... the bad news'

He is coaching the Perpignan team down in the south west of France and he works for Adidas.

'So God knows who this poser is.' Silence from both of us for a second or two. Andy broke first and said,

'It's just occurred to me, what was the imposter going to say to me if we had met at Goldenacre that day I couldn't make it after the Welsh match?' Another pause from us both as we considered that wee puzzle.

'What would his reply have been after I had said - you are not Jo Maso?' Andy exclaimed loudly.

Now that is an intriguing thought because, as I said earlier, Andy had met Jo a few times in very recent years and would not have been fooled as so many others were.

I think it's fair to say that all of us bar Ian McRae who had met "Maso" in Aberdeen, would not have met the real Jo Maso before and would only have seen him from at least a hundred yards away at either Murrayfield or Stad Colombe, which was vast. Spivvy McRae although playing against the man in Paris, was, after all, in the heat of the game and not really paying attention to his opponent's facial features. Also it was fifteen years previously. Additionally, and I don't know if this was the case with Jo Maso, but I have heard that, sometimes, not all of the French players attended the après game dinners. So it is possible Spiv never clapped eyes socially on Jo before the scratch game in Aberdeen.

I gave Rosemary the news that night when I got home. Realising our holiday was possibly now pie in the sky, and despite it being only mid-April, she phoned the Gite. There was someone there. Oh dear! The lady had never heard of us and so there was no booking. Rosemary asked me for "Maso's" phone number and she called the man. He wasn't in and his girl said he was out purchasing new tyres for his car. Rosemary asked him to call back; he never did. A second call was immediately made to the Gite. Rosemary discovered that it was available for the dates we wanted and so she booked there and then.

To the embarrassment of a number of people, probably everyone that had come into contact with "Maso", the story reached the desk of the gossip columnist of the Aberdeen "Evening Express", sister paper of the Press and Journal. It had probably come from one of the number of employees of that paper who lived in Stonehaven. The gossip merchant dug pretty deep but was careful not to name any of the better known celebrities in his column. He found out the imposter's real name, we will call him Monsieur Pimpernel.

Despite causing me embarrassment the Evening Express man inadvertently did me a favour. I took the story with me to our family holiday at the Gite on Domains Des Olivier.

As it turns out no harm was done financially to anybody but it would appear strange to rugby followers nowadays that so many people could fall for such a Grande Phantom as the one we had on our hands. He was very convincing though and had a lot of nerve. With today's professionalism in the game of rugby, Google and the social networking that goes on we would probably have found our man out very quickly. I am glad we didn't because this amazing story, which isn't finished by a long chalk yet, would never have unfolded.

The season well and truly ended, the school summer holidays beckoned as did our Gite, a vineyard in Beziers.

After a few days of driving with stops throughout the length of France we arrived at Domains Des Oliviers and were greeted by the owners, the Moreaus. They were keen to know more about the story behind our trip and so we told them an abridged version. They knew very little about rugby and certainly nothing about Phillipe Sella or, for that matter, Jo Maso. Mme Moreau had a brother-in-law who was a member of the Beziers rugby club and she thought that a meeting with him in her house might be useful. His name is Serge and he and the two props from the Beziers club came along also. Rosemary had a good grasp of French, Serge had some English, the props had none but, the language of rugby being universal we all got along famously as we drank some of the wine produced by the Moreaus. Serge and his two front row friends all worked locally. Serge got the gist of the story about the imposter and the real Maso and asked if we would like to meet Jo. What an unbelievable turn up. Yes of course I would like to meet the real Maso and tell him the story.

We gathered again at the Beziers club and merchandise shop in the town centre. Whilst Serge was talking to some fellows in the club I managed, with a lot of help from Rosemary, to have a conversation with the two props. I asked if they got paid for playing rugby. They said no, but they got time off during the working day to train with the Bezier's XV. They said their employers paid their full wage whilst they were at these training sessions. So you *are* paid to play for Beziers. 'Non, Non,' they protested. 'Aye that will be right,' I replied with a knowing nod and as big a grin on my face as they had on theirs.

Serge came out of the club and beckoned us in from the warm sunshine. He had Maso on the phone. Serge had given Maso the gist of the story and Jo asked to speak to me. I had a bash but his English at that time was not too great and my French was basically non-existent so Rosemary had a go in French. Her excellent attempt to explain the story and who we were was good enough to tempt the French superstar to meet us.

Maso arranged to meet us in a car park at an exit point on the Route de Sud near Perpignan. We Bruces were standing on a baking hot day soaking up the rays when a white Mercedes Benz appeared, mirage-like, in the shimmering sun at the far end of the car park.

Maso stopped his car quite a bit from us and got out. With the sun behind him he started to walk towards us. Gradually he came into focus and we could see he was wearing gold rimmed shades, a light blue shirt e shirt, denim trousers and sandals. He had longish golden hair and swarthy handsome looks. Rosemary, I think, was quite taken with the man. The

looks of British international rugby players was nothing like this gorgeous Frenchman. "Gorgeous" was her description not mine.

This godlike creature looked nothing like Monsieur Pimpernel! Maso introduced himself to us, politely shaking our hands and including those of our young daughters. It became clear to Rosemary and me that all of this meeting in the middle of nowhere, parking yards away from us was probably Jo's way of taking time to size up the situation without being stuck with a bunch of nutters. Our genuine looking little family group seemed to relax the man and he referred briefly to the story of the imposter and said that we must follow him to his apartment to meet his wife and then we could tell them the story in greater detail over drinks. After a shortish trip into Perpignan we arrived at the Maso's apartment. Annie, Jo's wife, was waiting for us. She seemed genuinely pleased to meet us and was immediately taken with our kids aged twelve and ten at that time. Jo left the room and brought back some presents for the kids and drinks for all of us.

As we sat enjoying our drinks, Jo and Annie listened attentively to the story of Msr Pimpernel. I gave him a copy of the Aberdeen Evening Express story about the Maso imposter which he had a quick look at and then he explained in broken English that he didn't like the story about this imposter. I asked him why and he explained with a smile on his face that he thought the Pimpernel was not much of an imposter because he didn't make any money from using the Maso name. Jo explained that his name was regularly used in scams, mostly by people kidding Parisian hotel staff that they were him and scarpering without settling their bills.

It was quite a feeling sitting in this famous man's living room and having his full attention. Annie seemed to be enjoying the company of Rosemary and our girls. She showered Kirsten and Sarah with little mementos of our visit and Jo looked out the very last of his photographs of his old playing days and autographed them along with a message on each.

The imposter story over, I spotted a glass display cabinet on the wall which had an array of International jerseys from, it seemed, all over the rugby playing world. There were two that caught my eye. One was a Scottish jersey; Jo told me it belonged to Chris Rea, a Scotland and Lions centre 1968/71. The other jersey was a Lions one. I was pretty sure the Lions had never played France and so I asked Jo the history. He said to me:

'Av you erd of Barry John?' Good God this was a Lions jersey from the 1971 tour of New Zealand. One of the pictures Jo gave us showed Maso and Barry John on a beach near Perpignan. Jo is wearing Barry John's Welsh jersey and Barry John is wearing Jo's French jersey.

Ever since that visit to the Maso's home we have exchanged Christmas cards and a year or so after our meeting the Masos had their first child, a daughter, Fannie.

CHAPTER 16

Fun with A Bear

Rosemary and I had a lot of fun during the International seasons, much of the time with Iain Milne. Iain would arrange to meet us at the door of whatever hotel the team were entertaining the opposition at and, indicating to the bouncers that we were his guests, in we would go for a few hours of, often, very hairy entertainment amongst the players, committees and their wives and /or girlfriends.

I think the most embarrassing time for me was after an Irish International at the Carlton Hotel. As usual Rosemary and I pitched up at the prearranged time, Iain met us and we were in. I was always just happy to stand and blether to the famous players of either side and enjoy a drink or three with them. This time was to be completely different. Iain insisted that we go up to the function room where the traditional après match dance was takivng place. Now I knew only too well that the SRU were pretty snooty about this dance and only those members of the home and away squads of players, their girls/wives and the respective committees, ex-presidents and their wives were permitted to attend. Iain insisted that we followed him into the dance. Of course at the entrance I met with human barriers who insisted that I turn round and go away. I made to do so but noticed that Iain and his girlfriend Marion had been welcomed with open arms and to my astonishment Rosemary was ushered in with them. Iain protested about the discrimination to the men at the door. Doug Smith, the then SRU President, came upon the scene. Iain, tongue in cheek, explained to the manager of the famous 1971 Lions that if I wasn't allowed into the dance he would never play for Scotland again. The legendary Smith said, 'Okay in you come but please keep a low profile, others may not be so keen to have the company of your friend.' So, effectively I had been invited to the dance by the SRU President. I was still ill at ease as I entered the main body of the kirk. There were Rosemary and Marion dancing with the Scottish players - I think it was a Gay Gordons. I thought to myself isn't this ironic, me a committed rugby man, president of my club and I am about as welcome as a bad smell in a space suit, and my girl is dancing away there oblivious to the severe discomfort that I am suffering. I sat down in a corner keeping a very, very low profile as per the instructions from Doug Smith. Everything would have been okay had it not been for The Bear's next outrageous move:

'Dougie, would you like a dance?'

Before I could say a word Iain grabbed me and whoosh we were on the dance floor doing some sort of quickstep. I think if I had not been known by some of the SRU committee men, I would have got away with this piece of tomfoolery. You see, at that time, I was on the committee of the SRU's North District and was well known to many of the officials of that part of the Scottish rugby map. Some of those Northern officials were also on the full SRU committee and, sitting on their pompous high horses, they were agog as they saw me being twirled about by their beloved tight head prop. The SRU in those days was run almost completely on an amateur basis and many of those gentlemen that sat on the committee guarded that privilege vigorously. After I managed to get off the dance floor I sat with Adam Robson, the President of the SRU of three years earlier. I reintroduced myself to Adam - he had spoken at the Mackie Dinner a few years before. We were having a bit of a yarn as I kept one eye on Rosemary who was having the time of her life on the dance floor, and the other, more nervous eye, on one of the North District committee men who was also an SRU man. This fellow was beckoning Bill Hogg, the secretary of the SRU. I knew what was coming; poor Bill had been given the job of kicking me out. Iain protested but I said that I was perfectly happy to leave. As I did so I asked Iain if he would tell Rosemary what was happening and that she would find me in the main bar.

The pompous ones were not bothered in the least that Rosemary remained, in fact I am pretty sure that she was very welcome, otherwise what really was the point in having a dance as few, if any, of the Irish players had brought partners with them. Equally, hardly any of the Scots lads had their girls on their arms. So, ludicrously, women with no direct connection to the SRU were as entitled to be at the function as the core of Scottish International Rugby. Fellows like me who were a significant part of ordinary club rugby in Scotland had to be kept out of the precious dance at all costs. So much for men's lib.

As Bill Hogg saw me out a very, very drunk Scottish selector came after me wagging his finger at me and shouting:

'You sir, have made the biggest mistake of your life !'

What a lot of tripe. Anyway I figure that inner sanctum mentality has long since left the SRU and all for the best I say.

I was very sorry for Bill Hogg as he must have felt like a wee gopher as he carried out the dirty work for the North District man.

I actually knew that North fellow very well and I would have been perfectly happy to leave had he personally requested me to do so. I only hung around because my wife, oblivious to the pettiness of the SRU zealots, was still having a ball and knew nothing of my discomfort.

Some years later I came across the now late Bill Hogg in his SRU official capacity when I was secretary and general manager at Heriot's Rugby Club. A more charming and helpful man one could not wish to meet.

The Bear must have taken ages to let Rosemary know what had happened. As great luck would have it I had time to share a couple of beers with Donal Lenihan, the great Irish and Lions forward. He just happened to be at the bar and wasn't interested in attending the dance, so we got blethering. I had never met the famous man before but, being typically Irish, he was engaging and happy to share a half hour or so with a perfect stranger.

Eventually Rosemary, Marion and Iain turned up at the bar and had a good laugh at my expense. It was quite funny I suppose looking back on it now but, at the time, it seemed to be a major diplomatic incident.

Iain Milne has been a huge friend of Mackie Rugby Club over the years. In his playing days and immediate post playing days he used to look for things to do to help Mackie. Iain knew that we were constructing our new pitch and that it would have to be opened with as much publicity, pomp and circumstance as possible.

'Would you like me to bring a team of ex Internationalists up to Stonehaven one weekend to celebrate the opening of your new pitch?'

'My God what a great idea. The lads would love it but who would they play against?' I said.

'Mackie of course?' Came the reply from the Scotland hero.

'The lads would love that but good players though they are I don't think they could give ex Internationalists much of a game.'

'No problem, few of them are still playing seriously and we will have uncontested scrums.'

'Ok, but who are you thinking of including in your squad?'

'Oh, as many as I can get from the 1984 Grand Slam side!'

I was stunned at this and very quickly realised that the event would be marvellous for our young players. They would be able to mix with these famous caps after the game as well as play against them. Much needed publicity for the existence of our club and the possibility of making some money out of the event were just two of the spin-offs.

As it turned out the following players managed to form the bulk of the team which Iain called "The Scottish Survivors"

Alex Brewster, Scotland and Stewarts Melville; Peter Hewitt, Scotland B and Heriot's; Jim Calder, Scotland, Lions and Stew Mel; Jim Aitken, Scotland and Gala; Finlay Calder, Scotland, Lions and Stew Mel; Bill Cuthbertson, Scotland and Harlequins; Alan Tomes, Scotland, Lions and Hawick; Roger Baird, Scotland, Lions and Kelso; Peter Steven, Scotland and Heriots; Jim Hay, Scotland and Hawick; Ian McRae, Scotland and Gordonians; Dougie Wyllie, Stew Mel and Scotland and of course Iain Milne, Scotland, Lions and Heriot's.

The game was to be played on a Sunday and the majority of the Scottish Survivors came up to Stonehaven the day before. This meant that the Mackie lads on the Saturday night could entertain their illustrious guests in the Mackie club house which was situated in the centre of the town. This was wonderful and I got so much pleasure at seeing the Mackie members have such a good time with these famous players. Pro rugby still had not come about and so the Mearns town lads were having a taste of what used to be common throughout Scotland's division one clubs of a Saturday afternoon after a match.....mixing with International players.

In addition to the fixture itself, a great deal of organisation was undertaken by the Mackie committee, in particular Ewan Hunter who gave us all a master class in Marketing. Ewan could sell ice to the Eskimos and he made Mackie an extraordinary amount of money that weekend with some clever income generating wheezes.

We erected a marquee near the new pitch in which we installed a bar and café. The weather was not desperately kind but a thousand plus braved the elements to enjoy the on pitch entertainment. The Mackie lads put up a good show but were inevitably beaten by the experts. I had just as much fun as the Mackie players as I watched them try to compete with their heroes. I think the Stonehaven men just couldn't believe what was going on. In some cases they were mesmerised. Dod Thomson a former Mackie captain told me that at one point he found himself running alongside Jim Aitken, 'I was so busy saying to myself, "For God's sake that's Jim Aitken the captain of the Grand Slam team," that I forgot I was supposed to tackle him'

What a great day that was for the Club and one the Mackie players of that day will never forget. Iain Milne had done it again for the Mackie FPRFC. I asked him how he managed to gather together such a priceless group of Scottish players and he said it was reasonably easy.

'I contacted them on the phone and asked them if they would like to go on a two match tour, all expenses paid !'

'Two match tour !' I exclaimed.

'Yes, I told them the first part was the Hong Kong Tens and they all jumped at the chance and agreed to be committed. It was then that I told them that the second leg of the tour was to be in Stonehaven!'

He said all of that with the mischievous grin on his face that I knew only too well. These famous players had such a high regard for their Bear that they would have played in the North pole for him had he asked them.

Heriot's had sent a few teams up to Stonehaven under various guises. For a change, one year, we asked if we could play Heriot's in Edinburgh before a Murrayfield International.

The Edinburgh men, up to this particular encounter, had never been beaten by a Mackie side but the North east Boys were the victors on this occasion, much to their unconcealed delight. The visitors did not expect to do so well and were trying to make the most of the day by taking a light hearted view of the forthcoming proceedings.

Roy Bruce, one of the Mackie props and captain for the day, suggested to his team that they should emulate the All Blacks just before the kick-off by doing a Haka but, given they didn't know the actions or the words, they decided to transform that match challenge from the Maori version to that of the British Hokey Cokey. The Heriot's lads stood looking at this ridiculous rabble and must have thought that they would have an easy morning of it. They were wrong and lost the game

Two bears in our kitchen

Me and Finlay Calder in the Mackie Clubhouse. I am wearing Finlay's "Scottish Survivors" match jersey

CHAPTER 17

Withdrawal Symptoms of the Retired Rugby Player

My administration time at Mackie was drawing to a close; my playing days had long disappeared in the mists of time. Along with many other guys, I felt that together we had achieved quite a lot in the twenty odd years I had been associated with Mackie. Much had been done by the various committees to simply establish and maintain a rugby club in Stonehaven. The club had taken on responsibility to help in the community, eventually leasing a club house in the middle of the town giving the inhabitants a direct interest in the club. We had also steered some young lads on a course in life that might otherwise have taken a wrong turn to a disastrous destination.

There was something missing so far as I was concerned.

It took a while for the penny to drop. It was training nights that formed my missing link! Training usually started around 6.30/7pm- this meant leaving work around 5 pm to go home, change out of office gear, have a quick bite of tea with the family and head for the training ground. I had stopped training with the club around the age of thirty-five and had not realised how big a part of my life training had become. It was only when I started to become stressed at work for the first time in my life that I put two and two together.

I realised that my physical fitness was waning and that, I figured, was affecting me mentally. It dawned on me that for two nights in every week of a rugby season I left work at 5pm without giving it a second thought. Apart from my earlier days in my job in Aberdeen I was able to get away to training on time and without anybody hindering me. The whole business of training was an automatic regime. Never once did I have a conscience about stopping what I was doing around the 5pm mark so I could get down to join the lads on the training ground. After a good workout I had a couple of beers with the lads before heading back to the family, a late supper and news with Rosemary about the happy events of the day.

What I was now doing was stupid. Instead of clearing out of the office at least twice a week at 5pm, every night was finished well after 6/6.30pm and I would take the baggage of the day home with me. Training had caused me to forget about the stress of the day and so I would empty my mind of work related matters at 5pm twice a week until the next working day. It wasn't just the actual physical act of training, it was clearing off out of the office with another focus.

What to do, what to do?I had an epiphany: start a training group of likeminded people with the focus on escaping the office working day at, say, 5pm, twice a week, probably the same nights as rugby nights, with a goal to achieve physical and mental fitness, thus reducing, or better still, avoiding stress in the work place.

I explained my theory to some Stonehaven fellows around my age and they pictured clearly what was going through my mind. I also spoke to a couple of the local doctors who thought that in principal it was a very good idea but wanted to know where I would hold the sessions and what was my target age group. I told them that we would simply train under the street lights nearest the Mackie playing fields and the participants would be males over thirty-five. No need for any funds, private or public.

The GPs could see that a lot of good could be done here for the locals but a lot of harm was also possible. Could we have a gathering of all of those likely to be interested and they would quietly assess, in medical terms, the qualifications of the interested parties.

I decided I would call the training group "The Over Thirty-five's Keep Fit Club" and advertised a gathering in the weekly paper "The Mearns Leader". As usual the Editor, Bert James, looked after Mackie and gave my proposed meeting a huge spread in his paper as if it were news rather than an advert.

Dozens of men turned up at the meeting and listened to my story about stress, working unnecessarily late in the office, keeping physically fit and therefore mentally fit and so on. The Doctors also spoke to the audience and whilst endorsing the general benefits that could be derived they also warned the men of the bad that could come from membership of this new Mackie FPRFC offshoot. Those with certain health problems, which they highlighted, should not consider joining this new group. Whilst we all enjoyed a beer or two and some nibbles later, I noticed the Docs speaking quietly to a few of the men and I guess some of them were advised to stay at home.

The first session went extremely well. After a couple of weeks I was starting to feel really good and delighted that I had something that was drawing me away from the office at a reasonable time. However some aches and pains eventually started to shine through. I went to see Rosemary Clark, the local physiotherapist.

Rosemary put my painful body right and also corrected our warm ups at the Keep Fit Club.It was only a few weeks after the inception of the club that I got a telephone call from a very rude lady. She demanded to know why we had formed a male only club ignoring the female of the species. I explained to her that many of the men that attended the club were a bit overweight and obviously not very fit. They would cease to turn up at the sessions if they thought that women would be there to look at their wobbly beer bellies. Equally, I felt that out of condition women would not be comfortable exercising in front of men. The lady on the phone continued to rant at me and I suggested that if she was so keen to keep fit there was absolutely nothing preventing her from starting her own club for women. Apparently she didn't have the time!!

The upshot of that phone call was the birth of a "Women's over thirty-five's Keep Fit Club". The founder and leader was my Rosemary. My girl had been pestered by a number of women who thought they should get together and follow the lead of their men. The rude lady phone call was the nudge Rosemary needed to get the ball rolling for the Stonehaven women.

One of the very last major administration projects I had to take responsibility for was the sale of the social club house which was leased during the presidency of Bob Richmond.

Bob had worked hard on a business plan, presented it to our Bank Manager and it was approved with no difficulty. Forty-five members, including Bob and myself, each guaranteed the bank loan to the tune of £1000.00. The business was bought from a club member who ran it as a pub come pizzeria. The new clubhouse, situated plum in the centre of the town, was opened by Iain Milne and it was a roaring success for a few years. We needed a steward and I persuaded a fellow who was married to a friend of my Wife's to leave his job as a chef at one of the local hotels to take it on. President Bob Richmond developed a heart problem and had to stand down from the presidency. He asked me if I would stand for the presidency again which I agreed to do and was voted in for a second time. The club continued to thrive for a while then, like so many things in life, support started to wane. Many of the young lads wanted to go on into Aberdeen of a Saturday night after matches and the après beers and pies. The off season trade then started to dip badly. My committee and I tried absolutely everything we could to keep the place going; food theme nights were instigated and well attended, Burns' suppers, live bands, discos - you name it - but we were haemorrhaging money badly. Some of the business-men on the committee took me aside one day to explain that drastic measures would have to be taken if we were not to have a serious financial problem on our hands. I was going to have to make the full time steward redundant. I bit that bullet and told the steward he had to go. The fellow was very decent about it which made me feel ter-rible. We struggled on without our steward and even closed the club a few nights a week. In the end I had to accept that we had too much on our plates. We sold the business for what we paid for it thus saving all the guarantees. The relief in my household was palpable. I left the running of the Club in the capable hands of Alan Davidson my vice president and Peter Beatt, a future president. Both these fellows had been a great help to me over the years.

My time up at Mackie and at my office in Aberdeen too, I left for the Capital to take up my new position in our Edinburgh sales office. Rosemary stayed behind to sell our home of nearly twenty-two years.

I reflected on the great times I had at Mackie. Some of my expe-riences were to stand me in good stead later and some are best for-gotten. Some were bizarre, some were hilarious and some were serious. Rugby clubs seem to attract all sorts of characters, well at least Mackie did. Players of varying abilities came from many cor-ners of the world to muck in with us and, world class players graced our dinners. All in all it was a great twenty years.

CHAPTER 18

Edinburgh and Heriot's Rugby Club

My employers returned me to Edinburgh in 1996.

Amidst all the settling in at my new post and looking for somewhere to live, I attended an amazing evening at Goldenacre: The Three Bears Dinner. A number of Herioters got together, headed up by two of my Heriot's school pals, Ian Wright and Colin McCallum who are also close friends of Iain Milne. They organised a benefit dinner for all three of the Milne brothers. It was such a huge gathering of people that the event had to be held in a marquee of circus proportions. It was a dinner that was the talk of the town, both before and after, and a huge acknowledgement of the affection the rugby fraternity in Edinburgh has for these three brothers.

Just before we were all required to take our seats, my friend and past Heriot's president, Ken Hutchison, found me and took me to the top table to briefly reunite me with Gareth Edwards who was the principle speaker. What an unforgettable occasion.

After a season of doing nothing rugbywise I was asked by Fraser Dall, the director of rugby at Heriot's FPRC, if I would take on the role of social convenor and try to revive the social life at Goldenacre.

I began to organise a club social calendar with John Mackie. John had returned to Edinburgh from Stonehaven some years before me. We took on board a couple of the younger players just so we kept that age group in our sights. The young lads in question were Bruce Douglas a 2nd XV prop and Andy Grant, another prop from, I think, the 3rd XV.

John and I started the social ball rolling with a successful wine tasting. That sort of thing was right up the Bruce/Mackie street. The wine merchant we invited to conduct proceedings, brought enough open bottles for seventy-five tasters; only fifteen turned up. We got absolutely plastered and ordered case upon case of wine.

The social scene was off to a great start. We followed the wine frenzie with various theme evenings based on my experiences at the now vanished Mackie Club House. They were all pretty successful. Heriot's Rugby Club was back to being a reasonably vibrant place of a Saturday night.

Season 1997/98 was a very difficult one for the Club. It was a period when our team didn't perform well and we were staring relegation in the face. The way the league was set up, the second half of the season saw the bottom clubs battling for survival and for Heriot's to stay up we had to win every one of our remaining games to make a play-off, which we did and which we won.

Shortly after retiring from The Standard Life Assurance Company where I had been employed for a very happy thirty years, Fraser Dall approached me yet again, asking me this time if I would like to manage the club on a full time basis and with a salary.

I had been finding retirement at the age of fifty a fairly lonely experience. Being near the Braids golf course was a boon but even that was sometimes pretty lonely. The position Fraser offered me was a wonderful opportunity that I just couldn't turn down.

Season 1998/99 beckoned. It was a great feeling to be such an important official of my old school's FP rugby club which was in the top tier of Scottish club rugby.

I did have some reservations about what some of the club stalwarts might think about the fact I was to be a paid official, especially those who had previously filled the position of club secretary. Things were about to change a lot insofar as the duties of a Heriot's Rugby Club secretary was concerned. My job title was secretary **and** general manager and my duties had more of a commercial leaning than had been the case, traditionally. Raising sponsorship and hospitality money was the prime objective whilst administering pretty well everything apart from the pure rugby side of things. I even dealt with a fair bit of the treasurer's remit after the retirement of Douglas Hill, the Club's longest serving treasurer.

I was very fortunate at the start of my new career to have the late Graham Fraser as a president and Kenny Scotland as vice president. Both of these gentlemen were very supportive of me. Graham used to phone me early most mornings just so we could discuss our plans for the Club that day. Like me, he was highly motivated and was keen for the Club to flourish. The pre-season word in the press was that Heriot's were very lucky to survive the drop in the previous season but would not escape that fate this time around. Everybody in the club, led by Graham, was determined to prove the critics were wrong.

With much the same team in 1998/99 as had played in the 97/98 play off, the 1st XV team bus set off to Old Anniesland in the west end of Glasgow to play the first fixture of the season against Glasgow Hawks, an amalgam of some famous Glasgow Clubs. Heriot's had a new skipper: prop, Jocky Bryce. Jocky, it seemed, had been around

Goldenacre since George Heriot himself. From the kick off Heriot's were not the poor relations as had been suggested in the previous day's Scotsman. However, as I recall it was a nail-biting contest. I had vowed that I would keep a sense of decorum, be as calm as possible during matches and try not to get too carried away with the proceedings. You see, so far as sponsorship was concerned, much depended on the club avoiding relegation. It was especially so at the time of this story as the BBC was still covering Premier One games. That meant advertising boards were on the telly and, of course, logos on the players jerseys would be picked up by the cameras as a game went along. During that game and all other games, I was very conscious of the consequences of Heriot's dropping out of the top flight of Scottish club rugby. To be honest it bothered me that this great job I had could be under threat.

We won the day and all was well. To win our first game at Hawks after dodging relegation must have pleased our sponsors, Warners, the Edinburgh based solicitors. Fraser Dall brought that firm on board before I came on the scene and they had an agreement with us for three seasons. So, I wasn't going to have to worry about finding a major sponsor for a while. I did however spend time keeping Warners up to speed with what was going on at Goldenacre and gave them every chance to capitalise on their connection with Heriot's.

Whilst Warners were still our main sponsors, Hall and Tawse, a large construction company based in the west, started to show an interest in upgrading their modest financial support for the club. I arranged to meet Mike Levack and Paul McDevitt, the Scottish boss and marketing man respectively. I knew Mike Levack was a keen rugby man so I took Kenny Milne along with me for support. Together we got a much improved deal from them and a promise to upgrade even further when the Warners contract ceased.

CHAPTER 19

A Pre-Season Tournament; Embracing Sponsors;
Special Players; Fund Raising, Rosemary and
I Tour Paris and Rome

In the late summer of 1998 Heriot's won a fifteen-a-side tournament in Cumberland. Fraser Dall our director of rugby wanted to run such a tournament at Goldenacre. It was to include all the Premier One clubs in Edinburgh, Kirkcaldy RFC, Aberdeen Grammar FP and Glasgow Hawks. Hawick having been at the same Cumberland tournament were equally motivated by it so they organised their own event.

Hall and Tawse jumped at the opportunity to sponsor that tournament for 1999 and a further five years after that. The inaugural tournament included a men's and women's competition. Boroughmuir won the former and Murrayfield Wanderers the latter. Whilst I was disappointed Heriot's did not lift the silver that day in the men's competition I was chuffed that our daughter Sarah scored two tries in the women's' final to help Murrayfield Wanderers lift their silverware. To my immense pleasure Sarah's first try was in the exact spot where I scored my first touchdown for the School XV thirty-five years earlier. Not long after that game Sarah was included in the Scottish Women's International squad. Sadly, like her dad, she had suspect knees and never managed to play for her country.

Mike Levack, his marketing man, Paul McDevitt and I had a great working relationship. Both Hall and Tawse and Heriot's thrived from it. Hall and Tawse were later to be taken over by Mansell Construction who continued to support Heriot's for a number of seasons. Mike, now the Chief Executive of the Scottish Building Federation, remains a member of the Club and continues his friendship with me and many of the club members that were around on that first visit he made to Goldenacre.

Warners also benefited from their relationship with us as we were doing so well on the pitch. Their logo, emblazoned on the front of the 1st XV jerseys, was often spotted on the telly. The BBC were broadcasting games at that time and Bill McLaren was usually the commentator. Their pitch side advertising board was even more obvious on the telly and, of course, there was a lot of newspaper coverage for the Edinburgh Law firm. This was right up the street of the, then, senior partner Brian Warner who, apart from having a genuine interest in Heriot's school and its former pupils, was keen to derive as much publicity for his firm as possible and help put them firmly on the Edinburgh legal map. We would not let him down as the 1st XV skippered by Jocky Bryce, coached by Donald MacDonald and Gareth Davies went on that season to win the league. We had proved the rugby pundits well and truly wrong.

As the Warner contract moved through the seasons I was able to persuade them to invest in the new Minis section which started up during their sponsorship period. In addition to winning the league in 98/99 the club had a host of players who represented Scotland at one level or another. Some of them, as predicted by Fraser Dall, would go on to play for Scotland namely Simon Taylor, Bruce Douglas and Gordon Ross. Jocky Bryce was Sportswriters Player of the Year and Simon Taylor was named Scotsman Tennents Player of the Year.

Although Bruce Douglas had not yet reached Murrayfield as a capped player he did eventually come out of his quiet spell during the early stages of our 98/99 Championship campaign and make a great social event and money raising suggestion. He said that we should have a 1000 pints competition. "What is that ?" enquired the remainder of the social committee.

'Oh it's dead simple we just tell the club that on a specified home game we, as a club, and our guests have to try and drink 1000 pints of draught beer or lager!' The idea was of course to have fun and boost bar profits with the minimum amount of effort. The best ideas are the simplest ideas!

I have to say this quickly caught our attention and imagination.

We decided to hold the event on the day of a home game against Melrose. That fixture always drew a large crowd. Posters were put up advertising the great trial of drinking strength and the cricket club very kindly lent us a portable score board to enable the Goldenacre barmaids to record the pints as they were bought. We lost the game against Melrose but more than defeated the 1000 pints target. We also lost to Melrose away at the Greenyards that year which didn't go down too well I guess, given we still picked up the championship trophy.

In the Spring of 1999 Scotland did the Nation proud by winning the last Five Nations Championship. They beat France in Paris by 36 points to 22 (five tries to three). Rosemary and I had travelled to Paris a few days before the match and stayed on for a week afterwards. We had a lot of fun exploring parts of Paris that we had never been to on our many shorter visits to that romantic city. I have to say that I didn't expect to see Scotland win in Paris, far less by such a huge margin, but win they did and I thought no more about it. England were heading for a win against Wales the following day, a Sunday, and that would have given them the Grand Slam. As it turned out Scotland hammered France and after the first Scottish try the fellow sitting next to me, a club mate, offered me a drink out of his not insubstantial hip flask. I accepted, of course, and my drinking companion said,

'We will have a pull each time Scotland score a try!'

Well of course we got five of them. What a night we had. The following night I took Rosemary for a River Seine dinner dance cruise on one of the fabulous glass covered Bateaux Parisiens. A table companion on our bateau happened to mention that Wales beat England earlier in the day and that just made the whole weekend complete; Scotland were the very last Five Nations champions.

In the Spring of 2000 Rosemary and I travelled to Rome to see Scotland play Italy in the new Six Nations Championship. It was the first season of the new style competition and the Rome test was the debut of Italy in the new European international rugby competition. It was going to be a wonderful few days in The Eternal City for us and we were joined by my old team mate, Fraser MacRitchie and his wife Linda, from London. We, as a rugby Nation, were a shade arrogant about our chances in the match as we entered the relatively small Stadio Flaminio. There was only one seated and covered area and the rest was all standing. It reminded me of a miniature Murrayfield before it was roofed and seated throughout. Although it was an early Spring day there was warmth in the sunshine.

There was little warmth in the Scotsman sitting behind and a wee bit along from us. He seemed to have taken a terrible dislike to

Kenny Logan. His feelings towards Kenny manifested themselves in a constant heckling of the Scottish winger.

'Logan you are the worst player in the team and that is saying something.'

'Logan would you please go away home, NOW.'

'Logan you are a disgrace to your country.'

'Logan you ought to be ashamed of yourself having the nerve to pull on that jersey.'

And so it went on until somebody said:

'Look my friend we and, when I say we, I include Kenny Logan, we have all got the message, could you please now shut up.'

Our man did as he was bidden until just before the end of the match which we were now obviously going to lose. An Italian player grub kicked a ball through the Scottish defence, Gordon Bulloch the Scottish hooker went to gather it but knocked it on in goal.

Our loudmouth friend leapt to his feet and in defiance of his previous acquiescence shouted :

'Och Bulloch ya stupid blankety blank, that's the sort of thing Logan would have done!'

I think it would be fair to say that nobody in the Scottish team that day had a game they would want to remember. It was not all Logan's fault.

During that trip to Rome Rosemary and I took a guided tour of the city. All of the most famous buildings and landmarks were included in this

day long tour. Our visit to St Peter's and the Vatican was probably the highlight for various reasons. St Peter's was huge, as one would expect and the history attached to that building is breathtaking. As I positioned myself to take in the magnificence of it all, I got a severe ticking off from a security man for leaning disrespectfully against a tomb. As I moved away from this not very remarkable sepulchre I saw it was where Bonnie Prince Charlie had been laid to rest together with his Father and Brother. You learn something every day. From within St Peter's we went to the Vatican to see the Sistine Chapel. We seemed to walk for miles in the Apostolic Palace and the entire ceiling throughout that walk was covered in paintings, so it was a little bit of an anti-climax when we got to *the* Michelangelo fresco in the Sistine Chapel for it looked to my inartistic eye much the same as the other works.

As we Scots tend to do, my fellow countrymen and I were looking quietly for some humour in amongst all the surrounding monasticism. There was humour in there, somewhere. Sure enough, in a bar later that evening I overheard a fellow Scot holding court with some friends, he may even have been Kenny Logan's fan from earlier in the day at the Stadio Flaminio. He was regaling his pals with a joke, a rather irreverent joke about the Apostolic Palace and the Pope. Apparently the Pope was having a birthday and he was taken to see his birthday present. It was unveiled to the Pope's cry of "Oh no, no another ceiling!"

*Alex Dunbar meets his old friend and Hawick rugby
foe, Bill McLaren and his wife Bette*

Alex organises his "Squadron" at Heriot's clubhouse

Our Sarah and Jilly McCord representing Edinburgh University's Women's XV in the final of the British Universities Rugby Cup Final played at Twickenham 1997

Mike Levack then of Mansell Construction, meets Bill McLaren at Goldenacre

CHAPTER 20

In Which Touchline is Born, Championship Win and Civic Reception

Although by this time in the history of Heriot's Rugby Club much was being made of modern technology, club websites, emailing members and so on, many of the non-playing members at Heriot's were from an age that had no experience of a home computer. Browsing websites and communicating by email were actions completely foreign to them. I decided that it was time the club had a regular newsletter in order to keep everyone up to date with what was happening. I started a newsy publication called "Touchline."

The job of stuffing hundreds of Touchline newsletters in envelopes on my own was a bit monotonous, so I wrote to all the members of the club over the age of sixty and asked them if they would like to come down to Goldenacre to help me. I got a tremendous response and roughly every quarter my squad of stuffers did a great job for me whilst blethering with their old school chums over a cup of coffee and a biscuit. I realised that these guys were mostly retired and some had lost their wives, so they loved to get out of the house and do something useful for the Club.

Talking about these fellows: during one of our stuffing days I happened to make a remark to some of the gang round my table about my father being in the RAF during the war. This pricked the ears of a member called Alex Dunbar. Alex was Heriot's captain in the seasons 1949/50 and 50/51. In 1949, Alex led the Heriot's seven to victory at the famous Twickenham sevens. To the delight of every Herioter Alex Dunbar's talented seven were the first side to take the Kinross Arbour trophy to Scotland.

Alex sought me out after our next home game. We got chatting about his wartime experiences and those of my father's that I knew about. I discovered in that wee chat that there were a number of RAF World War Two veterans in the club and suggested to Alex that they should get together in a slightly more organised but informal way and have a wee club within the club. Alex got cracking on that. On home game days the wartime flyers could be seen swapping books, cuttings and yarns. I like to think these wee gatherings were helpful to these blokes in ways that those of us who had never been in a war could never understand. I know from the look on his face that Alex got a lot of pleasure from those gatherings. Sadly Alex has now gone as have, I think, most if not all of his wartime Heriot RAF colleagues.

Alex or Dunners, as many of his contemporaries knew him, loved to go to away games with the 1ST XV. Even though there was a huge age gap between him and the players the lads loved to have him on the coach with them. The feeling was mutual, I can tell you, because Alex never lost the knack of having fun!!

In the early days of my time as secretary my youngest daughter, Sarah, along with some of her university friends, helped man our bars. They were adopted as a group by the lads and given the name

272

the Goldie Barmaids by the players. They occasionally interviewed players, coaches and managers for a column in Touchline. This was a sort of light-hearted way of informing the Touchline readers what was in the minds of the interviewees so far as the interests of the club was concerned, but often more personal matters were touched upon - nothing risqué. Older members were amazed at some of the content but they seemed to enjoy it nonetheless.

Rugby writers from The Scotsman newspaper often contributed to Touchline. They had a free hand as to what they wrote about but latterly their views on what was going on at Murrayfield were quite an insight. This was part of a sponsorship deal that Paul McDevitt and I struck with that paper in connection with the Mansell Cup. Such contributions gave a professional feel to the publication.

Many readers will know that Heriot's FP Rugby Club members are known unofficially as the "Nails". When the Club won the Championship in 98/99 a lot of merchandise was produced for sale. Included in the collection of jerseys and so on was a tie which had a repeat of a joiners nail throughout the cloth. This tie, though produced tongue in cheek, unintentionally offended a few of the older members of the club. They protested that the description Nails was usually meant as an insult to the Club and actually referred to toe nails not the nails as depicted in the tie; not that they wanted a tie covered with images of toe nails.

A lot of rot was talked about the Nails I was told, at the time of this tie business, by the late David Edwards, an Honorary President and former International cap, Captain and President of the club. Much claim had been given to two theories as to why we were called Nails. One is that a toenail is the lowest one can get i.e. it is in close proximity to the ground, and the other popular one is that a toenail is the last thing you see of a person as he disappears up the backside of another person!

'Both were completely wrong!' David insisted and went on,

'The reason we are called Nails is because a fellow in the FP 1st XV back in the fifties used to cut his toenails in the team dressing room!' He gave me the blokes name at the time but I have forgotten it now.

Often I find, and you probably do too, that the real explanation for something is nowhere nearly as romantic as the popular legend. Given some of the feet that I saw in many a dressing room I can't think of anything more unromantic than a pile of toenail clippings.

I never printed David's story in Touchline because it was around the time of the 98/99 championship win and I figured it would be like telling a kid that there is no Santa Claus. The young lads liked the myth and they especially liked other clubs' members calling them Nails. Dougie Lee, a close friend of mine in the Club, said that these nail callers were just jealous and he quoted from someone, I can't remember who, 'Detestation of the high is the voluntary homage of the low.' Absolutely spot on. On that theme, I remember the manager of one our caterers telling me a story about the Stewarts Melville Rugby Club who were based a mile or so west from us. I had been explaining to him the great rivalries between all the Edinburgh rugby clubs and he told me with a look of realisation on his beaming face that the Stew Mels regularly sang about the Nails in a not very complimentary way. I have to say I was delighted to get that piece of news as it only bolstered the Heriot ego in me!!

George Heriot's School Headmaster, Alistair Hector, took a great interest in what we were up to at the FP Rugby Club, and I have no doubt that he and the Head of the junior school, Stewart Adams, were very pleased when their FP Rugby Club were Scottish champions or Cup winners . I like to think that I got on pretty well with both Alistair and Stewart. They did everything possible to help me and the club wherever they could and I thank them for that. Whilst

I enjoyed a really good and productive relationship with Alastair and Stewart I also had a similar experience with Mike Gilbert the Chairman of the School Governors, and indeed all the other governors that I came into contact with. Mike Gilbert was a great support. I had no fear of approaching him about any concerns that I had in connection with the School and the FP Rugby Club. Every quarter the Rugby Club President, Vice President and I met with the School Headmaster, the Chairman of the School Governors, another governor, usually Jimmy Fiddes, one of a long line of dedicated Herioters and the Head of the PT staff, Douglas West. This to my delight was usually held in the Council Chambers in the old school building. What a magnificent room and such a wonderful piece of Heriot and indeed Scottish history. Now over three–hundred and fifty years old that room is still in working order. Our eldest daughter Kirsten was married to John Rogers in the School Chapel by the School Chaplain, Ailsa McLean. After the ceremony Ailsa invited the main wedding party to join her in the Council room to sign all the legal documents. Very grand.

The season ended in the usual way with the club dinner. Strangely the date of that function coincided with our last game of the season which was an away fixture. Our opponents were Stirling County. We needed only a bonus point to clinch the Championship title and that was accomplished reasonably early on in the game. Sadly I didn't get over to Stirling as I had to stay behind in the club house to help our caterer set up the room. However, I was so confident that Jocky and his team would win I had ordered up a huge banner to hang up above the bar which declared we were:"Heriot's, Scottish Champions 1998/99."

To cap everything for me in this amazing debut year of mine, the Club was invited by the Lord Provost of Edinburgh, the Rt Honourable Eric Milligan, to a civic reception in the City

Chambers for a celebration of our 98/99 Premiership Division One Championship.

To be honest I thought it amazing that a Labour Lord Provost of Edinburgh could even contemplate inviting a club to the City Chambers that had former pupil connections with a fee paying school. Especially a provost who is the son of a Labour ex-Edinburgh Regional councillor, Duncan Milligan. He, along with George Foulkes (now Lord Foulkes) and others in the mid-seventies, tried, unsuccessfully, to shut down Heriot's, as it was known and loved, and integrate it into the State system.

On the evening of the reception Provost Milligan was extremely gracious and complimentary to Heriot's Rugby Club. He was clearly delighted that it was Edinburgh clubs that had won the two major Scottish trophies. Boroughmuir, Lord Provost Milligan's own team, were also present that evening as they had won the Scottish Cup that season.

A very proud Heriot's Rugby Club President, Graham Fraser, replied to the Provost's kind remarks and thanked him for the beautiful commemorative crystal bowl that he presented to us on behalf of the City Council. Heriot's attended the City Chambers twice more as a guest of Mr Milligan and on another occasion the Heriots Rugby Club Committee were entertained at Boroughmuir Rugby Club by the Provost. It seems by that time the bridges between Heriot's, the Milligan family and the Labour Party in the Local Authority had been well and truly re-built and in the nicest possible way. Rugby has a habit of mending bridges and doing other good deeds.

The 1999 AGM of the Club was all part of the feel good factor at Goldenacre. The Club Treasurer, Dougie Hill, also a school governor, reported that gate receipts were up 100% on the season before and that fifteen-hundred more paying customers came to watch Heriot's. We had played a very attractive style of rugby and that no doubt brought neutrals along and returning members who had hitherto been absent. Dougie was delighted to be presenting such a bright picture to the members. This treasurer was himself a treasure. At the time of this AGM he had been in the job for over thirty years. He was to Heriot's administration as, say, Kenny Scotland was to playing full back for Scotland and that, all those Herioters who have had the privilege of knowing Dougie will agree, is no exaggeration. His wife, Lillian, has been a great support to Dougie through the years and therefore to the Club, too.

CHAPTER 21

Lord MacKay and the SRU; Grumpy Ground
Staff and Irritating Interruptions

Around January 1999 the structure of the SRU had been reviewed by Lord Mackay, an eminent FP of George Heriot's School. President Graham Fraser asked me to arrange a discussion on the subject in the club house and he would chair it. Amongst a host of other things, Lord Mackay suggested that there should be two super teams and the old special representatives made up from the districts should be abandoned. The latter effectively did away with the queue of committee men waiting their turn to be the president of the SRU. The face of Scottish rugby was to change fundamentally thanks to this report but many more radical changes were to follow in the next two or three years.

Finding myself geographically at the hub of most things sporting so far as Heriot's was concerned, major and minor matters, extraordinary or routine there was always something that held my interest.

Generations of Herioters who found themselves, for whatever reason, at Goldenacre often remarked how irascible the ground staff seem to be. I discovered why the demeanour of the guardians of Heriot's playing fields was, to put it bluntly, a bit off colour, that is until you got to know and understand them. Being based alongside them I was able to see what made them so liverish and indeed I empathise with them. I am sure they won't really mind me describing them so, especially as I can clear up for them their side of the story.

Quite a great deal of difficulty is caused for the ground staff through being, as it were, miles from anywhere whilst performing some of their duties, and, unlike the teaching staff, they don't have a fully staffed reception office or janitors to direct and otherwise deal with visitors. Often they would find themselves attending to, say, the 1st X1 cricket square right at the far eastern side of the grounds when, for example, an unscheduled lorry driver on foot, after a very long trek, would approach them to ask if they could please go to the main stand door at the furthest western extremity and open it because he had a load of whatever for whomsoever. This entailed a downing of tools and a foot traipse of about a mile round just to open a door.

Not long after I took up my job at Goldenacre and the club phone number was inserted in the BT Directory above that of the groundsman's number I began to get first-hand experience of this type of interruption. Monday mornings were taken up with phone calls from people who had left something after a Saturday match in the club or perhaps in the stand, or the stand toilets or the pitch. Both sexes were equally capable of this forgetfulness.

RRRRRRiiiiinnnng.

'Heriot's Rugby Club, Douglas Bruce speaking.'

'Oh hello, I am Mr/Mrs Pain in the neck. I am the first of about ten similarly irritating calls that you will get in the next few hours. I was at Goldenacre on Saturday morning/ afternoon and I left my coat/ jacket, umbrella, kit, keys, dog, son, daughter. Have you seen it/them/ him, him or her?'

You can imagine my frustration when, after a fruitless scouring of the large building for ten or fifteen minutes per call, hunting for whatever, my return call is received with an absent minded:

'Oh, yes sorry, eh thanks for calling me back. I no sooner put the phone down when I remembered I was at Inverleith(a ground near Goldenacre) on Saturday watching Stewarts Melville 2nds. being beaten by Heriot's 3rds. I knew Heriot's were involved somehow !'

You can perhaps now begin to see my point about grumpy ground staff.

One evening at about 6.30 pm I got a call from a Mrs Terribly Worried Mummy. I happened to be in the club at that time. I was busy organising the place for a very important meeting which the President of the Edinburgh District Union was chairing. I had by then assimilated into my very soul, a very strong sense of the boundaries that should be kept when asking for help from ground staff, especially when it was well after the end of their working day.

Mummy wanted to know if her twelve year old son had left his homework books somewhere, possibly at Goldenacre, after he had played rugby. I explained:

'I am really awfully sorry but I am unable to help with that sort of thing because you have called the FP Rugby Club, not the School. If you are sure the missing homework is at Goldenacre could you possibly come down to Goldenacre tomorrow morning and speak to the School's ground staff then?'

Not very deep down I knew that was not the answer Mrs Terribly Worried Mummy was hoping for. I also knew that the ground staff would have scoured the dressing rooms for property that had been left. Anything found would have been locked up in the "bothy" as the lads called their office. I had no access to that hallowed place.

'Oh dear,' sighed Mrs Terribly Worried Mummy 'How is my Rupert going to get his homework done?'

'Well I am really so sorry, I can't help you. I have no means of gaining access to the school lost property office and the ground staff have gone home for the day!'

I knew this outcome was not satisfactory but I thought that Mrs TWM at last appreciated the position as it stood at that time. The conversation ended just as the meeting was about to start and the dignitaries were assembling at the top table.

The meeting was well under way when I spotted through the glass doors a woman with a worried look about her. Oh Good Lord, it was Mrs Terribly Worried Mummy. She was dithering around outside the meeting room. Before I could do anything about it she was in. Mrs TWM approached the VIP's table with a Kamikaze look now added to her already worried face.

'Please help me locate my son's homework books NOW?'

George Jack, the District President and all the others at the top table including Todd Blackadder, the one-time All Black Captain and then Edinburgh Captain, were flabbergasted. I, by this time, had made it to the table and politely explained to Mrs TWM, sotto voce, that nothing had changed since I spoke to her earlier and, whilst I admired her concern for wee Rupert, and, as much as I would have liked to help her, there was nothing I, or indeed anybody, could do to help her until the next day when the ground staff were around. She went away eventually and said she would be back the next day. She came, but there was no sign of the books!! I wonder how young Rupert got on in life without his mummy. I was going to suggest to Mrs TWM that Rupert use the time honoured, tried and tested excuse: the dog ate my homework Miss, honest. I thought better of it, teachers are much wiser nowadays.

One summer Friday afternoon, the ground staff's half day, I watched a man drive a pickup truck into Goldenacre from that most easterly gate near the cricket square and then head for the 1st XV pitch (which was laid out as the first bend of an athletic track). He stopped at the Warriston Gardens end of the pitch and, in the shadow of the south stand, proceeded to unload an enormous pile of what I thought at first was coloured plastic tarpaulins. He then spread the tarpaulins out and started up a small petrol generator. A long pipe was attached between the tarpaulins and the generator and after a few minutes, lo and behold, a huge bouncy castle manifested itself. The wee man then started to unload all sorts of other kiddie inflatables and was about to start to blow them up when I thought I would have to abandon my desk, go down and ask him what it was all about. He was just about to inflate some other rubbery thing when I got closer to him and asked him what he was doing with the castle and whatever else he was about to assemble.

'It's for your fete tomorrow pal!' he said with great authority and that wonderful Edinburgh familiarity.

'What fete?' I enquired.

'Your Stewarts Melville School fete pal. I was told to blow the stuff up, anchor it and leave it at the sooth end of your stand, ken!'

'Well this is actually Heriot's School playing fields, Stew Mel is about a mile and a half further up the Ferry Road,' I explained, trying hard not to laugh.

'For F...s sake, what a f...ing waste of fu....g time.'

Pallopp

Z z z z z z z z z z z z z z z z z z z z z z z z s h h h h h h h h h h h h ssssshshshshhhhhhhhhhshhhzzzzzzzzzzzz. He pulled out the huge stopper and the castle started to wilt.

The man returned the writhing and still deflating castle to his pick up and made off for Stewarts Melville's grounds still cursing very loudly.

My most alarming time at Goldenacre was the Friday night before my last Mansell Cup. Glancing out the window that looked onto the 1st XV pitch and beyond I saw about two hundred metres away a gigantic sort of Chinese Dragon worming its way above and across some of the junior pitches. I had to do a double take before I realised that the dragon was the lengthy beer tent which had been pitched for the next day's tournament. I ran out of the club and raced across the 1st XV pitch just in time to grab the tail end of the "dragon" before it gained any more height. The rising tent dragged me face down along the ground and we were about to wreak terror and destruction on the citizens of Warriston when Big Ken, an assistant groundsman, came on the scene. Between us we managed to decelerate the tent's south easterly progress. Suddenly the breeze dropped, the tent stalled and came quickly to ground. We tore the canvas off the tent's steel frame before the whole thing decided to take off again.

Such a lot can happen in a working day at Goldenacre and the dynamics of the goings on in a twenty-four acre workplace can be staggering. Simon Theurer, our head groundsman, and I often swapped our latest Goldenacre stories. My favourite Simon tale involved a one-time Scottish National team coach, Matt Williams, who had phoned to request the use of Goldenacre for some training.

'No problem, come on down right away and I will show you around,' Simon said.

While Simon waited he thought that he would shoot some of the pigeons roosting in the Grandstand. Just as Matt drew up in his car Simon fired a shot from his air rifle, missing his target but hitting the metal roof of the stand with a very loud bang. Next, Simon saw a fleeing car burning rubber. His mobile phone rang. It was Matt,

'Simon do you know there is a madman with a gun in your grandstand shooting at us?'

'No that was just me,' our gun slinging groundsman replied, 'but I happen to be a crap shot.'

Simon forgot to add that he was only shooting at pigeons not Scotland rugby coaches. Needless to say Goldenacre never saw Matt again!

CHAPTER 22

World Cup 1999; Springboks, Samoa and That Man Bill McLaren

Although Wales hosted the Rugby World Cup in 1999, many of the games were played throughout the UK and France. The South Africans and the Samoans trained at Goldenacre prior to their games at Murrayfield. This was another facet of my job that I loved. The World champions training right on my doorstep, could life be any better? I was able to share all this fun with my friends Graham Fraser, the Club President and Dougie Lee. These guys were the liaison officers for the South Africans and the Samoans respectively and so I had a lot of contact with them, especially in the early stages of the Cup. Additionally, Ken Hutchison, a past club president and Mike O'Reilly, a past club secretary, were involved as the Scottish Regional RWC Manager and the Scottish team liaison officer respectively. So Heriot's Rugby Club was at the hub of the RWC!

About six months before the World Cup took place and during the off season, a Springbok's manager Arthrob Peterson came over to the UK to check out the various training venues that had been allocated to the Boks. Arthrob met up with me and Simon Theurer, head groundsman. Arthrob was suitably impressed with the magnificent playing fields, especially Simon's beautifully green grass but he was not happy with the club scrumming machine. Mr. Peterson spoke to the SRU and arrangements were made for an alternative and, presumably, better foil for the Bok forwards. By the looks on the faces of the Bok coaches, it was clear that even the SRU machine was not good enough when the South Africans got to Goldenacre in early October 1999. Rugby Union fans have a fair idea how important the game is to the South Africans, especially the white South Africans; a fact that Nelson Mandela recognised so crucially at the time of the RWC in 1995. I learned just how important the game of rugby is to them when their coach, Nick Mallet, decided to have their own scrumming machine flown over immediately to Edinburgh and then delivered to Goldenacre on a huge truck and trailer. The Bok's machine was called the "Green Mamba" it was massive. In fact it was so ridiculously big it had to be lifted off the trailer by a crane, then up and over the trees at the south east perimeter of Goldenacre and gently laid down on to the playing fields. There it stayed until the Boks left Scotland after their group match against Spain.

They sent the Green Mamba on to Richmond in Surrey to await their triumphant return from Paris where they beat England in a quarter final match. The amazing Mamba, I believe, is still in England, the property of some South West coast club who bought it from the South African Rugby Union. I guess the cost of taking that beast of a machine back to South Africa was prohibitive. I wonder if the new owners can shove the thing?

The Boks just seemed to get everything that they asked for, and not only from their own Union, but also from the SRU and Heriot's. The very first day that the Boks were to train at Goldenacre,

Nick Mallet didn't like the pitch that had been allocated for the International sides that were to use the Heriot's facilities - he preferred the 1st XV pitch. It was, of course, bigger and I wonder if he felt that it had more of a big stadium feel about it. Anyway he asked me if he could switch and I explained that it wasn't up to me and we should go and ask Simon Theurer. As usual Simon was very helpful and agreed to the change of plans.

Well, all of that was fine so far as the Boks were concerned, but, it wasn't okay for the agents acting for the many and varied RWC sponsors, Guinness being the major player in that connection. A representative of the RWC advertising agents called me up and expressed his concern about the ramifications that were bound to follow on from the training area switch. He said he would arrange to move the boards. He never did- at least not until the RWC was over and I never heard from him again. I guessed that there was no contingency budget for this upheaval.

Funnily enough, according to an independent study of the 1999 IRB Rugby World Cup conducted by Performance Research Europe, Guinness managed to take advantage of their official sponsorship position with more than half of the fans polled reporting Guinness to be involved with the RWC 1999, whereas Coca-Cola and BT had a poll response of only 26% and 21% respectively. The research showed that so far as most of the other sponsors were concerned there had been an over reliance on stadium signage!! Well, as it turned out, the public training sessions at Goldenacre didn't give the sponsors a signage advantage at all. I have a feeling that it's really much more simple than that. In any given year, never mind a RWC year, the average Rugby player and fan drinks quite a lot of Guinness and probably proportionately very little of any kind of fizzy soft drink ; furthermore, BT, so far as I know, don't make anything at all to drink!

When the Boks were training at Goldenacre, as with all the teams, they were obliged to give the press the opportunity to see them in action. Officially the journalists and photographers were allowed only about thirty minutes then they had to leave, but Nick Mallet was a wee bitty flexible on that point. However, when it was time to go Mallet left it to his PR man to ask the media to leave. During one of the sessions, and just after the public and the press had departed, I took a wander round the perimeter of the pitch. I was actually going to change the next home game sign for the club but thought that I would take the signage the long way round and have a chat with my nephew, Andy McGee. Andy, a Germany under-18 cap, was temporarily employed as an assistant to the ground staff whilst playing rugby for the Club . He was sitting eating his sandwiches on a touchline bench whilst chatting to Os du Randt, the famous Springbok prop. Andy was, like me, in his element being so close to the World Champions. I joined in on the chat with the huge Bok who was nursing a minor injury but who expected to be okay for the next game. He wasn't however for an extended conversation and went back to pawing the ground with his huge feet like some massive prize bull. I bade him and Andy farewell and went about my business. Suddenly I was set upon by the Bok's jobsworth PR man who abruptly and fairly disagreeably demanded my exit as the public session was over. Conscious as ever of the Heriot Motto "I Distribute Cheerfully" I smiled and introduced myself to him as Heriot's Rugby Club manager and welcomed him and the Springboks as guests of George Heriot's School and my Club. I told him that I was, in fact, carrying out some of my normal duties and not spying on his team. As I was apprising him of my, up until then, pleasure at watching the World Champions train on my Club's pitch, I caught Nick Mallet's eye. Turning away from the rude little PR man I wished Mr. Mallet a good afternoon - a greeting that he reciprocated - but before I could get into my stride His Prissiness interrupted and told Mallet that he thought that there was a couple of guys standing back from a window in the upstairs part of the clubhouse and spying on the Boks. Mallet sighed and said that he had noticed them going into the building a half hour or so earlier.

'Oooooooh oh oh did you!' said the PR man, slight pause 'I'll go up there and ask them to leave immediately.'

To my relief Mallet replied disdainfully,

'No, no just leave them alone, I am not bothered. They must think we are stupid. This goes on everywhere we train.'

I was relieved because I had let these "spies" in to the Club. Without warning, they just turned up at my office during the public session. They told me they were from the SRU and hoped it would be okay if they could observe the Boks from the President's room during the open session. They had binoculars and a notebook each. I recognised the fellows anyway and so was not worried that our trophy cabinet would be robbed or that our bar would be broken into.

I wished Nick Mallet all the best and carried on about my business. When I got back into the clubhouse I entered the Presidents' room without knocking and one of the spooks got a fright and threw away his notebook as if it had suddenly turned into a snake. I told the guys that they had been spotted by Nick Mallet but he didn't seem to be too bothered. They carried on as they were but in a much more relaxed fashion.

I have watched numerous International teams practice at Goldenacre including the All Blacks, the Springboks and the Wallabies and not once did I see any of them do anything that seemed all that special or top secret to me.

One very remarkable Springbok memory from another time was when I met a very famous Bok during the Mansell Cup at Goldenacre in the late summer of 2001. Francois Pienaar was Captain of the 1995 Rugby World Cup Champions and a book has been written and a film made of that amazing time in South Africa. Pienaar was coach of London Saracens who played Edinburgh in a pre-season warm up game during the Mansell Cup.

During the weeks running up to the 1999 RWC I got a call from a Heriot's Rugby Club sponsor who sold expensive, fast cars. Although his company supported the Club he didn't know all that much about the game and asked me if a particular Scottish player was "any good?" I told our sponsor that the famous player was excellent and had awards for being so. That was all I told the fellow but I asked:

'Why do you want to know ?'

'Oh his agent has been on the phone and has asked me if I would be prepared to lend his client one of our very special, top of the range cars for the duration of the World Cup in Scotland.' The sponsor told the agent that he would consider it and get back to him.

I was obviously part of the consideration.

The sponsor thanked me for the information and I left it at that. Later in the season the fast car man was at Goldenacre having lunch and I asked him if he lent the player the super-duper car.

'Oh no, we wouldn't even sell a car like that to a guy as young as that!!!"

Age before fame and fortune, I guess.

After the Springboks left Goldenacre it was the turn of Samoa to train at Heriot's. They got on to the main pitch too and after the public session was over, Brian Williams, the Samoan coach and one time All Black winger, did not display any of the flexibility that Nick Mallet granted to the Press: he ruthlessly ejected them. Bill McLaren was not even watching the session but was trying to make sure his pronunciations of the Samoan players would be precise. He was merely checking the names with a member of the Samoan coaching party. Brian Williams went over to Bill and demanded that he left Goldenacre immediately. I was a bit surprised at the treatment Bill got from Williams and I ran after the famous broadcaster to offer some sort of sympathy. Bill explained that he wasn't interested in the secrets of Samoan rugby but simply wanted to do justice to their players when he would be naming them in his BBC radio commentary a couple of days later. I suggested to Bill that he come up to my office, have a cup of coffee whilst watching the Samoans from the window. It wouldn't really have solved Bill's problem but he thanked me very kindly for the offer and explained that he couldn't take advantage of such a grandstand seat as it wouldn't be fair to all the other journalists who had long since left the premises - typical of the man, full of integrity and a kindly manner.

CHAPTER 23

More from My Office Window;
Touchline and the Back Office

It was not always International teams that I had the pleasure of watching from my office window; sometimes the likes of Gordon Ross would come down to Goldenacre for goal kicking practice when he was playing for Heriot's 1st XV and, later, when he was playing for the Edinburgh pro side. Most afternoons Gordon would spend ages kicking accurately ball after ball from different angles and distances. As a warm up to his session he would lay aside a corner flag, place the ball where the flag was and aim his kick at the upright whilst allowing for a slight draw. He rarely missed. As Gary Player, the great South African golfer, once reacted to a suggestion that luck played a big part in his golfing success he said, 'Yes, that's true, the more I practice the luckier I get.' Gordon Ross was a key player in the Heriot's championship sides of 98/99 and 99/2000. His kicking was priceless not only for Heriot's but also for Scotland. It is such a pity that Gordon had so few caps for his country. He deserved many more.

The Friday afternoon before a Scotland /Ireland International match David Humphreys and Peter Stringer of Ireland came to Goldenacre to do a bit of goal kicking practice. Simon, the grounds-man told me to look out for them. They arrived with their kicking coach who was carrying a couple of old fashioned forces kit bags stuffed full of rugby balls. The two Irishmen kicked ball after ball at the goals and, worryingly from a Scottish point of view, they never missed. When it looked like they were packing up I ran down stairs with a spare match ball and asked the guys if they would kindly autograph it. They did with great pleasure. I asked them if they would like to wait for their car in my office. Peter Stringer said,

'What car, sure its ok we will take the bus.'

Off they went and right enough they stood at the nearby bus stop to wait for a Lothian bus to come along. I was astonished that, in the age of professionalism, there was no chauffeur-driven limo waiting for them.

Whilst all the general excitement of the RWC was going on and especially the action at Goldenacre with the Springboks and the Samoans, my job managing Heriot's continued. We, as a club, still had a season to complete and a Premier One League Cup to retain.

In the spring of 2000 Scotland played against Italy in Rome as previously mentioned. Scotland lost spectacularly. However, on the bright side for me and my fellow Herioter's, Bruce Douglas and Simon Taylor were selected at U21 level for their match against Italy U 21s, which they won. Also, in that season Gordon Ross and Graham Dall made it to the Scotland A squad. Graham Dall, like Gordon Ross, was playing full time for The Edinburgh Reivers. A few of our players joined Graham Dall in the odd game for the Reivers. All in all Heriot's were doing their bit for Scottish rugby and it was a great feeling to be part of this success, albeit from the back office!

Talking about back office: "Scottish Rugby" magazine had a regular feature called BT Club Watch. Each month Club Watch focused on a couple of club matches. The January edition featured Heriot's v Glasgow Hawks in the Premier One division and Watsonians v Kelso in the Premier Two division. To say that I was pleased with what was said about Heriot's would be an understatement.

"Having developed a professional looking backroom team and approach to the senior team, Heriot's are creating a desire to remain at the top of Scottish Rugby!"

Heriot's 1st XV played eighteen league games in season 99/2000 and won fifteen of them. The title was ours again and we were off to the City Chambers for another civic reception. Although he had put in a development programme for existing players, Fraser Dall, our director of rugby, was already working on the recruitment of new players. He was casting his net as far and as wide as possible. Players were to join us from New Zealand, Canada, and England as well as from much nearer home. As a club we were determined to maintain our membership of top flight Scottish club rugby. Building on our success in 1998/99, including making a promotional video produced by a marketing company called "Marketing Advantage" with whom we made a reciprocal sponsorship deal, we marketed ourselves as a club that was a gateway to professional contracts for promising young players. The video was widely distributed and had a positive effect regarding both the recruitment of players and of sponsors. John Beattie, the BBC broadcaster, Scottish Internationalist and one time no 8 for Heriot's, agreed to take a part in the video and this added a bit of muscle to the production. Warners, our main sponsors, also appeared in the production telling viewers how helpful their connection with Heriot's had been. Like Mansell, Warners felt that supporting a big successful Edinburgh rugby club would and did raise their profile in the city.

It was a very busy summer therefore for both the playing side of the club and the administrative areas. The Mansell Cup took up a great deal of my time off season and I met regularly with Paul McDevitt of Mansell to keep him up to date with my progress. Paul did a great deal of work himself on the Cup. Conscious the whole time that the tournament was another vehicle for promoting Mansell, Paul never missed a trick. Both Paul, and his boss Mike Levack, were unhappy with the press coverage of the first tournament and blamed the fact that the tournament was called The Edinburgh Cup. Their company, then Hall and Tawse, was barely mentioned. Paul asked me if we could change the name to The Hall and Tawse Cup. I was only too pleased to help and with the support of the Club Committee the profile of the tournament took another turn towards mutually beneficial commercialism. The name was further changed to The Mansell Cup when Hall and Tawse were taken over by Mansell. Paul spent time with the marketing people at The Scotsman to make sure we got as much publicity as possible. We had photo-shoots before every tournament that would be of interest to the average rugby fan as well as the ordinary person in the street. These photo-shoots included pictures of Edinburgh pro players, and on one occasion, we persuaded players' representatives from the clubs participating in the tournament to come up to Heriot's School lawns and terracing dressed in their rugby kit.

Some also wore gladiator outfits and sported spears (the trademark of Mansell). Lord Provost, Eric Milligan came along and the press took a picture of him with the Cup, surrounded by the players. Shrewd thinking by the Mansell marketing man. The newspapers were now compelled to call the competition "The Mansell Cup."

The club prepared for the coming 2000/2001 season as early in the summer as was decent. Things at Goldenacre were really on a high at the time of the new millennium. It was such a great feeling to be involved in success. How long would it last?

Heriot's receiving the 1999/2000 Premier 1 Championship Trophy at Myreside

The team that won pictured capering before the official photographer arrived
Standing Left to Right:
A Binnie, B Douglas, T McVie, S Taylor, D Boswell, A Dall,
C Capaldi, G Lawson, A McLean, D Proctor
Seated Left to Right:
S Walker, D Short, I Stent, G Lawrie, J Bryce (Captain),
G Ross, C Keenan, H Gilmour, D Fowler

VIPs who are sadly no longer with us at a Civic Reception at the Edinburgh City Chambers for the 1999/2000 Scottish Champions. Left to Right:
Lindsay Stewart, Hon Vice President Heriot's Rugby Club, Bill Hogg, Secretary Scottish Rugby Union, Graham Fraser, President Heriot's Rugby Club

CHAPTER 24

Kenny Scotland and Pies; The Job Just Gets Bigger; How Mean Can Supporters Get

The New Millennium saw Heriot's Rugby Club with a new President, Kenny Scotland. One of the greatest Scottish rugby players of all time was now my boss. I was really thrilled to be in this position, actually working with THEEE Kenny Scotland, my boyhood hero. Additionally the likes of coaching legend, Jim Telfer, would occasionally enter into my working day. There were endless meetings with the brass at HQ and Jim was often there, usually promoting the pro game and in that connection Ian McGeechan was never very far away. In the number of meetings I attended when Telfer was there and which had the future of Scottish club rugby on the agenda, I always had the feeling that he never quite grasped the mood of the amateur clubs. To use the American phrase, he just didn't get it. It's either that or he couldn't allow the feelings of the clubs to cloud his determined pro rugby vision.

Top players from clubs all over Scotland who I looked up to in my early FP days were now popping up here and there as committee men or coaches of their clubs. I found the Borders clubs' committee rooms full of ex-players some of whom had been capped, for example: Alastair Cranston of Hawick, Roy Laidlaw of Jedforest, John Jeffrey of Kelso and Finlay Calder Stew Mel, but at that time Finlay was coach of Gala. I found that the Borders' committee rooms were the most atmospheric after a game, the home committee always being very fair in their comments about the players and the way in which the match was played. I think because all of the Border clubs had such history and traditions, the game of rugby itself was much bigger than whether their beloved teams won on the day.

My job just got bigger and bigger. I took on a part-time assistant, Moira, a mum and a single parent of two Heriot kids. Moira being a Heriot mum understood a great deal about the ethos of the Club and was a great help to me. She took away a lot of the routine day to day, time consuming jobs which were nevertheless very important to the success of our department. This left me to get on with looking after the existing sponsors, procuring new ones and also doing my best to fill up the programme and the pitch perimeter with advertisements. Corporate entertainment was vital and I tried to fill as many tables as possible at home games. We had two excellent caterers in my time at Goldenacre and I reckon that as a club, we did a really good professional job in terms of hosting and the provision of first class meals. My first president, Graham Fraser, asked me early on in my appointment if it would be possible to serve up something to our visiting committees that was a bit more appetising and professional looking than greasy pies and sausage rolls. I said I would look into it and asked the first catering company that I had hired what they could do that would not break the bank. I was amazed when, at the first chance they got to impress me and the committee, they brought out huge platters of grilled prawns, chicken livers, all sorts of delicious canapés, the tastiest little pork pies and many other delicacies not to be seen in any other rugby club committee room.

We enjoyed this gourmet spread at a very reasonable cost throughout the two years of Graham's presidency. When Kenny Scotland took over he asked me if I thought that our committee room "snacks" were not a bit too ostentatious. Would we not be better just offering pies and sausage rolls? Kenny, because of his previous experiences of caterers in a former business life, had an excellent understanding of how this form of catering worked. The majority of the cost was having staff in the club in the first place. They were there not only to provide our committee with the traditional après hospitality but also to cook and serve the lunches on offer to members and their guests plus, of course, all the meals for the players after their games. But still, given all of that, Kenny wondered if I could see what could be done. I spoke to the catering manager, a nice helpful lad who said he would look into the matter but explained that sometimes some of the more exotic titbits were from other outside catering functions that had been cancelled and which we were either not charged for or were sold at discounted prices. I explained that our president was really concerned not only with the cost but the over the top look of our "snacks". He said that he understood and had got the picture okay.

Whilst entertaining the very next visiting committee I spotted that the first trays to come from the kitchen contained scotch eggs. Kenny looking at the tray from a distance congratulated me upon arranging a more down to earth offering and turned away before any more food came out. I dashed over to thank the catering Manager and he said into his cupped hands,

'Don't thank me yet, at least not until you've had a wee taste!'

I took a plate over to the buffet table and lifted up a couple of scotch eggs; I took two because they were quite small eggs. I bit into an egg and realised that they were not your usual battery, caged hens' eggs; the caterers had given us a batch of scotch eggs the main ingredient of which had been produced by dainty little quail!

Kenny seemed to drop the idea of committee snack change after that and the committee room guests continued to enjoy the delicious Heriot's offering. Truly we upheld the Heriot's motto "I distribute cheerfully."

The next "Touchline" after Ken Scotland's election to the presidency of Heriot's RC included part of an article from the School end of term magazine The "Herioter" June 1960. The contributor wrote about Ken's success in the 1959 Lions tour to Australia and New Zealand. Although the Lions only won the last of the four tests in New Zealand 9-6, The tourists came close in two other victories. One of those was the first test in Christchurch. The Lions scored a goal, three tries and a penalty goal for a creditable 17 points (a try then was worth only 3 points). Don Clarke the powerful All Black full back however kicked six penalty goals for 18 points and the game. If we had played that game today the score would have been Lions 25 / New Zealand 18.

Later in Ken's presidency the School XV had a fixture with an Australian school XV. The FP committee thought it would be a good idea to invite the teams, parents and teachers of both sides and, of course, our committee to the Club for lunch after the game. The Aussie contingency arrived early and I was already there with some of the committee. I introduced myself to the Aussie parents. One dad decided to have a blether with me. It turned out that he was actually a New Zealander who had moved some years before to Australia. He was mad keen on rugby. As we stood gazing out of the window, beers in hand, the converted Kiwi suddenly stopped chatting about his past and asked,

'Is that Ken Scotland walking along the path out there?' Kenny was actually a long way off at this point but the Kiwi dad spotted him. I confirmed it was Ken and the fellow got terribly excited; it seemed he could not believe his eyes. He explained that when he was a wee boy in 1959 he was sitting in some log cabin somewhere in New Zealand with his dad listening to the test in Christchurch on the wireless. The match had apparently been very exciting and all Kiwis had been so relieved to have had the boot of Don Clarke in their weaponry.

My new found friend asked,

'Do you think I could speak to Ken ?' as if our beloved full back was a god,which of course Ken is to many at Goldenacre.

I said that it would be a pleasure for me to introduce him to Kenny. Kenny, as I have previously indicated, is a shy sort of guy normally but he got on like a house on fire as he went through that Christchurch test with this eager fan, blow by blow, tackle by tackle, try by try, penalty by penalty. It was one of those very warm occasions that rugby at Goldenacre often experienced and which gave me such a lot of pleasure.

In the early part of the new millennium season our away support at Heriot's was really very good so I started to run supporters buses for our members. This was appreciated not only by my club but also by the opposition treasurers as Heriot's helped swell their bar takings and their catering profits.

During my tenure at Goldenacre I found the attitude to monetary support that a minority of club members gave to the game in general pretty miserly. The Scottish Cup was a prime breeding ground for cheap and mean behaviour. The way the finances should have worked at Cup ties was meant to be fair to both clubs involved. Home support had to pay for entry to a Cup game just the same as away supporters. Even committee men had to stump up. Usually there was trouble over this and all sorts of smart Alecs would try it on. In my experience of home ties, some meanies would turn up well before the turnstiles were opened, sneak into the bar and lie low. Unless a home club official caught them at it quite a lot of gate money would be lost and, remember, that affected both clubs. This practice was rife at Cup games and sometimes at other types of fixtures.

Another common ploy was to sneak in with the team bus and if anybody questioned the sneaker in he/her would claim to be any one of the following :president of the opposition, bus driver, committee man, doctor, physio, bag man or mascot!!! This particular ploy was perpetrated at any type of match. Some away supporters at Cup games just couldn't understand or perhaps care about the monetary damage that they were doing to their own club never mind the home guys.

I discovered the dodges that could go on at the very first Goldenacre Cup encounter I was officiating at. The next one was going to be properly policed. Along with a number of our stewards, committee men and turnstile operators I got down to the club extra early. The opposing club obviously had a hardworking, dedicated, and ambitious committee. They encouraged travelling support that would have been the envy of Manchester United. Coach after coach arrived in very good time so we had to be very alert to catch the dodgers, who I reckoned, were not regular supporters of their club. I lost count of the number of presidents, general committee men, physios, doctors, bag men and so on that this club apparently had at its disposal. I explained to each of the chancers that any away club was entitled free entry for one physio, one bag man and two coaches. The rest, under the agreed terms of the Scottish Cup, had to pay to gain entry. I told them that I had even paid for entry and I was the full time manager of Heriot's. Some of the miscreants agreed it was a fair cop and some were pretty disagreeable about it. It was a constant puzzle to me where some so called rugby club supporters thought the money came from to keep the game alive for them to enjoy.

CHAPTER 25

The Losing Battle to Keep Membership Numbers Up; More Experiences with the Three Bears

In the December 2000 issue of Touchline I reported the successful dinner my club held in recognition of Treasurer Dougie Hill's devoted service to the Club. Dougie had served on Heriot's committee without a break for thirty-three years. His wife, Lillian's, contribution to the club by way of the huge support that she gave her husband was also recognised. Lillian often fielded some bizarre phone calls. Her favourite was a mum who called to see if the treasurer had any idea where her son was now living as the stupid boy had not bothered to advise his family of his move. I had a similar call from an Irish dad just a week or so before the end of a Christmas term. He hadn't heard from his Edinburgh University student son since the start of that term and he wondered if I had any word of his son. The young man had not moved without telling anybody but just never answered his mobile or returned any calls. The dad explained to me that he couldn't really care less because his son was only following in his footsteps but he would be grateful for a clue if only to stop his wife nagging him.

In the summer of 2000 the Club and the British Lions went on a tour to Australia. I was going to go with them but my Rosemary spotted that the date we were due to return was only a couple of days before our eldest daughter's wedding. Mrs B put it to me that not only would I not be around to help with all the organisation, I was liable to miss the wedding altogether should there be any flight delays. I had to agree with her, well come on I did, didn't I ?? So I missed out on a wonderful trip and of course the chance to see the Lions in their test matches but it was worth it as our daughter's wedding day was wonderful. That was the last tour the club embarked upon and I hae ma dooots about any other tours. They are massive projects to organise and fund over and above all the other huge commitments a club has to bear.

However, those who do go on such adventures swear that the bonding and so on that occurs is wonderful for club and team spirit. Certainly the smaller tours that I went on with Mackie to Denmark and Sweden bore that out. I won't be covering any tour events as it is law, the breaking of which is punishable by firing squad, that what goes on tour, stays on tour, unless of course you are the English National XV who have a nasty habit of getting caught on cameras capering about on boats and in night clubs; the latest being in a New Zealand Bar during RWC 2011 where they took part in a dwarf flinging competition!!! Mike Tindall the Captain at the time was additionally caught in the embrace of a young lady and I guess he had to do some explaining to Zara, his bride of only a few months, and she aint a dwarf. I wonder what his grannie and grandpa in law had to say about it all?

As the Spring of 2002 hove over the horizon the SRU were marketing, as hard as they could, that season's BT Cellnet Cup Final. It was important to have as many people attend the game at Murrayfield and so to make it as easy as possible they gave all clubs a deal that we simply could not refuse. The ticket price for a day's entertainment at Murrayfield was £10.00. However, clubs were allowed to keep all the cash for tickets sold and that was a huge incentive for committees to get selling even if their own club would not be participating in any of the final matches. We had high hopes at Goldenacre for an appearance in that season's final but it was not to be. We lost to Glasgow Hawks at Anniesland in the semi-final; what a disappointment; well there was always next year. In the Spring issue of Touchline I was able to report good news from the representative playing front: Three of our players made it to the U21 National team, one to the U19 side, nine to the Edinburgh District XV, Edinburgh under 20 side sported two Herioters, Caledonia U20, one and Caledonia U19 also had one Herioter. That impressive list included Rory Lawson, Geoff Cross and Ander Monro all of whom, at the time of writing, are competing in World Cup 2011 along with Nick Deluca who joined Heriots later. Ander Monro is, of course, a Canadian cap. By the Spring of 2002, Simon Taylor and Gordon Ross were in the full national squad, Simon had already been capped and indeed was a Lion on the 2000 Australian tour. Graham and Andy Dall were in the A Squad.

By the summer of 2002 Heriot's had supplied seven players to the pro ranks. Pro rugby was still a thorn in the side of club rugby. Heriot's did its best to co-operate with the paid ranks if only because it was really too late to do otherwise. We had lost the huge support on the terracings that we used to enjoy and I think a lot of that was due to pro rugby and the perceived demotion of the importance of the amateur game. There were all sorts of reasons and it was a matter of trying to identify them and see what could be done to halt the rot. We had tried, with some success, to improve the travelling support for important games by arranging coaches for our members so it was time to really try and address the poor home support. One particular generation seemed to have been completely lost. These were the guys who were young dads and their working wives were mums. I think that group of members were having a totally different weekend to the generation just above them and beyond i.e. "Right dear if you want to go to Goldenacre to watch the boys you will have to take wee Jason and Emily with you!" If you have ever tried to do that sort of thing you probably did it just once because it's impossible. I know!!!

I thought that having a properly run crèche at Goldenacre would perhaps help some of those poor husbands get out and watch the boys and maybe even have a beer or two. I took a straw poll of the likely beneficiaries of such an enterprise and they seemed to think it would be a good idea, one even recommended a suitable company. I interviewed a very nice young lady who was a director of the recommended child minding company and I nearly choked to death when she told me the likely costs of such a venture. It was all perfectly reasonable when she explained the health and safety and environmental health issues, the wages of her staff and the cost of insurance. That idea was binned.

By this time Warners had completed their sponsorship contract which had been worth a great deal, I believe, both to that very successful legal firm and ourselves. Mansell were now not only to be sponsors of the annual fifteen-a-side side tournament but the main backers of the Club. Their motives for backing us were similar to those of Warners; they hoped that being associated with a club like Heriot's, which was a household name in Edinburgh, would help them raise awareness of their firm amongst the Edinburgh public.

At around this time Kenny Milne and our back-to-back Championship Captain, Jocky Bryce returned to the playing side of the club. Kenny had already assumed the position of Director of Rugby but was now also to coach our development side. Jocky, having had a season coaching Hamilton RFC, was to bring what he had learned from that period plus some of his hard playing experiences to bear on Heriot's 2nd.XV. Jocky, as well as being a tough no nonsense player, has a light and very likeable side to his character. The combination of these qualities plus his loyalty to Heriot's endeared him to all members of the club.

Having such a well-known rugby star as Kenny Milne on our committee in any capacity was a big deal but to have him back in the centre of our rugby development was priceless. On the one hand Kenny would not only be part of a positive and successful decision-making process playing wise; on the other no tiddly wee job was beneath this Heriot stalwart. Kenny was however a bit of a worrier; like me, I guess, he would get himself a bit down if we lost a game, especially one that we should have won. Kenny would phone me at the club of a Monday morning after a game on Saturday and, win or lose, we would dissect the game piece by piece. If we lost it was a hard and kinda depressing conversation but if we had won then it was imaginary champagne time. In a way I was humbled on the one hand and chuffed on the other that this famous rugby star would even think that I could contribute anything worthwhile to the conversation.

After an International against Wales at Murrayfield, Rosemary and I met up with Iain Milne at the Balmoral Hotel (formerly the North British Hotel) where the teams were relaxing at the bar after the usual après match dinner. Iain got bored with the whole thing and asked us if we would like to go into town for a drink. Rosemary wanted to go to the Oxford Bar which you will no doubt know is a tiny wee pub with loads of character, and where at least two famous people regularly haunt, namely Ian Rankin, the author of the Inspector Rebus series of novels and, of course, The Bear, himself. One of Iain's International jerseys is framed and hanging on the wall of the bar. I can honestly say that being in the company of the Bear can be a fairly bumpy ride; what is coming next is a complete lottery.

The three of us left the Balmoral Hotel and stepped out onto a windy and very wet Princes Street. We just got to the corner of Edinburgh's main thoroughfare and North St Andrew Street when we were besieged by a group of Scottish rugby fans. The rain was heavy. Iain, dressed only in his dinner suit, stood out and couldn't help but draw attention to himself and also to Rosemary and me. From out of the crowds on the Princes Street pavement came a cry:

'Look everybody, there's a couple of the lads that were playing today. Let's get their autographs.'

They stopped to chat to us. Iain was used to this sort of adulation and knew how long such encounters could take; so, because of the foul weather conditions, he kept walking whilst tugging Rosemary by the hand. I was surrounded, indeed trapped, by the autograph hunters. I was chuffed to bits that they thought I was one of the Scottish team and didn't want to disappoint the fellows. Whilst explaining that I didn't have a pen, I wondered who the devil I was supposed to be? The guys all started to rake their pockets whilst their girlfriends were rummaging in their handbags. Thank God, none of us had a pen, or anything to write on for that matter. I was looking up for some bear-like help but he and Rosemary were well away. I could hear the Bear in the distance, howling with laughter.

Mercifully, one of my fan club announced with an air of resignation:

'Oh well, never mind maybe the next time. Sorry the team lost today but you had a great game!'

I caught up with Rosemary and Iain a few minutes later. Iain knew full well what had happened. I think my dear Rosemary was quite impressed that I was mistaken for not only one of the guys in the team but one who had played well.

It was fun being a cap even though it was only just for a few minutes. I have often wondered who I was supposed to have been, did I go on to win more caps, maybe even a Lion's place?

Standing by Heriot's well stocked trophy cabinet.
Left to Right, Jocky Bryce and Geoff Cross (Heriot's Edinburgh and Scotland) exchange dark front row secrets

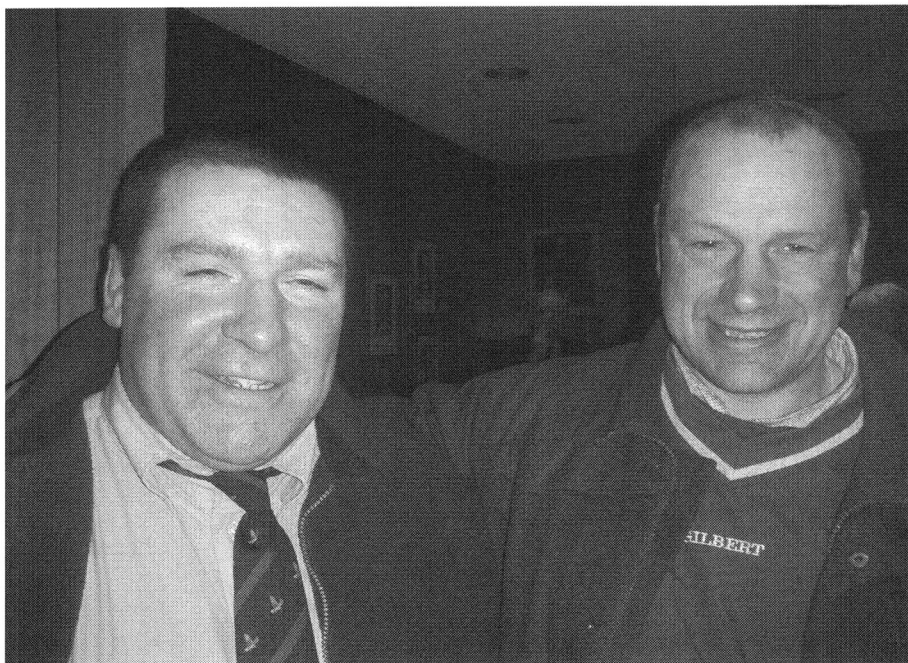

Two Scottish Lions roar together at Goldenacre, Left to Right, Peter Wright and Kenny Milne

CHAPTER 26

New Coaches; Sir George Mathewson; Local Residents

So, Kenny Milne was back in the heart of Heriot Rugby. Whilst he and Jocky Bryce were coaching the lower teams, Phil Smith who had previously played at stand-off for us, had returned to Goldenacre to take over the 1st XV head coach job from Donald MacDonald. Phil had a fair amount of success as coach so far as the Leagues were concerned and he coached the 1st XV to a glorious Cup win in 2003, more of which later.

Whilst there were changes on the playing side of the club some fundamental moves were being made in the admin department. My helper, Moira, had been a wee Godsend but we needed more automated assistance. Since our treasurer Dougie Hill had retired the club was finding out just how much the stalwart had done for us. The fellow that took over had difficulty keeping both his full time job and Heriot's books going and so he had to resign. Colin McCulloch CA, an associate member and FP of the Academy (Brechin that is !!), took over most of the Accounts work but Moira and I did a lot of what I believe CAs call "secretarial work." This included the gathering in and recording of subscriptions, sending out fixture cards, banking, invoicing, debt collection, bill paying and the sale and distribution of International tickets. To help us with what is a huge amount of work I asked an old school chum, Big Dave McDougal, an IT man and ex Heriot's 1st XV lock, to see what computer assistance would be useful to help us accomplish the foregoing and take the drudgery out of it.

I used to get a lot of phone calls from rugby players' agents and from players themselves, both at home and in my office, from New Zealand and Australia, sometimes at ridiculous hours given the difference in time zones. Most of the conversations were equally ridiculous. During the late nineties and up until I retired from Heriot's in 2005, it seemed to me that Antipodean rugby players and their agents thought that all they had to do was call up Scottish rugby clubs to tell them that they and their clients were from the Southern hemisphere and were therefore automatically excellent. The players were ready and willing to come and play for Heriot's or whomsoever for some sort of financial gain, usually not sweetie money. Their idea of remuneration was in the form of either a direct wage or some other financial benefit. One Australian player called me himself and suggested that a good way to make it easy for us to put him in our side would be to fly him and his wife over to Scotland, find them both jobs and give them an apartment, all for the duration of their stay. Oh, and the return fare to Cloud Cuckoo land could be included in the deal. It really was as astonishing as that. We were expected to assume that any southern hemisphere player would be of first class quality and a massive benefit to our club's playing performances. After the very first call I received on more or less those lines, I asked the guy to give me an email address so I could get back to him at a time that suited us both. I spoke to Kenny Milne about it and he said:

'Reply to the fellow along these lines: get yourself over here at your own expense, arrange for your own accommodation and we will be happy to give you a trial after which we will let you know if we are interested'

Kenny then said that that was to be my stock reply to everybody, no matter who, and I had his permission just to get on with that policy. Kenny was not for wasting time and money on phantoms.

Needless to say I never heard again from any of the callers who wanted that kind of open ended deal. I did have a call out of the blue from an Aussie hooker who had made it under his own steam to the UK. He was staying at the Y and asked if he could come along to the club and join. It turned out that his call coincided with a training day so I invited him to come and join the boys. There was no indication at first from the lad that he was looking for any financial benefit. However, when he joined the lads at the training grounds, he brought the subject of remuneration up with Kenny Milne who told the hooker that he would speak to him later, in private. It turned out he had all sorts of expectations. Kenny thought his performance at that training session was reasonable but he was not a match for our first and second choice hookers. Kenny advised me later that the lad was told thanks but no thanks. Our first choice hooker looked out for Kenny later that evening and found him in my office. The very much in form front row no 2, just a young lad, expressed his concern that we were going to take on an Australian fellow just like that. It turned out that our visitor had been suggesting to those at the session that night that he was coming to the club and would be joining the 1ˢᵗ XV squad. Kenny put our man at ease immediately and told him that that would not be happening.

Standing on the touchline at the very next Premier One game which was away but within the Edinburgh area, I spotted the Aussie hooker in the middle of the opposition front row. Heriot's have, over the years, fielded a number of overseas players, all of whom were nice guys and up to standard. None of them called the tune about financial benefits.

As I worked my way through this wonderful job I felt privileged to be in regular contact with not only our home-grown rugby stars, but many from other clubs and businesses, such as Scott Hastings who, along with his brother Gavin, ran a marketing company called Hastings International. Amongst, no doubt, myriad other matters, they looked after the daily affairs of the business relationship between BT and the SRU. BT were the main sponsors of Club Rugby in Scotland at the time.

I would often find myself in conversation with the great rugby journalist, Norman Mair, in our committee room after games and many of the committees that were our guests included members who had played for Scotland. When we played Hawks in the early stages of my appointment at Goldenacre, Sir George Mathewson, the then head of the Royal Bank of Scotland, and his delightful wife would join us for a drink in the committee room. Sir George's son played on the wing for Hawks at that time. On one such occasion I reminded him of his playing days for Aboyne Rugby Club umpteenths when he was Chairman of Scottish Enterprise and based in Glasgow. He used to get up to Aboyne of a Friday evening and run out for a game on the Saturday, sometimes playing against me and John Mackie when we turned out for Mackie FP. The memory brought an embarrassed smile to George Mathewson's face as well it might, for he, John and I were not exactly putting any Scotland Caps in fear of losing their place in the National side!!

Whilst the good news on the playing front kept coming in during my period of office there was always the mundane stuff to deal with. I just could not get away from neighbours who seemed to feel their week was not complete without some complaint or other being made to me about the Club, often via the local Conservative Councillor, Allan Jackson.

Virtually all the complaints were of a stupid nature. I don't really know why any of them got as far as me and were not stopped dead in their tracks by the councillor. I think one of my favourites was when some elderly people had an audio problem. They were sitting in the garden of their sheltered homes that look on to Heriot's playing fields and were being irritated by a constant cracking or slapping noise just over the wall. Councillor Jackson asked me to look into it for him. I asked him if he could let me know when the noise next sounded and I would go and investigate. When I got the relevant call, I had a look from Heriot's side of the wall. The disturbance turned out to be the noise of occasional cricket balls upon bats; leather upon willow. I called him to tell him about the cause of the so called disturbance and explained that the School had been making that kind of noise at that very spot every summer for about a hundred years and would not be inclined to stop!

CHAPTER 27

Bad Weather; The Cup; Sympathy for Hawick; Gala
and Dod Burrell; Matt Williams and Todd Blackadder

In the winter of 2002/3 we experienced some bad weather; the BT
leagues were badly disrupted causing three league matches to be
postponed. This was fortunate in some ways because injuries that
occurred earlier in the season were, by the Spring of 2003, on the
mend. The BT Cup was in full swing and by this time we were
looking forward to playing Jedforest. In the November of 2002 we
had played Orkney in our third round. I missed that day because
Rosemary and I were in South Africa for our "Summer" holidays.
Although we beat the islanders 115 to 6, both sides had a great après
match celebration. Accies were our fourth round opponents and
we beat them 50 points to 7. So we were on the march again in the
Scottish Cup, would it be our season? All the time we were successful on the pitch the future of club rugby was starting to look pretty
gloomy. Seven of our 1st XV were included in the Edinburgh Pro
team back up squad and two were in the Borders pro back up squad.
We had strength in depth as our seconds were doing extremely well

in their league competition. Bruce Douglas, Gordon Ross and Simon Taylor had all appeared for their country in the Autumn Tests at Murrayfield. Seven of our 1sts. were included in Roy Laidlaw's Scotland Seven's squad. Thanks to congested fixture lists and age group representative rugby our own Seven's tournament, always played in March, was cancelled for the second season running. In fact the tournament was never played again. The age group rugby commitments were affecting many clubs throughout Scotland.

April 2003 saw Heriot's win the Scottish Cup. What a day that Final was. I have never been so nervous at any rugby match as I was that day. We had the works. First the game was at Murrayfield; second we were playing against our old rivals, Watsonians; third the whole thing was televised. Additionally, I had to arrange hospitality at Goldenacre before and after the match for our members and their guests . You can imagine the clamour for tickets for that event. Whilst we were all enjoying a hearty lunch Kenny Milne settled our nerves by giving us his thoughts on how both sides were likely to tackle the game. Naturally, Kenny summed up with the expectation of a Heriot win although it would be tough. Well it was pretty tough but we won 22/11 which was good enough for me. Mansell were delighted that Heriot's had this magnificent achievement whilst on their sponsorial watch. They were also genuinely delighted for us. I had already experienced being involved with the club when we won the league 98/99 and 99/2000 and here I was again in the middle of something historic for the Club. At Murrayfield our support was phenomenal as was 'Sonians. I was on the edge of my seat for the boys and Rosemary was on the edge of her seat for me. What a day at HQ and what an evening at Goldenacre ! The cheer was deafening when Rory Lawson, Club Captain, brought his team back to celebrate with the members and guests. Filled with natural confidence Rory made a short speech thanking his team and us for making the win possible. Now there was a Scotland skipper in the making. Bryan Mackie, our President, praised the team and urged us all to have a great evening to mark the very special Heriot day. Bryan is a quiet, reserved bloke and usually hides any emotion; but, that day he was palpably over the moon, as was his supportive wife, Elaine. Many of our older members present at Goldenacre as well as at Murrayfield were thrilled for these young lads who had come up behind them under a different sort of regime to the one they had been a part of as players. By this time the Club had been open to non-Herioters for about thirty years whereas before it was closed to anybody not educated at the school. The future was no longer certain unlike the era in which they had played when there was no Cup, no leagues and, crucially, no demotion. Pre leagues, Heriot's FP Rugby Club's glittering fixture list was sacrosanct!

I prepared a special colour edition of Touchline.........to hell with the expense; this was an important day in the history of Heriot's Rugby Club. The club dinner was held only a few weeks later and it was a humdinger. Kenny Milne asked Gareth Chilcott of Bath, England and the British Lions to be our principal speaker; he was a riot. What a finish to the season.

The Club was bound for The Toon Cooncil's City Chambers for our third civic reception in five years.

It was 2003 and my first Touchline of the 2003/04 season reported emphatic wins against Hawick, Stirling County and League Champions Boroughmuir. In fact our score of 51 to Hawick's 6 was a record tally against the Greens. Their committee was shell shocked. I was with the late David Edwards, an Honorary President of our club, when he spoke to the Hawick President and told him that he was sad that Hawick had taken such a battering that day. He added that our National squad was always at its best when there was a strong Hawick side to pick from. I don't know if it was much consolation to the Hawick hierarchy but I do know that David's remarks were heartfelt. The strength of Hawick, or indeed any of the senior clubs, had been important to the National selectors in the seasons prior to 1995/96 but so much had changed since then. Hawick, like every other club, were now having to lose their best players to the pro sides before they would get anywhere near the National side.

That amazing victory over Hawick prompted me to run a feature in that particular Touchline about our rivalry with Hawick. Looking into the past it is clear that Hawick were held in awe by Heriot's over the seasons. Until the traditional New Year's day match in 1966 we had not beaten Hawick at Mansfield Park since the Second World War. That situation changed in the 1966 game when we won 11/3. Prop Ian T. Lawrie was so pleased about the win he and his wife named their daughter, Julie, born on Hogmanay, Julie Mansfield Lawrie. Ian went on to become a Lions' selector. In the pre-season Mansell Cup, Boroughmuir won the Tournament taking the Cup back from us which we won in 2002. Bill McLaren very kindly presented the Cup to the winners that day and he and his lovely wife, Bette, had lunch in the Club's Presidents' room with the committee and our wives. A wonderful experience relaxing with the great man and his charming wife.

As 2003 ended we bowed out of the Scottish Cup having been beaten narrowly at our bogie ground, Netherdale, by a determined Gala team. The late George "Dod" Burrell, Scotland full back and International referee was at his beloved club that day and was as mischievous as ever with his wicked sense of humour. We Heriot's committee men, were furious that day at the dreadful decision making on the park. Early on in the game we rejected a couple of kickable penalty opportunities and booted for position instead. Nothing came of either of the ensuing lineouts and so six points went up the spout. We lost that day by I think two points instead of winning by a margin of four at least. Standing at the bar one of our committee suggested that more time should be spent dinning it into our players that correct decision making was imperative and kicking easy points was a must every time, no question etc. etc. Dod, a wonderful after dinner speaker, listened to the chat and gleefully suggested that now that we had Saturday afternoons off there would be plenty of time to do it. It was really difficult not to laugh as Dod had such a droll way of putting his throw away remarks.

Whilst we were still licking our wounds after the Gala Cup defeat we were welcoming back our young players who had been contracted to The Edinburgh Gunners throughout the World Cup.

On the International front, Scotland appointed an Aussie, Matt Williams, as coach, who, in turn, recruited Kiwi, Todd Blackadder, to his coaching team. Todd, an ex All Black skipper, was captain of the Edinburgh Gunners at the time. Because of his connection with the Gunners I often had the opportunity to talk to the great man. Todd, though a quiet, mild mannered fellow off the park realised his importance in the world of rugby and how much of an influence he could have on us Scots over our attitude to pro rugby. He therefore had a high profile at meetings both official and casual. He put himself about and came to the Mansell Cup in 2004. Mingling with the teams, he chatted to the players and later socialised with us in the club house ; crucially he sat with Rosemary and some other wives and charmed the boots off them. He was the subject of a few Bruce conversations over meals for a few days after that, prompted by Mrs B I might add.

Shortly after his appointment as Scotland coach Matt Williams came along to Goldenacre to take a training session which our guys seemed to enjoy very much. I was on holiday when Matt was at Goldenacre so I never got a chance to meet him and I believe it was the next time he planned to be at Goldenacre that Simon our groundsman accidentally scared him away when Matt heard him shooting pigeons but though that he was the target.

*Graham Fraser, Rosemary and Todd Blackadder captain
of Edinburgh and former All Black's Captain*

323

CHAPTER 28

Reunions; SRU Changes Again!
Another Mackay Leads the Way;
Radical Changes Planned at Goldenacre

Reunions of players from different decades were organised each season at the Club. This was good for the bar and gave us an opportunity to persuade some ex players who had been lost to the Club to come back on a more regular basis.

Another style of reunion took place in December 2003 when I invited a trio of Heriot International referees to lunch in our Presidents' room with me and David Edwards our Honorary President. The refs were Brian Anderson, Jake Young and Douglas McMahon. Brian was actually a Royal High School man but was now on the school games staff. He was on the International refs panel in the eighties and included a World Cup in his CV, Jake was a seventies ref and Douglas McMahon hailed from the sixties. Many readers, especially of my vintage, will remember the BBC Rugby Special programme of the seventies. As the catchy tune in the introduction to the programme started, the opening shots showed a hostile Bob

Hiller, the England full back face up to Jake and Jake dismissing him with a confident flourish. What was going on? Jake revealed at our wee lunch time gathering that a high ball had gone up, Hiller marked it, Jake was unsighted and neither saw nor heard the call for the mark. Hiller was promptly buried by the French forwards. After recovering from the onslaught Hiller rushed up to Jake and shouted,

'What about the "bleep" mark ref?'

'What mark ?' was the reply from Jake as he dismissed Hiller. So now you know.

Asked about the current top referees throughout the world and in particular the southern hemisphere, none of our three lunching refs had much time for the Super 12 Antipodean refs but they thought the South African arbiters to be excellent; Andre Watson came in for particular praise because he stuck firmly to the Laws of the game.

A few club members gave me some questions on the Laws to put to the refs and Brian kindly answered them for me. The burning questions at the time were about touch judges; the Laws governing advantage and the use of fourth officials. I asked Jake what sort of player made a good referee. Jake without hesitation said, 'A player who disliked refs and who always questioned their decisions!'

Whilst clubs and pro rugby were getting back to sailing on an even keel after the 2003 World Cup, changes were blowing in the wind at the SRU. Scotland's Director of Rugby, Ian McGeechan, was doing his best to stimulate debate in Scottish rugby. He was banging on about the importance of the link from the National team to the pro teams to the clubs. He wanted the club game to be vibrant and clubs to be encouraged and supported if they chose to be top clubs in the country and to develop that dynamic environment. It needed to be all linked together. McGeechan had a number of ideas which I published in Touchline and the one that stood out for me was the suggestion that salaried coaches should be introduced to clubs. We Herioters, along with probably all of the Premier I clubs, were already paying our coaches some cash but not enough for them to live on. I can only presume that Geech, as he was known, was looking at paying our coaches considerably more. But if that was the case then I have no idea where he thought the money was to come from, unless of course he had the SRU coffers in mind. His other suggestions were mainly about making the game more competitive and giving ambitious clubs something to aim for. That was tempered a bit by his feeling that there should also be social rugby.

Whilst McGeechan was making his feelings clear the, then President and chairman of the newly formed Unitary Board of the SRU, Bert Duffy and David Mackay respectively, were also announcing plans that they hoped would advance our game. A Strategy Development Group was to be formed who would be assisted by strategic management consultants. This Unitary Board, recently formed by David Mackay, was to replace the Executive Board which had been formed after the earlier Lord Mackay investigation into the game in Scotland. This all sounds like a maze of committees and I hope you are not lost in it already.

Before the Executive Board broke up David Mackay, as its President, spent about three months investigating Scottish rugby and he found a lot that he didn't like. He duly sacked Bill Watson the SRU Chief Executive and scrapped the Executive Board. The new Unitary Board was formed by Mackay with the blessing of the Union's General Committee. Following on from this, more power would be given to the Murrayfield executives so far as the day to day running of the SRU was concerned.

Matt Williams, the National coach, chucked his tuppence worth into the pot when he announced his plans for changing the look of rugby in Scotland. The first edict was to exclude players from the National squad who refused to play their club rugby in Scotland. Wow! That was a bold move. Imagine if the likes of Fiji, Samoa and Argentina were to restrict their National squad to their home based players; they might find it very, very difficult to raise even a sevens side. At least their respective Unions wouldn't have a gigantic wage bill like the SRU has for our two pro sides.

Oh boy, I thought, here we go again after the Lord Mackay investigations of the Union there are to be more committees, meetings, consultants blah blah blah. However, I must say I was reasonably optimistic for the future of Scottish rugby at this time. David Mackay was, is indeed, a proven top class business man and to my mind he was on the right track with his determination that, as a rugby Nation, we should all be working together, pros, amateurs, players, non players, women's rugby, everybody.

The SRU was to go through much more pain than hitherto experienced. The night of the long knives was not far off.

When all of this upheaval was going on President Bryan Mackie and his committee decided that we should have a root and branch look at how we ran things at Goldenacre. We set up a think tank and employed a professional facilitator. The Think Tank met for the first time on the eve of the Cup final which we won. Was this to be an omen. A great deal was accomplished that night and a number of little action groups were set up to turn the ideas into reality.

Much could be done immediately. The first was to call ourselves publicly, Heriot's Rugby Club so far as day to day business is concerned. Many felt that the whole handle of our constitutional name, George Heriot's School (FP) Rugby Club, was too much of a mouthful. There was another important reason for that change. We had heard that one of the other city clubs, when trying to recruit the same players as we were, had made suggestions to these lads that joining Heriot's was stepping into the past as we were primarily a stuffy, snobby and elitist fee paying school former pupils club. Whereas they were a modern fully open set up. In fact Heriot's Rugby Club, while closely associated to George Heriot's school and its Govenors, is not an elitist organisation and has been a fully open club for many years. The School Governors have nothing to do with the day to day running of the rugby playing side of the club. I know, however they would have something to say if the rugby club did anything to bring the name of the School into disrepute!

So that simple wee name change began immediately and with no opposition from the FPs within the membership. A number of the other proposed changes were delivered over the next few years but sadly the most important goal of 2008 members by 2008 has not been reached. I guess most other major clubs are struggling to increase their membership.

Heriot's International Referees
Back row Left to Right, *Brian Anderson, A N Match Referee, Jake Young*
Seated,*Douglas Mcmahon*

CHAPTER 29

Clark Cup; Summer Rugby; Pro Rugby and Our Lights; Possible False Dawn at the SRU; The Truth About Numbers of Players in Scottish Rugby.

Our last home game before Christmas 2003 was against Boroughmuir. George Clark, a solicitor and Boroughmuir RFC secretary, had sons at George Heriot's school. George called me one day and asked if, given his strong connection with Heriot's, he could present a cup to the winners of the first encounter each season between Boroughmuir and Heriot's Rugby Club. The committee were all for it. After delays caused by weather postponements, the first Clark Cup game was played in March 2004. Boroughmuir were victorious and were therefore the first recipients of the Clark Cup. The theme for that day was the fiftieth anniversary of the very first encounter that Heriot's 1st XV had with Boroughmuir 1st XV. One interesting little snippet from that day was my discovery that Bob Proudfoot, a Boroughmuir prop and present at this Clark Cup game, weighed in at 12st 7 lbs. in that first encounter with Heriot's game back in 1953.

I reported that wonderful celebratory lunch in Touchline. Also in that edition, I was able to tell the members yet again of a number of Heriot players who were enjoying representative rugby for Scotland at U19 and U21 level plus another list of four players who had gone on to secure pro contracts at both the Borders and Edinburgh sides. Heriot's were also sporting four players in the national squad, Simon Taylor, Bruce Douglas, Andrew Dall and Gordon Ross.

Our one-hundred and fourteenth season was winding up: we were fifth in the league and looking forward to the three R's: recovering, regrouping and recruiting. Amongst all the palaver at the SRU and the development of pro rugby, both on the park and in the "pro terracings", there was the question of summer rugby. Moves were afoot to have summer rugby at least considered. I think that a number of clubs would support sunny seasons. Who, these days, really wants to play rugby in the bucketing rain, freezing temperatures, mud and gloom? Graeme Morrison, rugby correspondent for Scotland on Sunday, called me that summer, on my mobile, to talk to me about Heriot's opinion on Summer rugby. I was sitting at a pavement table outside a sun blasted bar in Luxembourg at the time enjoying a particularly fine, thirst quenching beer. Did I think it was a viable proposition to play rugby at Goldenacre in the summer? I said that I thought there would be no opposition from my club but the School might have something to say about it; the pitch belongs to The Heriot Trust. Edinburgh University and Heriot's Rugby Club had a formal association with each other at this time and their coach Dale Lyon wrote in our Touchline that summer rugby raised serious worries for all University teams given that exams and then summer closure of the Universities would probably put their teams out of business.

I wrote a few sentences ago about the palaver within Scottish rugby so far as the running of the SRU was concerned; well, in addition to all the frantic changes in the administration at the top of Scottish rugby there had previously been a constant shuffling about of our pro team's venues. When the pro game started in Scotland there were no pitches for them and they sometimes used club pitches. At one time the Hibernian FC ground at Easter Road was the home of Edinburgh Pro Rugby. Compare all of that with the generally easy time English Rugby had with the introduction of the pro game.

At an informal meeting with the original Edinburgh pro side's management, it was put to me that we could possibly secure the Edinburgh pro sides fixtures permanently at Goldenacre, if only we would install floodlights - at our expense of course. It looked on the surface like quite a good proposition from the revenue point of view: our income would be likely to increase dramatically. I investigated the possibility of installing the necessary lights. Firstly, the Club's neighbours nearly had a fit when I told them that we were applying for planning permission to erect the lights; secondly, no matter which way we looked at the funding of the project, the cost to Heriot's RC was prohibitive. So, it was a dead duck; although, at the time of writing this book, our application for planning permission is still within the statutory limits for consideration by the Edinburgh Council Planning Department.

It seemed to me and probably everybody else that the SRU had not thought the whole pro thing through properly. Frankly they just didn't have the cash to give any Scottish Pro side a decent stadium, never mind one that was floodlit. I don't think the Scottish pro game will flourish until their sides have proper homes of their own.

David Ferguson, chief rugby writer at the Scotsman wrote in the last Touchline of our one-hundred and fourteenth season that he, and all the other Scottish rugby journalists, were sick of reporting "another false dawn" after our national side seemed to be forever looking like they were about to blossom into a world beating side when down they would crash.

Ferguson went on, 'There is a very different air now with David Mackay and Phil Anderton steering the ship.'

The former was the Chairman of the Unitary Board and Phil Anderton was the Chief Executive Officer of the SRU.

I thought David Ferguson was right; there definitely did seem to be a light at the end of the tunnel. The Scotsman rugby writer also made comment in his contribution that the clubs had, for too long, hidden the true numbers of adult playing members on their books. Frankly, most clubs told porky pies about their membership rolls because, to tell the truth, they would have lost valuable accreditation cash from the SRU.

Cash for points basically. Clubs were credited with points for the number of players they retained each season and increased their points if their playing membership also increased. I had to fill an accreditation form up every new season. In addition to the playing compliment of the club more points were awarded if we could show we had a mini section, supplied referees to our District Referee's Society etc. etc. It's fair to say the average club secretary would have had difficulty in ascertaining an accurate figure with regard to playing numbers for all sorts of reasons and I was no different. Firstly players would come and go. The coming bit was okay but so far as the going bit was concerned I could never be sure if we had seen the last of players if they had not been around for a while. It was rarely any use asking their mates or sometimes even the coaches. Secondly, and this used to drive me up the wall, vast swathes of players would try to avoid paying their subscriptions. Heriot's, like practically every other club, didn't have the courage to kick players out of contention for a place in any of our fifteens if they didn't pay their dues on time. So much pressure was on clubs to win or, more to the point, not get demoted, that it was paramount that the best possible team would be picked regardless of whether the players were paid up members or not. I eventually sorted out our problem, I set Kenny Milne on to our debtor players!

The SRU eventually called an amnesty on the matter of player numbers in the Scottish club game. Clubs duly carried out proper audits to arrive at the truth. I had already worked out for myself that the actual number of senior rugby players in Scotland was around six to seven thousand, about half the thirteen thousand the SRU thought played the game. Ferguson finished his contribution by saying that he thought that rugby was just as popular a sport to new generations as it was twenty or thirty years before, it's just that other sports have caught up. I guess he was right but, so far as Scotland and all its available sporting activities is concerned, I think far too much emphasis is placed on the round ball game. I would further venture to suggest that most countries throughout the world suffer similarly.

First Clark Cup
*Bill Macmillan, one time Scottish sprint star, comically describes
his mazy run to score the winning try for Heriot's in the first
Heriot's 1ˢᵗ XV v Boroughmuir encounter in 1953*

CHAPTER 30

SRU's Strategic Advisory Group; Fund Raising; BBC Rugby Special at Heriot's; Pro Rugby Blamed for Rift in Scottish Rugby; Andy Irvine and the Moonies!!

The first meeting of David Mackay's Scottish Rugby's Strategic Advisory Group had been held in January 2004. Members of that group included Grand Slam 1990 Captain, David Sole, Ian McGeechan and Susan Deacon MSP. One of the outcomes was to hold a meeting at Murrayfield, quote: "where the whole of the Scottish Rugby Community would have a chance to be involved positively in crafting our direction!" Whilst this sounded admirable, I had been involved in so many of these sort of brain storming exercises over the years, I smelled trouble.

David Mackay called the gathering an "Open Space Meeting". Heriot's were represented by President, Bryan Mackie, Vice President, Jock Millican, Treasurer Colin McCulloch, and me. A set discussion kicked-off proceedings: where would we like our National side to be in world rugby in four years' time? After the 2011 RWC our National team was six places on the wrong side of that!

An outside company called Genisis facilitated the event and they also recorded all the findings that were arrived at by little sub meetings. These findings would form the basis of what was to be known as "The Genisis Report" and that would be put to a Special General Meeting of the Scottish Rugby Union, more of which later. I think they must have needed a large lorry to take all the paper away. At the end of the day's proceedings David Mackay highlighted the fact that no mention of the Scottish Rugby Union finances had been made by anybody in the room. He put that down to the possibility that the Scottish rugby community was happy to leave that subject to the SRU itself: that in my humble opinion was to be a mistake. During one of the wee meetings within the main meeting that day, we discussed what kinds of fund raising went on in clubs. I was amazed by the representatives of some of the smaller clubs when they told our group their methods of raising money. Heriot's and probably all the bigger clubs rely upon bar takings, dwindling gate money, subs, sponsorship, advertising, and if all that fails, members are asked to put their hands into their pockets. I used to run large hospitality events at Goldenacre on the days of Home Five/Six Nations Test matches. We made huge amounts of money from that. However, the big problem with that is very few members are actually involved in the organisation and running of the event - no team work involved. To me it is crucial that the membership rolls up its collective sleeve and grafts for its funds as evidenced by many smaller clubs. I was astonished at the efforts put in by the likes of Orkney RFC and Mackie Academy FPRFC in Stonehaven. They gave us master class lessons on how they had activated the memberships of their clubs to get on and make money. Their imagination knew no bounds. Mackie, for example, have an Annual Cow Dump (literally and lavatorially). On a piece of paper, they draw a pitch to scale, square it off and number each of the squares. The club members have fun selling corresponding numbered tickets all over the Mearns and in Aberdeen. The sheer basic crudeness of the project really appealed to the targeted market. Every ticket holder and hundreds of other spectators stand around the pitch to witness a cow wandering about with a full tummy or is it tummys. Eventually the cow will evacuate her bowels on a square and the owner of the lucky ticket wins the prize. It's a win/win situation, Mackie make loads of money and they get their pitch grazed and a small part of it fertilized!! Hilarious and actually much easier and more fun than stuffy raffle ticket sales or pestering members for hand-outs. Where have all the Rugby Club Jumble sales gone?

The 2003/4 Six Nations matches were seen by the BBC as an opportunity to revive Rugby Special networked from club houses. Heriot's was chosen to send out the Scotland v France Rugby Special. This required a lot of input from me, but the number of BBC personnel involved was incredible. It was however produced very professionally and I was chuffed when the director asked me, I suppose because I was kilted, together with some random French bloke to "introduce" the show. We just had to stand in front of the camera with a drink in our hands as if we were making a toast. Nevertheless, fame at last. John Inverdale hosted the programme, Johnathan Davies and Andy Irvine talked about the game and other teams in the competition. Bill McLaren very kindly accepted our invitation to be our special guest.

After the broadcast I took Rosemary and my family for a drink to a pub in the nearby Canonmills area of Edinburgh. Some of our daughter's German cousins (were with us) who had come over from Berlin to attend the match at Murrayfield. We made up quite a big crowd at the pub bar. Rosemary was standing back from the bar with most of our group and our eldest daughter, Kirsten, was with me. After a while a pretty looking young woman approached me and asked me if I would like to go off with her. It dawned on me, after my initial astonishment, that her scantily clothed shapely body indicated that she was a prostitute. I got rid of her and realised that in the heat of the moment Kirsten had witnessed the whole scene. She was in stitches at my discomfort. We got over that bit of excitement eventually but not until after Rosemary had heard about it and had finally stopped laughing. Half an hour later, blow me, if you can excuse the pun, did the bloody woman not come back again to see if I had changed my mind. I told her I had something else planned and would she please go away, or words to that effect. She asked me what it was that I was going to do and unable to think of anything else I exclaimed 'I am going home to my friggin bed!' This pretty well finished my daughter and, later, everyone else.

Season one-hundred and fifteen, 2004/5 saw Heriot's RC with its first ever president that had not been educated at George Heriot's School. President Jock Millican created a bit of history at Goldenacre. As well as all the other important duties that Jock had as our President, he attended the SRU review meetings which were sponsored by the Unitary Board. The financial and playing status of the Union was being scrutinised with a microscope. Jock told us that big changes throughout our game were coming, top to bottom; they were not an option, we had no choice.

Meanwhile at Goldenacre we had to make changes of our own. Kenny Milne recruited Iwan Tukalo as head coach to replace a retiring Phil Smith. Iwan was, of course, a member of the 1990 Scottish Grand Slam team. The influence that Kenny had on, and for, Heriot's was immeasurable. The Club also relied upon Kenny to recruit good players and this he did for us both in quantity and quality. Changed days since the pre nineties. Keeping a 1st XV together year-in-year out was becoming very difficult. Edinburgh Gunners continued to flourish helped along with the supply of Heriot's players. Those Herioters contracted to the Gunners were to play most of their rugby for the Club; but, in the event of injuries within the pro club or because of absences caused by International matches, the pros would have first call on them. Yes, the club game was moving a million miles away from when I first joined Heriot's FP as a school leaver. Professional Rugby Union were three words that should never go together was the feeling amongst many interested parties . It was a difficult time for club committees. In some instances pro rugby split whole clubs, Heriot's lost some of our older members who simply walked away from the game altogether in dismay. Some hung on and did their best to go with the flow. Even some younger members deserted but there were many complex reasons for that, some of which I explained earlier, but I think fewer would have departed had it not been for the changes in the game as a whole.

Mansell stood down as our main sponsor and were replaced by Cape Promise Wines, part of the wine and Spirit arm of brewers Scottish and Newcastle. Mini rugby was developing rapidly at Goldenacre and senior schoolboys were forming an older age group section. Efforts were being made to widen the net to catch non-Heriot schoolboys. Outstanding players in their time, Iain Milne, brother Kenny, Iwan Tukalo, Andy Irvine and Peter Hewitt were all involved in coaching these up and coming kids. Sunday afternoons at Goldenacre were busy times.

Still the ordinary back room work kept me very busy with all sorts of non rugby matters. I had a call from a wife of one of our members who wanted to hold a Sunday birthday party in the club for her wee girl. I explained that it was not possible as the club house was given over on Sundays to Andy Irvine and his Minis. 'oh, ooooooohh,oh..... I see!' said the puzzled lady. 'Well thank you anyway!' and we hung up.

The next day the same lady called me back and she said,

'Mr Bruce, my husband and I were discussing over dinner last night what you said yesterday about Andy Irvine. We were wondering........ when and why on earth did Andy join the Moonies!'

When I explained it was the Minis I thought her next "oh,oooooooh,oh I see!" was mixture of embarrassment at her error and relief that her hero was not in fact a member of that most unusual movement.

My last Touchline included a piece written by David Ferguson of The Scotsman on the mood of optimism at the AGM of the SRU in June of 2004. He went on to say however that the feeling was changing and it looked like the SRU had taken cold feet at the proposed bold changes. The decisions on the changes were due to be made in the September of 2004 but had been put back to October and then it was the December of 2004. Ferguson ended his piece with the "hope that the delays were caused by getting the complex details for the changes correct and not a softening of the will to change!"

Alan Tomes (Hawick, Scotland and British Lions 1980), Kenny Scotland (Heriot's, Scotland and British Lions 1959), Iain Milne (Heriot's, Scotland and British Lions,83),Andy Irvine (Heriot's,Scotland and British Lions 74, 77 and 80). Between all four of these players they had 175 caps for Scotland

CHAPTER 31

Community Rugby; My meeting with Harlequins CEO at the Stoop; Friends of Scottish Rugby; The London Caledonian Club and My First Plateful of Partridge; Mini Cab Fiasco in London.

Earlier I wrote about our own club review in 2003 which our committee hoped would put us on a stronger footing. Much was promised, or at least hoped for, but little of that list was delivered in the seasons immediately afterwards because of a plethora of legitimate distractions. In the latter part of the summer of 2004 I embarked on another initiative.

For some time I had been considering widening our parish for want of a better description. Goldenacre, George Heriot's school playing fields, seemed to me to be a sealed off compound within a large community. What potential rugby talent could be hidden in North Edinburgh, from Granton, along the shoreline to Leith and back towards Goldenacre. Talk had often been heard about mergers of the North side clubs but nothing had come of it. Mini rugby had been started at most of the clubs on the North side of town and the intention was to have a completely open door for anybody and everybody of the right age living in the area and even beyond. Why not also fling the net over older boys and young men. I was sure that given the opportunity, lads from the areas described would grab the chance to take up the oval ball.

I determined to pursue the ideas that had been running around in my head and spoke about them to a non-playing member of the club, Ian Nimmo. His son was playing for our 1st XV at the time, also called Ian. Ian senior is a successful businessman who has valuable contacts all over the UK . He was keen to help out his son's new club and he could see a future for my idea. He suggested that I might benefit from talking to the then chief executive of Harlequins, Mark Evans, with whom he was friendly. Ian arranged the meeting at The Stoop Memorial Ground. It was early summer and well short of the start of Quin's season. What a huge ground the Stoop is! I found the admin section, negotiated my way round desk after desk, each manned by huge blokes who had mountains of paperwork in front of them. They were nearly all ex-players, many former Internationalists of different anthems. Eventually I got to Mark Evans' room. Ian Nimmo was already there. We got straight down to action. I explained that we wanted to increase our membership and his solution was simple:

'Get involved in the community at all age levels. Youth rugby is one of the keys to success in the community.'

Mark explained that, for many years, Harlequins had relied on players coming to them from other clubs and had not had a youth policy. Quins looked at themselves and became so involved with the community and the youths therein that the RFU were going to them for help and advice. I left the meeting determined that Heriot's would become less insular and imitate the great Harlequins project.

Later in the year Ian Nimmo snr invited me to join him as his guest at a luncheon run by the Friends of Scottish Rugby in the

Caledonian Club, London. There I met the president, treasurer and other committee members of Friends of Scottish Rugby (FOSR). They were interested in what I had to say about the development of youth rugby and explained that if the SRU approved of Heriot's plan they would help us financially. FOSR is a wonderful organisation which exists primarily to help fund projects like the one I was hoping to promote. An amazing set up with tremendous money raising ability and influence in all sorts of places. After we had all eaten a very elegant and delicious lunch, with appropriate wines for each course, in a magnificently, regal dining room we were treated to an after lunch speech from Catherine (Kate) Letitia Hoey MP. Ms Hoey was a Sports Minister in the Blair government and one time Northern Ireland High Jump champion. She spoke eloquently and very knowledgably about sport in general.

Having been apprised of what information the FOSR needed from me I headed off down to the bar with Ian Nimmo and a few others from the lunch. The Caledonian Club is a magnificent building with an air of old money affluence about it. The members all seemed to be very far north of the poverty line. Standing at the bar I spotted one member who had nothing whatsoever to do with the FOSR. He was itching to find out what had been going on. He asked me in a very plummy Sandhurst accent,

'I say, wots all this abite old boy?'

After I had outlined what had been going on and how much I had enjoyed my sumptuous lunch, highlighting the fact that I had never had partridge before, Colonel Blimp looked at me aghast and said,

'Good God man, were you brought up in a cinecil hice?'

Returning to Goldenacre I started to write up a plan. The main ingredient of this plan was to hire a full time, salaried development officer. First on the agenda was to invite a representative of

Perthshire Rugby Club to come to talk to my committee and to representatives of the school and the Governors. Iain Nimmo was also present. Perthshire were already heavily into the exact same programme as I had envisaged for Heriot's and their man gave an excellent presentation. Everybody present approved, so it was a matter now of pulling together others who had the dosh to help me, along with the committee, and deliver the finished article. I was fighting against time. Rosemary and I had decided, in September 2004, to retire and move to Skye in the March of 2005 to start a completely new life; it was now November 04. I had to get more done so that whoever took over from me could have a seamless continuation.

Shortly after the meeting with the Perthshire representative, the chairman of FOSR contacted me and invited Heriot's to take a table at their annual Christmas dinner fund raiser. It was an opportunity to make money for the club. Provided we took a table, FOSR would invest a sum of money in the club. This was an additional funding opportunity for the club and very useful whilst I was drawing up a plan for the bigger picture. Ian Nimmo invited a number of his contacts along to the dinner and very generously underwrote the table costs for us. So, off Jock Millican and I went to a massive function hall in the City of London which was a brewery at one time. Jock was already in London on business but I had to get down specially for the function. I flew down the day before and stayed with my daughter, Kirsten, in Richmond. I called up a local mini cab company and made arrangements with them to take me to the dinner. Big mistake!!

The cab driver, who had little English, was obviously not local and not even British but timeous and very polite. My first impression of the fellow was that he looked as though he knew what he was doing. My heart sank immediately after I told him where I wanted to go; the look on his face was priceless. I wasn't sure whether it was because we were going far too near the centre of London and likely to come across lots more traffic than one would find in Richmond, or whether he had no idea how to locate our destination! I had made a good allowance for the likely driving time so there was room for a wee error or two. Everything was going well until my driver seemed to lose confidence around the Houses of Parliament. Now I knew that the city centre is on the left side of the Thames if one is travelling down to the mighty sea which we were, but to my horror my driver turned right and headed over Westminster Bridge taking us to the wrong side of the Thames; furthermore, not to mention worryingly, we were now smack dab in the middle of the London rush hour with about an hour to the dinner kick off. The driver got us back over the river to the right side at the next bridge and I started to relax when, did the mad bastard not go and cross the river again! Some of the bridges around there were one way and it seemed ages before I could get my driver back on the correct side again. My confidence in my man had forsaken me by this time and I said to him,

'Just please get into the heart of the City and we can ask the way!'

Driving just anywhere except of course back over the Thames in a southerly direction I got my man to stop so I could ask someone for directions. 'Stop!' I commanded and he quite literally screeched to a halt in the middle of the street. I had seen a couple standing in a shop doorway sheltering from a heavy downpour and hoped that they could help. They looked a bit surprised as this biggish fellow dressed in full Highland evening wear bore down upon them. I asked the startled couple if they knew where my dinner venue was and they told me. It was back down the street, left for a bit and left again for a few hundred yards but after that they were not sure but it wasn't far they hoped!! So did I.

I turned to get back in the cab. In that movement I saw why the girl with the helpful bloke was looking back up the street with a "I wonder what the hell is going on here with this kilted person and his driver" look on her face. My cabbie had fled the cab and was standing in the middle of the road trying to thumb a lift. In the name of the wee man. Thanking my astonished Good Samaritans whilst running towards the deserter I shouted at the top of my voice,

'Hoy, what the blankety blank are you doing?'

'I am trying to get you a black cab sir, he will know where to go!!'

A taxi driver hailing another taxi; I had never heard the likes. I was starting to feel like Donald who had just come down from the Isle of Skye!! I shouted again, this time with good news,

'I know where to go, get back into the cab and I'll direct you.'

Well we slowed up at the point where my shop door direction advisor had said he couldn't be sure about the fine tuning of our journey. There were a lot of policemen about. I asked my driver to hold on whilst I asked a pretty lady bobby for the final directions. It seemed that we had blundered into the middle of a crime scene and all this gorgeous copper wanted us to do was bugger off quick because she and her Met colleagues were very busy. You couldn't have made this all up. I was now at the end of my tether and pleaded with her for help. Thank God.... she told me and off we went to finish the adventure. We got to the door of the ex-brewery and I told my man to wait whilst I checked we were at the right place. We were, and also just in time. I marched back to the errant cabbie who was by this time constantly running his eye over me. It dawned on me that his sly sideways glances were not of admiration for the way I looked, he was checking to see that my sgian dubh (small knife) was firmly tucked into my right leg stocking! As I got to his open window I told him we had made it . He seemed relieved and indeed overjoyed. Sarcastically, I asked him how much he thought the whole fiasco was worth.

'Nothing sir !' and sped off into the night. I doubt he had a clue where he was or where he was going.

I found my host, apologised for my tardiness and had a quick beer at the bar. It was a great dinner for FOSR from the financial point of view as well as the social side of it. I could see how the numbers worked out as there were heaven knows how many raffles, auctions, general knowledge quizzes and so on that everybody had to take part in! FOSR, as I have explained, had influence in all sorts of places and I was not really too Surprised, therefore, when Angela Rippon the famous TV presenter suddenly appeared beside me during a break in proceedings. We had a chat about this and that and then just as suddenly as she appeared so she disappeared.

I think the FOSR raised their bank balance by a five figure amount that night and all of it was bound for good Scottish Rugby causes.

CHAPTER 32

SRU Meltdown, Jock Millican to the Rescue;
A Dream Vanishes; Skye Beckons

When I got back to Goldenacre it was on with the run-of-the-mill club stuff with an eye on the forthcoming Six Nations and all the International style hospitality. I kept my community rugby development project as close to the forefront as possible. Jock Millican, Ian Nimmo and I kept that ball up in the air as much was to be gained by bringing it all to fruition. However, as we were about to enter 2005, all the bold targets that the SRU Four-year Strategic Plan had set were to start looking like a big pie in the sky. My dream for community rugby, if that's not too slushy a description, was about to falter as a result of the doubts coming from Murrayfield. The SRU was heading for meltdown and when the Chairman of the Unitary Board, David MacKay, was dismissed by the SRU committee, closely followed by Phil Anderton, a senior employee of the SRU called me with an SOS plea. He asked me to speak to Jock Millican, my President, and encourage him urgently to contact his fellow Premier One Presidents to step in and try to halt the rot that was rapidly eating its way through the Union. I called Jock to tell him that he had to intervene in the troubles that beset our game at the top. Community rugby in the shape I had hoped for was necessarily put aside; no SRU meant no community rugby.

After I contacted Jock Millican he contacted Bill Hogg, the long standing Secretary of the SRU, by phone and email to reassure the Murrayfield staff that the clubs held them in high esteem and that they would be supporting them. It was the General Committee and the way that they were behaving that the clubs had concerns with.

The Premier One clubs met later that week and agreed that a small team made up of Jock, and representatives from Glasgow Hawks and Hawick should produce a proposal to try and rectify the situation. This was late December 2004 and by early January 2005 the small team had put forward a motion to a SRU Special General Meeting to be held later that month and called originally to discuss the Genisis report but now the agenda was the very future of Scottish Rugby.

The Hawks and Hawick representatives both had long holidays booked for January /February 2005 so it was left to Jock to carry the matter forward and to present the motion at the SGM. Those vacations were partly responsible for the motion becoming named "The Heriot's motion".

With the help of the Premier One clubs Jock contacted as many clubs in the Union as possible to talk through the motion and per-suade them to vote for it. In order to gain wider support he arranged for clubs at different levels of the game to officially second and sup-port the motion. Jock also kept the Union Secretary, Bill Hogg and Gordon Dixon, the SRU President aware of what was going on and underlined the need for Dixon to control the General Committee.

The meeting came and Jock proposed that the Heriot's motion be considered first - a number of club representatives, including

Jock, spoke to the motion, no one spoke against it and so probably the most important motion at either an SRU Annual General or Special General Meeting was carried.

What was the motion? In summary, it stated that the governance of the Scottish Rugby Union will be through an Executive Board accountable to the clubs through a new Scottish Rugby Council, (bye bye general committee). The Board's main role would be to administer Scottish Rugby on a day to day basis, to propose the strategic direction of Scottish Rugby and then implement it after approval by the Council.

The Council would be made up of a President, Vice President, representatives from Premier One, Two and Three and the National Leagues ensuring each major region is represented as well as our schools and women's rugby. The President and Vice President would serve, normally, one year terms and the councillors, two years. The Scottish Rugby Board would consist of a 50/50 mixture of executive and non-executive members.

The carrying of the motion led to the formation of what was known as the Dunlop Committee. They proposed the new governance and structure of the SRU, which is still in place and which other sporting bodies look on with envy. A major change, and I believe a most welcome one, was the time limits for those serving on the Council and the non executives on the Board. In the old days some of the committee were on for fifteen or twenty years and the only way off was by becoming President!! The President in those days also had responsibilities for running the organisation, as did the chief executive, and it was unclear who was in charge. So the Dunlop Committee proposed that the President's role should be ambassadorial and that people should be encouraged to stand for President from outwith the Council, or from the old Committee, and this has happened. So, peace and quiet at Murrayfield at long last. What a carry on it had been from 1995, when the game turned professional, until common sense prevailed ten years later through Jock Millican, Heriot's President, and his small team of Kenny Hamilton of Glasgow Hawks and Malcolm Murray of Hawick.

My days at Goldenacre were drawing to a conclusion. I saw out the International lunches which were as successful as ever on many levels. March 27th 2005 and the Isle of Skye beckoned Rosemary and me. Quietly I left the club and the centre of Heriot's rugby. Sadly the rugby club on Skye cannot find enough players to make a team nowadays. Shinty is the top game here!

Although I have no rugby to watch on Saturdays nor pints of beer to sink with club mates I still support Heriot's, Mackie FPRFC and my other clubs, rejoicing in their wins and worrying when they lose. As for Scottish Rugby in general the new set-up appears to be working well and club rugby has developed, particularly at the top level with a Premiership of ten clubs. This size of league together with the cup competition and the cross border British and Irish Cup allows a sensible number of games during the season. Professional Players not involved for Edinburgh or Glasgow are drafted to the Premiership clubs – again raising the standard.

The challenges facing the club game are common across the Home Countries - maintaining and increasing playing numbers, numbers of games being played, club finances, ageing committees, allowing talented players to progress upwards.

Newspaper reports on Premier One games constantly tell readers how exciting club rugby is, so, hopefully, the game I know and love is secure and has a great future. Long may Heriot schoolboys and perhaps schoolgirls run up Clark Road to the Red Pavilion for their first taste of the greatest team game on the planet.

Acknowledgements

Back in 2004, Rosemary, my dear late wife, suggested I write a book about my rugby experiences. This is in stark contrast to how she felt about my involvement in the game when we were engaged to be married in 1969! It didn't take too long, however, for her to see that rugby is fun and so she decided to join me on the social front and, crucially, support me solidly when I was twice President of Mackie Academy FP RFC and when I was general manager at Heriot's Rugby Club. After I retired from Goldenacre with only the first few chapters written, work on the book slowed down because our new bed and breakfast venture on Skye took up so much of our time. I managed a few more chapters in the dark winter nights on the Misty Isle before Rosemary died very suddenly in January 2009. Our daughters, Kirsten and Sarah, encouraged me to finish the book. Rosemary, of course, never saw the finished article but, if she had, I like to think it would have made her laugh.

"Wrapped in Rugby" is not meant to be a history of any of the clubs I was associated with but they, and rugby in general are a big part of my humble history. I must thank, not only those clubs for whom I played for allowing me to be a part of them, but particularly many of the members of Heriot's Rugby Club and Mackie Academy FP RFC for helping me piece together much of the book. A special thanks goes to George Heriot's School for including me in their pupils' roll and letting me remain there to complete my education! The late Donald Hastie, Heriot's first games master and my hurdles mentor, is a big influence in this book and I am indebted to him for inculcating his sporting values into my daily life.

The following individuals at Mackie FP RFC where I spent most of my senior rugby life and who have directly contributed to my story are as follows:

Doug McConnell, Bob and Rod Richmond, Peter Beatt, the late Bob Lewis, Alan Davidson, Neil Westland, Raymond Pittendreigh and Brian Thomson.

Those Herioters that not only helped with the book but me when I was secretary and general manager at Goldenacre make a long list and they include:

Alistair Hector (Headmaster), Mike Gilbert (Chairman of the School's Governors) Kenny Scotland, Derek McCracken, Douglas Hill, Ken Hutchison, John and Bryan Mackie, the late Graham Fraser, the late David Edwards, Simon Theurer head groundsman and his staff, Andy McFarlane (also of Aberdeenshire) and last but not least, Colin McCallum and Alan Brown organisers of the original Heriot Cavaliers.

I also need to make a special thanks to Peter Mitchell, formerly of the Aberdeen Press and Journal who has been a great help to me not only with regard to rugby but many another part of the lives of the Bruce family and, of course, Iain The Bear Milne who has kindly written the foreword. Jock Millican not only helped me with my book but, as you will see from the last chapter, he, along with Kenny Hamilton of Glasgow Hawks and Malcolm Murray of Hawick literally saved the SRU from extinction and therefore rugby as we know and love it in Scotland.

People say when a prospective author doubts whether he or she can actually write a book "Oh just get it down on paper, an editor will sort it" I tried to do a bit more than that but I still needed a good editor and I found one in Linda Henderson. A London Wasps supporter from birth, now living on Skye, Linda took on the job of making my book readable and I thank her from the bottom of my Heriot heart. My lovely niece, Jane Lee McCracken, gathered and edited all the illustrations which are in the book and the excellent cover which she also designed. I am so pleased with that and grateful to Jane for making such a great job of it and especially for being a wonderful niece.

Printed in Great Britain
by Amazon